Practicing College Learning Strategies

Third Edition

Practicing College Learning Strategies

Carolyn H. Hopper
Middle Tennessee State University

HOUGHTON MIFFLIN COMPANY
Boston   New York

Publisher: Patricia A. Coryell
Senior Sponsoring Editor: Mary Finch
Associate Editor: Shani B. Fisher
Editorial Assistant: Andrew Sylvester
Associate Project Editor: Kristin Penta
Editorial Assistant: Lisa Sullivan
Senior Production/Design Coordinator: Sarah Ambrose
Production/Design Assistant: Bethany Schlegel
Senior Manufacturing Coordinator: Marie Barnes
Marketing Manager: Barbara LeBuhn

Cover Image: © Joe Fleming/images.com

Printed in the U.S.A.

Library of Congress Control Number: 2002116644

ISBN: 0-618-33350-9

123456789-CRS-07 06 05 04 03

CONTENTS

v

2   Critical Thinking *37*

3   Setting Goals *49*

6 Processing Information from Textbooks *123*

9 Managing Stress *221*

10 College Essentials and College Etiquette *235*

11 : Principles of Research *253*

Appendix: Principles of Studying Math 273

PREFACE

Many people think that because they have survived high school and are in college, they know how to study—but the skills needed to survive college cannot be left to chance. Most students have never been taught "learning to learn" strategies. In *How People Learn,* John Bransford points out that the goal of education today is "helping students develop the intellectual tools and learning strategies needed to acquire the knowledge that allows people to think productively about history, science and technology, social phenomena, mathematics and the arts." Taking a learning strategies, study skills, or college survival course is probably one of the best things you can do to ensure success in college. *Practicing College Learning Strategies, Third Edition* reflects the belief that students can be taught how to learn more efficiently; they need to be told why these strategies work. They also need hands-on reinforcement of what they learn in class. The activities in this book are designed to enhance a learning strategies, study skills, or university orientation course by providing a concise presentation of materials and including practice opportunities to complement class discussions.

The most obvious change in the Third Edition of *Practicing College Learning Strategies* is the **change of title.** An increased emphasis on **learning strategies** reinforces what has always been the goal for this text: teaching students to learn how to learn. Central to the text has been finding and practicing strategies that work toward making students successful. The best way to achieve this goal is through hands-on classroom testing, and this textbook has accompanied me throughout my own learning strategies courses. This continual process of review has prompted the addition of information on what **brain research tells us about *why* these strategies work.** In keeping with the straightforward style of the text, I have added enough neurological research for a basic understanding of how the memory works (in Chapter 4), in order to empower students by providing them with the tools necessary to make maximum use of their memory and thereby improve their job performance, school achievement, and personal success.

xiii

What Does The Book Cover and Why?

One of the unique features of *Practicing College Learning Strategies* is that it begins with a Survival Kit that provides the most basic skills that students need to be productive from "day one." Before delving into the details of learning strategies, students are armed with basics in note taking, test taking, reading, reviewing, and logging assignments, in addition to tips for the first day class and finding technology resources. **The Survival Kit has been updated** to include **Jensen's Optimal Learning Equation** and Dr. Ralph Hillman's **The BREATHE System.** Neuroscientist and educator Eric Jensen synthesizes the findings of brain and learning research by presenting the following equation for Optimal Learning: He says that attention must be given to *Personal History* (beliefs, experiences, values, knowledge), *Present Circumstances* (environment, feelings, people, context, goals, moods), *Input* (five senses—visual, auditory, kinesthetic, olfactory, or gustatory), *Processing* (learning preference states, left/right hemisphere, abstract or concrete), *Meaning* (connecting experience, data, and stimuli to form conclusions and create patterns that give our lives meaning), and *Responses* (multiple intelligences). Instead of concentrating on any one area of learning, we must fit the pieces of the puzzle together to include all. Throughout the Third Edition of *Practicing College Learning Strategies,* each area that Jensen says is necessary for optimal learning is addressed.

The three main strategies in The BREATHE System—paying attention to posture, relaxing shoulder and neck muscles, and taking deep cleansing breaths—give students a way to realign their focus and get more oxygen to the brain and thereby perform other strategies more efficiently.

New! A Brain Byte feature appears throughout the margins, providing bite-sized factoids highlighting what brain researchers have discovered about learning.

The first three chapters of the Third Edition will help students adjust to the new environment of college. Chapter 1, Applying the Principles of Time Management, addresses time-management problems inherent in a college student's schedule and sets in place an individualized time management plan to help each student meet the demands of a college schedule.

New! *What's Your Advice?* follows each chapter summary—a new exercise requiring students to synthesize and evaluate what they have learned in the chapter in the form of providing advice to fellow students.

Chapter 2 introduces students to the critical thinking skills that they will need to be successful in college. Each subsequent chapter has critical thinking activities to practice the new techniques. In Chapter 3 students are given guidance on setting goals and determining their locus of control.

The next four chapters are centered around basic learning strategies that students must master to be successful in college. In Chapter 4, Memory Principles, the discussion of *what* memory strategies work for successful students has been expanded to include brain research show-ing *why* those strategies work. Building on what they have learned about learning, students then develop strategies for taking notes, read-ing textbooks, and taking tests through Chapters 5–8. The focus of these chapters is to support students' discovery about how they learn and process information, and highlight the need to utilize the strategies that work for them. The Learning Styles chapter, Chapter 7, introduces sen-sory modes, hemispheric dominance, and multiple intelligences—three elements brain researchers say are necessary for optimal learning. In-ventories are included to help students determine their preferences and practical strategies using those preferences are practiced.

Although students experience stress and need to know specifics about their higher education environment during the first days of school, these chapters are specifically placed toward the end of the text. It has been my experience that students get a bit "antsy" at the begin-ning of the semester and want to learn skills they can use immediately. Having addressed those skills in Chapters 5–8, they are now seeking ways to practice the skills and deal with the stress and problems that higher education presents (Chapter 9). Discussions on College Essen-tials and College Etiquette presented in Chapter 10 mean more to those students who have already experienced part of a semester. The Princi-ples of Research information in Chapter 11 has been updated to include more technology and electronic databases. The appendix addresses some unique strategies needed for studying math.

New! Virtual Field Trips: Each chapter includes Internet assign-ments to supplement the text. The assignments are noted in the text, and the exercise is available on the *Practicing College Learning Strategies* web site. These interactive exercises take students on a guided journey across the Internet as they practice strategies from the text. You can visit these Virtual Field Trips online at *http://collegesurvival.college.hmco.com/students* and select *Practicing College Learning Strategies* under "Hopper." Additional interactive exercises, electronic flashcards, and practice tests are available online for students, too. Information about using the web site is available on the Instructor's web site for this text at *http://collegesurvival.college.hmco.com/instructors*. I maintain my own Study Skills Help Page which can be accessed online at *http://www.mtsu.edu/~studskl/*.

Additional Resources

Instructor's Resource Manual

An Instructor's Resource Manual accompanies *Practicing College Learn-ing Strategies, Third Edition*. Following the structure of the main text, the IRM provides additional activities and exercises by chapter. Answers to the chapter summary questions presented in the text are provided. Each chapter has a sample test to use in class or for homework.

College Survival Consulting Services

For more than fifteen years, Houghton Mifflin's College Survival consultants have provided consultation and training for the design, implementation, and presentation of student success and first-year courses. Their team of consultants has a wide variety of experience in teaching and administering the first-year course. They can provide help in establishing or improving your student success program. They offer assistance in course design, instructor training, teaching strategies, annual conferences, and much more. Contact College Survival today at 1-800-528-8323, or visit them on the web at *http://collegesurvival.college.hmco.com/instructors*.

The College Survival Student Planner is a week-at-a-glance academic planner available in a specially priced package with this text. Produced in partnership with Premier, The College Survival Student Planner assists students in managing their time both on and off campus. The planner includes a "Survival Kit" of helpful success tips from Houghton Mifflin Company College Survival textbooks.

From College to Career Success: A Web-Based Career Resource Center is a perfect way to invite your students to begin preparing for the future. Access additional articles online to further reinforce key workplace applications to the learning process. An E-token to access this on-line resource can be purchased as a stand-alone product or shrink-wrapped with *Practicing College Learning Strategies*. Access the Career Resource Center on the College Survival web site at *http://college-survival.college.hmco.com*.

Myers-Briggs Type Indicator® (MBTI®) Instrument*: This is the most widely used personality inventory in history —shrink wrapped with *The Confident Student* for a discounted price at qualified schools. The standard form M self-scorable instrument contains ninety-three items that determine preferences on four scales: Extroversion-Introversion, Sensing-Intuition, Thinking-Feeling, and Judging-Perceiving.

Retention Management System™ **College Student Inventory:** The Noel Levitz College Student Inventory instrument is available in a specially priced package with this text. This early-alert, early-intervention program identifies students with tendencies that contribute to dropping out of school. Students can participate in an integrated, campus-wide program. Advisors are sent three interpretive reports: The Student's Report, the Advisor/Counselor Report, and The College Summary and Planning Report. Forms A and B are available for shrink wrap.

Videos are available to supplement your in-class lectures, including two **Roundtable Discussions videotapes,** "Study Strategies" and "Life Skills." (All of these videos are closed-captioned.) Contact your sales representative or College Survival Consultant for an up-to-date list of available videos and for pricing information.

*MBTI and Myers-Briggs Type Indicator are registered trademarks of Consulting Psychologists Press, Inc.

Acknowledgments

I am indebted to many people for the preparation of this book. This text is the result of suggestions from students and faculty involved in the Developmental Studies courses at Middle Tennessee State University. The success of the learning strategies program at MTSU has been very much a team effort. I have benefited greatly from my association with the talented and caring members of the Developmental Studies faculty and staff.

Thanks specifically to department chair Carol Bader, academic advisors Terri Tharp, Barbara Hensley, Lewis Gray, Carla Hatfield, and colleagues Sheila Otto and Andrea Elliott, whose understanding of how crucial it is for students to learn how to learn has made the course successful for thousands of students. The students in my Summer '02 Learning Strategies class allowed me to field test the new material in the Third Edition and were invaluable in their feedback. These students are hard working and insightful. I know they have what it takes to do whatever they choose to do. Thanks to Chris Baker, April Brandon, Kurt Gahm, Tabitha Goldthreate, Carrie Hubka, Cindy Jarvis, Heather Jentzsch, Shane Jones, Erika Lawson, Athanas Martin, Jon Morrison, Robin Paugh, Kim Rogers, Cheryl Singleton, Hal Smith, Sylvia Thompson, and Carl Watts.

In addition, I want to thank Jean Rhodes, who—while finishing up her Ph.D. in English this summer—listened to me explain what brain research says so much that she began to use it to analyze the literature she was reading. I owe the on-line version of the hemispheric dominance inventory to Mark Templeton's expertise and patience.

Eric Jensen and Karen Markowitz at the Brain Store (*http://thebrainstore.com/store/*), Pierce Howard (*The Owner's Manual for the Brain*), and Eric Chudler (*Neuroscience for Kids, http://faculty.washington.edu/chudler/neurok.html*) were generous in granting permission to share their research about what brain research says about learning. A special thanks to Ralph Hillman, the Voice Doctor and friend, for sharing The BREATHE System. The brief introduction that I have included in this text does not do justice to this system. I hope you will examine it further at *http://thebreathesystem.com/*. Thanks to Laurie Witherow and Ginger Corley, who once again granted permission to use their wonderful "All I ever need to know I learned from my advisor."

I can't begin to thank the wonderful staff at Houghton Mifflin's College Survival for their vision, suggestions, and persistence. Shani Fisher is a marvel and Andrew Sylvester's assistance is invaluable. Special thanks to Sponsoring Editor Mary Finch and Associate Project Editor Kristin Penta for their work on this revision.

I would like to extend a special acknowledgment to the following instructors for their reviews of the text and suggestions for the improvement of this edition:

Evelyn J. Leggette, Jackson State University, MS
Dianne Stanley, Corning Community College, NY
Kathryn A. Trosen, Muscutine Community College, IA
Phoebe A. Wiley, Frostburg State University, MD
Janet M. Zupan, University of Montana, MT

Carolyn H. Hopper

Practicing College Learning Strategies

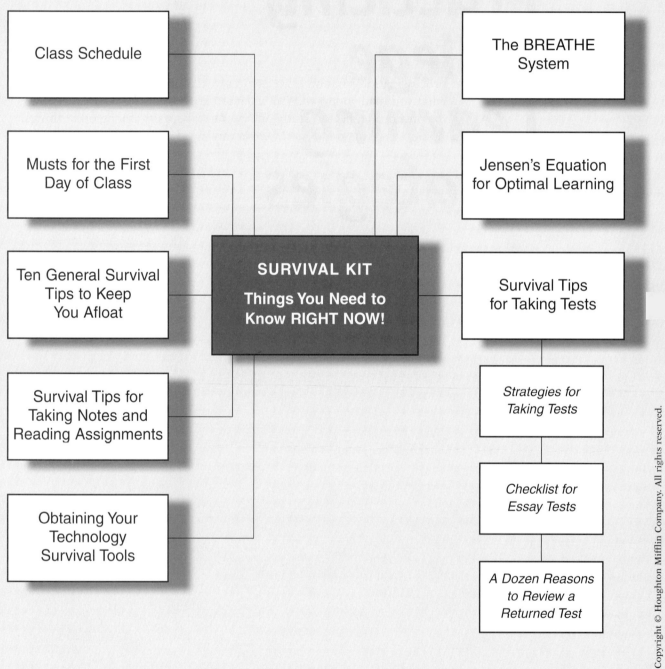

Class Schedule

Musts for the First Day of Class

Ten General Survival Tips to Keep You Afloat

Survival Tips for Taking Notes and Reading Assignments

Obtaining Your Technology Survival Tools

SURVIVAL KIT
Things You Need to Know RIGHT NOW!

The BREATHE System

Jensen's Equation for Optimal Learning

Survival Tips for Taking Tests

Strategies for Taking Tests

Checklist for Essay Tests

A Dozen Reasons to Review a Returned Test

Survival Kit

Things You Need to Know RIGHT NOW!

This is a learning strategies text. You will learn about note taking and processing information from lectures, textbook reading, and making what you read your own. You will learn how to control your time, how to concentrate, how to study, and how to take tests, among other things. If you are taking this course before you begin college, you probably have extra time to learn each skill. However, most of you are taking this course while you have already begun other courses. So you may need help now! You may feel yourself drowning. You may be behind in reading assignments or may have read them and don't remember what they said. If you have tests coming up, you already need to be taking notes. You can't learn everything you need to know in the first week, but here is a temporary survival kit equipped with information that will be covered in detail later in this book. This Survival Kit will keep you from treading water and give you something to hang onto until the lifeboat comes.

Name _____   Telephone number _____

Fill in the chart below with important information you will need for each class.

Class	Time/ Room	Instructor	Name of Another Student in Class	Student's Phone Number

Musts for the First Day of Class

1. **Be on time. Sit up front. Ask questions if you don't understand.**
2. **Take notes.** You will not remember what went on the first day of class without taking notes. Assume that everything that is said will not be repeated.
3. **Get a list of textbooks and material you will need for the class and have them all ready for the next class.** Don't wait until the next class period if there is a problem.
4. **Study the syllabus.** The syllabus should tell you the course requirements and objectives, what the instructors will expect from you and what you can expect from the instructor in the way of tests, assignments, grading policies, and absence policies. You cannot assume that all instructors have the same policies for late work, missed tests, or absences. Highlight anything you have questions about and ask as soon as possible. Check the syllabus for assignments that are due the next class period. Complete these assignments. Go overboard in doing your best. First impressions are important.
5. **Write** down the instructor's name, telephone number, e-mail address, and office hours.
6. **Get** the name and telephone number or e-mail address of at least two other students in the class.

Ten General Survival Tips to Keep You Afloat

1. If you haven't already registered, **try not to schedule back-to-back classes.** You'll wear yourself out besides missing the best times to study—right before and right after class.
2. **Begin the first day of class.** Know what's expected of you. Take notes on the first day even if it's routine stuff you think you already know.
3. **Establish a routine time to study for each class.** For every hour you spend in class, you will probably need to study two hours outside class. Study for each subject at the same time and in the same place if possible. Studying includes more than just doing your homework. You will need to go over your notes from class—labeling, editing, and making sure you understand them. Study your syllabus daily to see where you are going and where you have been. Be sure to do reading assignments. (Don't put them off just because there's no written assignment.) Read ahead whenever possible. Prepare for each class as if there will be a pop quiz that day.
4. **Establish a place to study.** Your place should have a desk, a comfortable chair, good lighting, all the supplies you need, and so on, and of course, it should be as free of distractions as possible. It should not be a place where you routinely do other things. It should be *your study place.*

brain byte

Dr. Judith Wurtman of MIT says that proper nutrition can boost thinking and learning. The brain's most basic need is for oxygen, but ingredients found in protein are critical to the brain. For mental alertness, three or four ounces of protein-rich foods should be a regular part of your diet.

5. **Do as much of your studying in the daytime as you can.** What takes you an hour to do during the day may take you an hour and a half at night.
6. **Schedule breaks.** Take a ten-minute break after every hour of study. If possible, avoid long blocks of time for studying. Spread out several short study sessions during the day.
7. **Make use of study resources on campus.** Find out about and use labs, tutors, videos, computer programs, and alternative texts. Sign up for an orientation session in the campus library and computer lab. Get to know your professors and advisers. *Ask questions.* "I didn't know" or "I didn't understand" is never an excuse.
8. **Find at least one or two students in each class to study with.** Research shows that students who study with someone routinely make better grades. You will probably find yourself more motivated if you know someone else cares about what you are doing in the class. Teaching a concept or new idea to someone else is a sure way for you to understand it. Yet studying in a group or with a partner can sometimes become *too* social. It is important to stay focused.
9. **Study the hardest subject first.** Work on your hardest subjects when you are fresh. Putting them off until you're tired compounds the problem.
10. **Be good to yourself.** Studying on four hours of sleep and an empty stomach or a junk-food diet is a waste of time. Avoid food and drink containing caffeine just before or just after studying.

The BREATHE System

Dr. Ralph Hillman has developed a program he calls The BREATHE System, a system designed to help classroom teachers train their students to reduce anger, control potential violence, and raise test scores. The program has some benefits for college students as well. The BREATHE System is a way to deal with low self-esteem, test anxiety, feelings of being overwhelmed, anger, and stress. Like much of what you will learn in this text, the system is relatively simple, but requires discipline. The BREATHE System is probably not something you would automatically think of as a learning strategy; however, you will find that it promotes concentration and clear thinking as well as routinely relieving stress. The BREATHE System involves knowing and consciously forming the habit of using what Dr. Hillman calls the Big 3 (reprinted from *Delivering Dynamic Presentations: Using Your Voice and Body for Impact* by Ralph E. Hillman. Copyright © 1999. Reprinted by permission of the author).

The Big 3 Are Posture, Neck and Shoulder Muscles, and Breath Support

Posture   Good posture allows the organs of your body to operate efficiently, to maintain good self-esteem, and to look like you can handle the events of each day. The six essential components of good posture are: 1. unlock your knees; 2. level your pelvis; 3. tuck your tummy; 4. elevate the rib cage; 5. shoulders back and down; 6. head up on top.

1. **Unlock your knees** while standing; if you "snap" or force the knees back, making your legs rigid, blood flow to your brain is diminished and the natural curves in your spine are exaggerated.

2. **Level your pelvis** so that the gentle arch of your lower spine is encouraged. If the pelvis is pulled too far back, the arch is exaggerated and too much tension is placed on the muscles necessary for efficient breathing.

3. **Tuck your tummy;** make a conscious effort to pull your belly button back toward your spine. Leveling your pelvis (#2) and elevating your rib cage (#4) will make this process easier. Most of us want tight abs but we are not willing to maintain the constant postural pressure on those muscles to allow them to be in position all the time.

4. **Elevate your rib cage;** keeping your ribs slightly elevated frees the thoracic cavity (rib cage) to move freely during inhalation and exhalation.

5. **Shoulders back and down;** if the previous four steps are in place, positioning the shoulders is a lot easier. If you are having trouble getting a "feel" for where the shoulders should be, try this: Put your back up against a wall. For most of us, our buttocks hit the wall first, then the shoulders, and finally the head. Put your hands up at shoulder level with the backs of your hands against the wall or as close to the wall as you can get them. Notice the pull in the muscles of your upper chest. We've been habitually walking around as a hunchback for so long that many of our good-posture muscles have shortened. Consistent practice can get them back in shape. As you are standing against the wall, with your hands by your sides, your thumbs should fall easily along the seams in your slacks or trousers. As your shoulders roll forward your hands will hang in front of your body and not along the sides.

6. **Place your head up on top** so that there is a straight line from the bottom of your ear to the top of your shoulder, to the top of your hip, and to the center of your foot. Keep your head level, eyes forward. If your body shape is deep through the thoracic cavity, putting your head against the wall may be too far back for you. The goal here is to have your body line up, whether standing or sitting. If the angle of the back of your chair is too far back, then don't lean all the way back. Push your lower back against it and then sit erect. Use good posture as your home position. Use it often, be consistent, and soon it will become your habit.

The second part of the Big 3 is the response of the **Neck and Shoulder Muscles.** Most of us are unaware that these muscles are inappropriately tensed much of the time. If you are experiencing frequent tension headaches, for example, your body is already telling you to relax those muscles. The next time you are experiencing a headache, do the good-posture check backed up against a wall, then execute calming breaths for several minutes. Most people report their tension headache is relieved in a few minutes. Neck and shoulder muscle is an awareness issue. Only by checking with a mirror, placing your hands on your neck, or using a buddy to check for your visible tension can you learn to feel when those muscles are tight and tense. You may be unaware that you tighten up when starting to inhale, when speaking, or when you've made a mistake. Some of us tighten up the neck and shoulder muscles before we make any other body movements, even walking. One of the biggest culprits is the habitual inhale. If your posture is not aligned, the muscles of the upper abdominal area and the thoracic area are simply not available to be used and you must tighten the neck and shoulder muscles to execute every inhale. At 12 to 18 inhales a minute, that's a lot of muscle tension. Like the home position with posture, this relaxation should be worked on until it becomes a habit. Once good posture is achieved and awareness of the additional tension is obvious, then we are ready to work on breathing.

The third part of the Big 3 is **Breath Support.** For proper breath support, you need to breathe using the muscles of your diaphragm which "attach at the base of the rib cage and hump up into the chest cavity." Dr. Hillman describes breathing as most efficient when the muscle activity and movement are around the torso, between the navel and the base of the sternum. The ribs should rise slightly and move sideways. You should keep the tummy firm from the navel down, expanding the rib cage sideways.

Hillman reminds us "to use the upper abdominal muscles without raising the shoulders or puffing out the lower abdominal cavity (our lungs are not down there)."

To obtain the most value from diaphragmatic breathing, use a deep cleansing breath: keep your posture erect and neck and shoulders relaxed (steps one and two of the Big 3). Now completely fill your lungs, allowing the air to enter through your nose, freely and easily expanding the rib cage sideways. Then, pursing your lips completely, empty your lungs by blowing the air out, keeping the exhaled air under pressure by using your diaphragm. To determine that you are getting the full benefit of a cleansing breath, place your hands around your abdominal area at the base of the ribs. You should feel this area moving in and out, and expanding sideways. Concentrate on slowing down your inhales and exhales. Practice by starting with 5-second inhales and 5-second exhales. Progress to 10-second inhales and 10-second exhales. A cleansing breath will make you both more relaxed and alert.

To help form the "breathing habit" in the classroom, begin class by taking a few minutes to breathe. You will find that The BREATHE System actually gives you an edge in practicing other learning strategies. The BREATHE System will be suggested as a strategy in several chapters. An overview of Dr. Hillman's BREATHE System is presented in Chapter 7. If you want to know more, you may want to read Chapter 7 of *Delivering Dynamic Presentations: Using Your Voice and Body for Impact,* Ralph E. Hillman, Allyn and Bacon, Boston, 1999. You may also log onto *http://thebreathesystem.com/* to find out more.

Survival Tips for Taking Notes and Reading Assignments

It's the first day of class. You know you need to take notes, but you're not sure how to record the important information. Examine the illustration titled "Notes That Save Time" on the next page. The label in the margin system is a great way to take notes and will be explained in detail in Chapter 5 of this book; meanwhile, know that your notes will be more useful if you set your paper up as illustrated on page 7. The left margin should be about $2\frac{1}{2}$ inches wide. Take your notes on the wide right-hand side. Don't write in full sentences. Write only the few words you need to help you remember what was said in class. Use the left margin to identify what each section of notes is about by writing a question or label in the margin as soon as you can after class. Use the bottoms of pages to summarize main ideas. Begin the semester taking notes like this, and when you get to the label in the margin system in a few weeks, you will be well on your way to learning how to process important information from lectures into your long-term memory.

Yes, I know that you already have reading assignments, too. Begin using the same system that you used for your notes. This is illustrated in the chart titled "Reading That Saves Time" on the following page. Chapter 5 will explain in more detail how to get the most from this system. Meanwhile, as you finish each paragraph, label the margin with a question and underline the answer before you go to the next paragraph. You will get more out of the assignment if you preview it first. Study the title, headings, bold print, summary, charts, graphs, and tables before you begin reading. Again, **keep up to date with your reading.**

Survival Tips for Taking Tests

Before You Begin

1. Preview the test before you answer anything. This gets you thinking about the material. Make sure to note the point value of each question. This will give you some ideas on budgeting your time.
2. Do a "mind dump." Using what you saw in the preview, make notes of anything you think you might forget. Write down things that you used in learning the material that might help you remember. Outline your answers to discussion questions.
3. Quickly calculate how much time you should allow for each section, according to the point value. (You don't want to spend thirty minutes on an essay question that counts only 5 points.)

LABEL IN THE MARGIN SYSTEM

Notes That Save Time

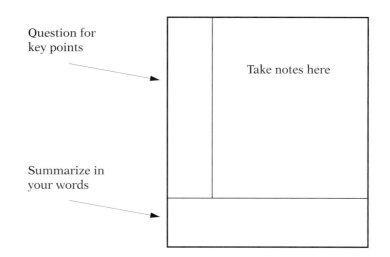

Question for
key points

Take notes here

Summarize in
your words

Reading That Saves Time

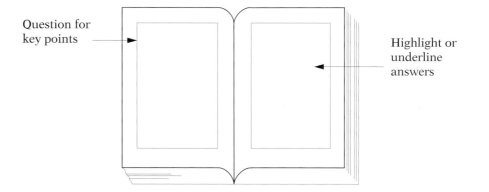

Question for
key points

Highlight or
underline
answers

Taking a Test

4. Read the directions. (Can more than one answer be correct? Are you penalized for guessing? And so on.) Never assume that you know what the directions say.

5. Answer the easy questions first. This will give you the confidence and momentum to get through the rest of the test. You are sure these answers are correct.

6. Go back to the difficult questions. While looking over the test and doing the easy questions, your subconscious mind will have been working on the answers to the harder ones. Also, later items on the test may give you useful or needed information for earlier items.

7. Answer all questions (unless you are penalized for wrong answers).

8. Ask the instructor to explain any items that are not clear. Do not ask for the answer, but phrase your question in a way that shows the instructor that you have the information but are not sure what the question is getting at.

9. Try to answer the questions from the instructor's point of view. Try to remember what the instructor emphasized and felt was important.

10. Use the margin to explain why you chose a particular answer if the question does not seem clear or if the answer seems ambiguous.

11. Circle key words in difficult questions. This will force you to focus on the central point.

12. Express difficult questions in your own words. Rephrasing can make it clear to you, but be sure you don't change the meaning of the question.

13. Use all of the time allotted for the test. If you have extra time, cover your answers and rework the questions.

Checklist for Essay Tests

Use the following as a guide when writing answers to discussion questions and as a checklist after you have written your answer.

_____   **1.** Do I really understand what the question asks me to do?

_____   **2.** Have I done any preliminary planning of my major points?

_____   **3.** Does the first sentence of my answer repeat the question and forcefully show the reader how I will develop my answer?

_____   **4.** Do the major points stand out?

_____   **5.** Are the major points supported with examples and facts?

_____   **6.** Are there clear transitions between the major points?

_____   **7.** Would someone who has not taken this class be able to understand the concept discussed in the way I explained it?

_____   **8.** Have I completely covered all major points needed to answer the question?

_____   **9.** Did I stick to the question?

_____   **10.** Have I concluded with a summary statement?

_____   **11.** Did I proofread for misspelled words, sentence fragments, run-on sentences, comma splices, subject/verb or pronoun/antecedent agreement errors, and other errors that might prevent the reader from understanding what I have written?

_____   **12.** Is my handwriting readable, and have I left enough space for comments or additions?

A Dozen Reasons to Review a Returned Test

1. Check the point total to make sure it is right. Look for mistakes in grading.

2. Know what questions you missed and why you missed them. The reason you missed these questions is often as important as the answer in terms of your performance on the next test.

3. Study the instructor's comments especially for essay questions so that you will know what is expected next time.

4. Figure out what kinds of questions (including tricky questions) the instructor likes to use.

5. See if the questions came from the text or the lecture. Concentrate more on that source when you study for the next exam.

6. Correct and understand what you missed. This is information you need to know. It may appear on a later test or the final.

7. Determine which type of questions you missed so you can review strategies for that type.

8. Review to get an idea about what kind of test the instructor may give next time.

9. Review to put information back into your long-term memory.

10. Ask questions while the test is fresh in your mind.

11. Review how you studied for the exam. Look for better ways.

12. Reviewing gives you a good reason to talk to your professors and let them know you want to improve.

Obtaining Your Technology Survival Tools

There was a time when you could begin college classes without needing technology any more complicated than a typewriter. Those days are gone. Here is the very least you should consider.

1. **Obtain an e-mail account.** You will need it for many of your classes for assignments and communicating with your professors and classmates. (It's also a cheap way to keep in touch with family and friends.) Ask your professor or advisor *now* what's involved in getting an e-mail account through your college. This may be as important as buying your textbooks.

2. **Find where computers are available to access the Internet and to use for assignments.** Are there computer labs on campus? Where are they located? What hours are they open? What's the best way to access the Internet on campus? Is computer use included in your tuition? If you live off campus and have your own computer, how do you access computer technology on campus?

3. If you are scared silly by your lack of computer skills, **find out where you can learn the basics.** Are there classes available? Are there classmates or instructors who will help you? You don't have to be a computer expert to use your class homepage on the Net or to e-mail your professor. Admit that you need help if you do, and don't look for excuses.

4. Ask each of your professors if the class has a **homepage** on-line. Many classes will have the syllabus, assignments, class notes, practice tests, supplementary materials, and the like on-line. Using the homepage for your class is a good way to learn the basics. Your college will have a homepage even if your class does not. Begin your on-line exploration immediately.

5. Do you need other technology tools such as a graphing calculator?

Jensen's Equation for Optimal Learning

When educators speak of learning, sometimes they emphasize one or two strategies as important. Neuroscientist and educator Eric Jensen synthesizes the finding of brain and learning research by reminding us there are many things we need to consider when seeking strategies for learning. The following equation lists areas you need to consider if you want to truly learn something.

Jensen's Equation for Optimal Learning

Personal History
(beliefs, experiences, values, knowledge)

+

Present Circumstances
(environment, feelings, people, context, goals, moods)

+

Input (5 senses)
(visual, auditory, kinesthetic, olfactory, or gustatory)

+

Processing
(learning preference)
states, left/right hemisphere, abstract or concrete)

+

Meaning
(connecting experience, data and stimuli to form conclusions and create patterns that give our lives meaning)

+

Responses (7 intelligences)
(verbal-linguistic, spatial, bodily kinesthetic, musical-rhythmic, mathematical-logical, intrapersonal, interpersonal)

=

Optimal Learning

Source: Eric Jensen, *Super Teaching*, San Diego, The Brain Store, Inc., 1998.

Assignment Log

Name _____

You may find it helpful to keep up with your daily grade in this study skills class by using the following sheet. Record the quiz or assignment requested to be turned in, along with the date due. Check (✓) whether you turned it in or not. When it is returned, record possible points *and* points that you received. Your daily average is determined by dividing the points you have earned by the points possible.

Assignment	Date Due	✓	Points Possible	Points Earned

Make sure you know how the grade for each assignment or test is derived. Check your syllabus to see how your final grade is determined.

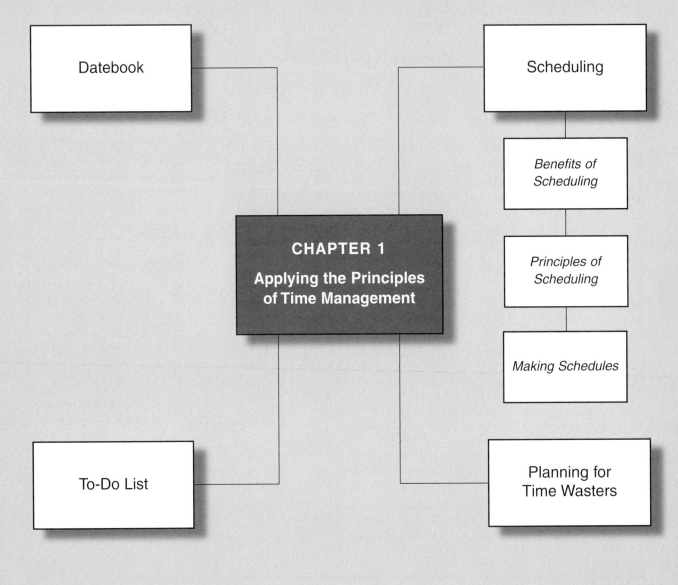

Datebook

Scheduling

Benefits of Scheduling

Principles of Scheduling

Making Schedules

CHAPTER 1

Applying the Principles of Time Management

To-Do List

Planning for Time Wasters

CHAPTER 1

Applying the Principles of Time Management

Now that you have started college, do you feel as though you have been caught in a whirlwind? Do you wonder where you will find the time to get everything done? Don't professors know you have a life? Time management is a critical issue for college students; how smart students are is less important to their success than how they manage their time. The demands on your time may be entirely different from anything you have previously experienced, and these demands on your time will force you to make difficult decisions. Most professors agree that you can count on at least two hours of outside work for every hour you are in class. Many add that those two hours of work may earn you only a C. Some classes require more time. How many hours are you taking? What other responsibilities do you have? What are you willing to give up in order to be a successful college student? There is just so much time. You can't continue to do all the things you used to do and add the job of being a college student without giving up something. You also can't have more than twenty-four hours in a day. **You can, however, make extra time in two ways: by doing the same task in less time and by making use of time that you previously wasted.** Throughout this course you will be seeking ways to do things not only faster but also more efficiently. One definition of study skills is finding ways to do things better in less time. However, few of the study strategies you will learn will work for you if you don't have time to use them.

The cardinal rule of time management is to *always carry pocket work*. Always have something that you can do while waiting. Make flash cards of what you need to study for an upcoming test. Make copies of homework assignments or just be sure to have a book with you. Those wasted ten, fifteen, or twenty minutes add up. And you will discover later that you usually learn more in short sessions than in longer ones. Program your mind; make it a habit to use wait time. The second most important thing is to *carry a date book*. You may think you will remember what your assignment is and when it is due, but you can be sure only by writing it down.

Let's quickly examine your present situation.

How many hours are you taking? Multiply those hours by two and add to the number of hours you are taking. (If you are taking 15 hours and study a minimum of 2 hours for each hour you are in class, that's 45 hours.) _____ These are the hours you are adding to your present responsibilities. Is there enough time to be successful?

List some things that you are willing to give up or spend less time on now that you are in college.

Give some examples of time wasted that you could fill with pocket work.

Purchase a date book today. In it, write your specific plans for tomorrow.

Critical Thinking About **Time Management**

Quarterback Peyton Manning uses a good analogy with money and time management that's worth thinking about before you work on your time-management strategies. Imagine, he says, that someone put $1,440 into your bank account each day with these stipulations:

1. There can be nothing left at the end of the day.

2. You lose what you fail to invest in worthwhile work.

What would you do?

You have, in fact, been given this. Instead of dollars, you have been given 1,440 minutes each day, and those same stipulations apply. You have no minutes left at the end of the day, and those not spent on worthwhile pursuits are pretty much lost.

What will you do?

Why is this a good analogy?

How do you determine what is worthwhile?

Scheduling: The Foundation of Time Management

Because many of you may never have been in a situation that required scheduling, you may be skeptical about the necessity for doing it. But the truth is, college students are too busy to leave things to chance. There may be other times in your life when you can get by without having a schedule of some sort, but the balancing act most college students are forced to perform makes it difficult to survive without a schedule. In fact, once you get used to being in control of your time, you'll probably never go back to random day-to-day living. For those who are still skeptical about the usefulness of a schedule, what follows is a list of the benefits of scheduling you may not have considered.

Benefits of Scheduling

1. Scheduling helps you avoid one of the great time wasters, procrastination, because it gives you a set time to accomplish each task. It gets you started and helps you avoid putting off doing things that you dislike.

2. Scheduling keeps you up to date and helps to avoid last-minute cramming. By keeping up to date and studying things as you come to them, you will learn much more efficiently.

3. Scheduling things that you need to do actually creates time to do things that you want to do. As a college student, you must be careful to keep a balance in your life. You need to have time for things other than studying. Scheduling takes away the guilt because it allows you to know you have a time for study and a time for play.

4. Scheduling keeps you in control. You are the creator of your schedule. You set your priorities and times to do things.

5. Having a schedule saves time. Yes, it takes time to devise a schedule, but that time is repaid many times over. Your schedule is a guide telling you what to do next and assuring you that everything will get done. Studying the same subject at the same time, in the same place, programs your mind to concentrate on that subject, and you complete your studying more quickly and more efficiently. That's what study skills are all about. You are seeking ways to study faster and better.

Despite these benefits, many students are still reluctant to use scheduling. Remember, however, that the job of being a college student is like no other job you've ever had. Scheduling may be your only means of surviving. At least try scheduling, and choose the aspects of it that help you the most. Let's now examine some basic principles of scheduling so you get the full benefit of this procedure.

Principles of Scheduling

1. **Make use of daylight hours.** Research shows that each hour used for study during the day is equal to one and a half hours at night. This means trying to make use of free hours during the school day. These are the most effective yet most often wasted hours.

2. **Study before a class in which discussion is required or pop quizzes are frequently given.** The material will be fresh in your mind.

3. **Study immediately after lecture classes.** You can enhance your retention and understanding by studying right after class. Use this time to fill in gaps in your notes and to review information you have just learned. When you become more familiar with the label in the margin system for taking notes and processing lecture material, you will find that the hours immediately after class are perfect for labeling your notes and that using them will save you valuable time. You will be able to complete your assignments faster and more efficiently because you don't have to refocus your concentration. (Do you see why scheduling back-to-back classes is a mistake?)

4. **Study at the same time every day.** You should have certain hours set aside for study that you treat the same as class. Having the same study time five days a week will soon become habit and therefore easier to follow. Since the mind is programmed by routine, it will be easier to get started and to concentrate on the task at hand. Studying in the same place also aids concentration. If you have family responsibilities, it's best to schedule your study time while you are on campus, if at all possible. There are just too many things at home that could interfere. If you have school-aged children, setting a time for everyone to study is a good idea, but you will accomplish even more if you can schedule study time on campus as if it were a class.

5. **Plan enough time to study.** The rule of thumb that you should study two hours for every hour you are in class is only a guide. Depending on your background or experience or the difficulty of the class, you may need to allow more. Start out by studying for two hours, but adjust according to your need.

6. **Space your study periods.** A study period of fifty to ninety minutes at a time for each subject is probably most efficient. You should then take a break for ten to fifteen minutes. Studying for longer periods of time often becomes counterproductive.

7. **List activities according to priorities.** By putting first things first, you will get the most important things done on time.

8. **Study during your prime time.** We all have daily cycles of alertness and sluggishness. If your work, classes, and circumstances permit, make use of this knowledge: Schedule your hardest subject at your most alert time, and schedule less demanding tasks during the day when you are less productive than you'd like to be.

9. **Leave unscheduled time for flexibility.** Packing your schedule with too many details will almost ensure its failure. Lack of flexibility is the major reason why students don't follow schedules.

10. **Analyze your use of time.** One cause of getting behind in college is failure to make use of short periods of time. By keeping a time log, you can see where you are currently wasting time. As noted previously, the time between classes and during the school day is the time most often wasted, even though it is the most efficient time to use for studying. Your time log may reveal a waste as simple as not responding to your alarm clock the first time or napping in the afternoon after classes.

Time Log Exercise

In order to use your time most effectively, it is necessary to analyze honestly how you normally use your time. Monitoring your time for a typical week should give you a basis for this analysis.

Directions: Carefully fill in the following chart each day to account for what you did each hour. You do not have to stop each hour to fill it in, but you will probably want to do it several times a day. Don't depend on your memory at the end of the day. In addition to noting what you did, indicate your alertness by using the following symbols:

+ "I really feel sharp!"   0 "I am functioning normally."   — "I am sluggish."

At the end of five days, write an analysis of your use of time and make a schedule that reflects the most efficient use of your time. How well do you know yourself? In the space below, predict what you think you will discover when you use the time log. For example, will you discover that you waste too much time napping or watching TV? Are your classes scheduled too close together? Is your study always too late at night?

Predictions

1. _____

2. _____

3. _____

4. _____

5. _____

Name _____

Time Log _____

Time	Day 1 Day ___ Date ___	+	0	–	Day 2 Day ___ Date ___	+	0	–	Day 3 Day ___ Date ___	+	0	–	Day 4 Day ___ Date ___	+	0	–	Day 5 Day ___ Date ___	+	0	–
6–7 A.M.																				
7–8 A.M.																				
8–9 A.M.																				
9–10 A.M.																				
10–11 A.M.																				
11–noon																				
Noon–1 P.M.																				
1–2 P.M.																				
2–3 P.M.																				
3–4 P.M.																				
4–5 P.M.																				
5–6 P.M.																				
6–7 P.M.																				
7–8 P.M.																				
8–9 P.M.																				
9–10 P.M.																				
10–11 P.M.																				
11–midnight																				

Time Log Analysis

After keeping the log for at least five days, answer the following:

1. Using your time monitor, fill in the chart below.

   This past week I:

   Slept _____ hours

   Attended or traveled to class _____ hours

   Ate meals _____ hours

   Worked at a job _____ hours

   Studied _____ hours

   Played _____ hours

   Was involved in athletics _____ hours

   Other _____ hours

2. At what times were you really sharp? _____

3. At what times were you the most sluggish? _____

4. What did you discover about your use of time? _____

Planning a Master Schedule

A master schedule should be made every time you have a major change in your use of time; for example, at the beginning of each semester or when you get a new job. *Use the list below and the master schedule worksheet on the following page to plan for this semester.*

1. First and foremost, note those activities for which *you have no choice about when to do them:* classes, labs, job, picking up children at school, commuting, weekly meetings.

2. Count the number of blank spaces. Yes, include Saturday and Sunday. Write this number at the bottom of the master schedule. These are the hours in which *you can choose what you do.* Note that the master schedule accounts for only the hours between 7 A.M. and midnight. You can create more choices by getting up earlier or accounting for hours after midnight.

3. Now, note in those blank spaces the activities that *you need to do but have a choice about when to do them.* Assuming that your first priority is school, begin there. For each three-hour class that you are taking, fill in three spaces with study time for that particular course. Don't just write *Study.* Write *Study math.* Make sure that you use what you already know about scheduling to make wise choices. Use daylight hours. Study right after a lecture class or right before a recitation-type class. *Treat these times as if they were classes,* as a part of your job! Miss them only for the same reason you might miss class or work. Even if you don't have homework to do, use these times to review or work ahead. This allows you one hour of study treated like a class for every hour you are in class. But for most classes you will probably need at least two, so also schedule enough additional hours of study time to total two hours of study for each hour you are in class. Scheduling one hour that is treated like a class for a specific subject and one hour at another time allows you to be more flexible and still establish routine study times.

4. Now, note the other things that you need to do: recreation, shopping, meeting with friends, time with family, laundry, cooking, eating, and so on.

5. Any remaining blanks are for whatever comes up without guilt!

brain byte

Not managing your time can, in fact, affect not only what you have time to learn, but also the types of learning that can take place. When a person is relaxed and in control, the parts of the brain that allow creativity, analysis, synthesis, planning, and problem solving are active. However, when a learner feels he is not in control, these parts of the brain shut down and the only learning possible is rote memorization or simple learning based on habit or instinct.

Master Schedule Worksheet

	Sun	Mon	Tue	Wed	Thu	Fri	Sat
7–8							
8–9							
9–10							
10–11							
11–12							
12–1							
1–2							
2–3							
3–4							
4–5							
5–6							
6–7							
7–8							
8–9							
9–10							
10–11							
11–12							

Putting Your Master Schedule into Practice

Now you are ready to make out a master schedule for the semester. You will probably need to continue to make a weekly and daily checklist also. Study your master schedule. Did you consider the following things in your planning?

Have you used daylight hours for studying? (For most people, these are more effective than nighttime hours.)

Have you scheduled study time immediately before classes?

Have you scheduled study time immediately after classes?

Have you scheduled either your most difficult class or your most difficult studying when you are the sharpest?

Have you scheduled either relaxation or exercise when you are the most sluggish?

Have you scheduled enough sleep?

Have you scheduled time for eating well-balanced meals?

Have you considered your work schedule?

Have you considered travel time?

Do you have a regularly scheduled study time for each class (even if you have nothing due for the next class)?

What will you do differently when you schedule your classes next semester?

Now it's time to try what you planned to see if it will really work. Use your planned master schedule to fill in the time-management log on the next two pages. There is a column for what you planned to do and one for what you did in reality. Keep the log for a week. Then make adjustments to your master schedule as needed. There is a clean master schedule following the exercise if you need to make adjustments.

Time Management

	Monday		Tuesday		Wednesday		Thursday	
	Planned	*Reality*	*Planned*	*Reality*	*Planned*	*Reality*	*Planned*	*Reality*
7 A.M.								
8 A.M.								
9 A.M.								
10 A.M.								
11 A.M.								
12 noon								
1 P.M.								
2 P.M.								
3 P.M.								
4 P.M.								
5 P.M.								
6 P.M.								
7 P.M.								
8 P.M.								
9 P.M.								
10 P.M.								
11 P.M.								
12 midnight								

Notes: _____

Time Management (cont'd)

	Friday		Saturday		Sunday	
	Planned	*Reality*	*Planned*	*Reality*	*Planned*	*Reality*
7 A.M.						
8 A.M.						
9 A.M.						
10 A.M.						
11 A.M.						
12 noon						
1 P.M.						
2 P.M.						
3 P.M.						
4 P.M.						
5 P.M.						
6 P.M.						
7 P.M.						
8 P.M.						
9 P.M.						
10 P.M.						
11 P.M.						
12 midnight						

Notes: _____

Master Schedule

Now you are ready to make out a master schedule for the semester. You will probably need to continue to make a weekly and daily checklist also.

	Sun	Mon	Tue	Wed	Thu	Fri	Sat
7–8							
8–9							
9–10							
10–11							
11–12							
12–1							
1–2							
2–3							
3–4							
4–5							
5–6							
6–7							
7–8							
8–9							
9–10							
10–11							
11–12							

Date Book

Your master schedule is your guide in planning, but you will need at least two other time-management scheduling tools. The first is your date book (also called an appointment book or assignment book). You should keep it with you at all times and write your assignments for each class each day. Consult it before you make any commitments of your time. Remember, this is your job. You are the manager of your time. (The manager of any efficiently run business would also schedule appointments.) Even though you may have a syllabus for each class, you need to bring your assignments for all your classes together in one place so that you can see all that you have to do and set priorities. Early in the semester you should examine the syllabus for each class and record the dates for major tests and assignments. This way, you know if you have two or three major tests or assignments due on the same day and can do some planning. Your date book will help you stay organized. In addition to assignments and appointments, you can keep track of phone numbers, addresses, and other important information all in one place. Most college bookstores will have several types of date books. Choose one that is easy to keep up with. You should not be without your date book any more than you would be without your wallet, watch, or ID card.

To-Do List

The second managing tool is your daily schedule, or to-do list. The easiest way to construct a daily to-do list is this: on an index card, before you go to bed at night or as soon as you get up, make a list of everything you want to accomplish during the day. That's the easy part! You also want to prioritize the things you need to do. Look over your list and decide which items *absolutely must* be done. These are your first priority. The second order of importance might be those things which *should* be done. The third order might be those things which you *would like to do* but which could be put off. You can also have a category for routine things. You can use any system you want to label your priorities. Some students color-code with highlighters; others use a 1, 2, 3 or A, B, C system to indicate importance. Since you will seldom make your list in order of importance, marking priorities is a must. Instead of an index card, you may want to make copies of the chart below and use it as your to-do list. Develop the habit of making the same type of list each day, and it will become easy and routine.

To-Do List **For Day**_____ **Date** _____

Priority Code	Job to Be Done	Time	Check When Completed

Time Wasters: Plan Your Attack

Because you are so busy as a college student, it is important that you stay in control. This does not mean you can't be flexible, but it does mean you need to have a plan. By analyzing your master schedule and time log, you will get some idea of just how flexible you can be. If you have a job, a family, or other responsibilities, you will have less time with which to be flexible. If something unexpected comes up at a time you already have scheduled, try to trade off hours and plan when you can accomplish your originally scheduled task. You want to be careful not to waste time doing something you really didn't want or need to do. On page 31 is a list of frequent time wasters for college students. There is a difference between allowing time to do these things and having them interfere with things you need to accomplish. Plan how you will avoid such time wasters should they occur. Probably the most frequent time waster is visitors dropping in unexpectedly, especially if you study in your dorm room, apartment, or home. One logical solution is to study elsewhere. Can you think of other solutions?

Afternoon naps are another real hazard for college students. Remember, what takes you an hour to do in the daytime may take you an hour and a half at night. Many students use naps as a form of procrastination. Getting enough sleep at night is one solution.

Virtual Field Trip:
Procrastination and Time Management

This is the first of many Virtual Field Trips you will take during this course. The web site for Virtual Field Trip Central is http://collegesurvival.college.hmco.com/students and select "Hopper," or go to http://www.mtsu.edu/~studskl/3evirtualfieldtrips.html. On this site you will find both the page number in *Practicing College Learning Strategies,* third ed., and a trip title. Your destination and itinerary will be just a click away. Bookmark or add this site to your Favorites for easy access.

Study the list in the first column. Give at least two possible plans in the second column to combat each time waster.

Time Waster	Plan A and Plan B What to Do When This Occurs
Drop-in visitors	Plan A Plan B
Phone interruptions	Plan A Plan B
TV	Plan A Plan B
Afternoon naps	Plan A Plan B
Family or friends making demands	Plan A Plan B
Surfing the Net	Plan A Plan B
Your biggest time waster not mentioned	Plan A Plan B

Critical Thinking About **Prioritizing Exercise**

For this exercise you need a partner or a group of three or four. Choose **either** John **or** Mary. It is not uncommon to find yourselves in a situation similar to John's or Mary's. Study the things John or Mary needs to do. Prioritize and rank each item in the order you think it should be accomplished. Number the items from one to ten. One is the item that should be done first.

John's To-Do List

_____ John's roommate just broke up with his girlfriend—needs comforting.

_____ 500-word English paper due tomorrow afternoon.

_____ Psychology exam tomorrow morning—is on the syllabus.

_____ Book report due tomorrow in history. He's read part of the book, but he's not really sure what's it about.

_____ It's his mom's birthday. He promised to go to dinner.

_____ Biology test announced as he left class today.

_____ No clean shirts. He hasn't done laundry in two weeks.

_____ History paper due in two days, but he has tickets to the big basketball game tomorrow and a date with that someone he's been wanting to date all term.

_____ It's not his day to work, but his boss wants him to come in for a couple of hours (probably means all night).

_____ Party tonight with a live band and free food.

Mary's To-Do List

_____ 500-word English paper due tomorrow afternoon.

_____ Psychology exam tomorrow morning—is on the syllabus.

_____ Book report due tomorrow in history. She's read part of the book, but she's not really sure what it's about.

_____ Son is having trouble with his math homework.

_____ Tomorrow is gym day and daughter's gym clothes are dirty.

_____ Biology test announced as she left class today.

_____ Out of milk and stuff for school lunches.

_____ Promised to help desperate friend study for algebra test.

_____ Daughter has spelling test.

_____ Message on answering machine to come in for part-time job interview.

1. What is your group's rationalization for the order they selected?

2. What are some ways John or Mary could have avoided letting so many things pile up?

3. Suggest a plan for managing upcoming commitments and assignments.

 ## Summary

If you have been using the label in the margin system suggested in the Survival Kit, you probably already have the following questions labeled and the answers underlined in your textbook. This is a good check to see if you grasped the major points of the chapter. To make a useful study summary sheet, fill in the following. When you have written your answers, cover them and see if you can recite in your own words the answer to each question. Each chapter will end with summary questions.

What are two ways to make extra time?

1.

2.

What is the cardinal rule of time management (give some examples)?

▶

What is the second most important thing to do when managing time?

▶

What is the foundation of time management?

▶

Explain the significance of the number 1,440 when dealing with time management.

▶

What are five benefits of scheduling?

1.

2.

3.

4.

5.

What are ten principles of good scheduling?

1.

2.

3.

4.

5.

6.

7.

8.

9.

10.

Explain how to create a master schedule.

▶

What are two tools in addition to your master schedule that are necessary in managing your time?

1.

2.

Name your three biggest time wasters and briefly explain your plan to combat them.

1.

2.

3.

■ ■ **What'ſ Your Advice?**

Philip is a junior at a major university. He is 24 years old, not married, and he lives in an apartment near campus with three other students. He does most of his studying there. This semester he is taking fifteen credit hours. He works twenty hours a week. He has flexible work hours and he chose to work on Monday, Wednesday, and Friday and schedule his classes on Tuesday and Thursday. He really wants to do well in school, but he has struggled to make Cs in his classes. He says he reads extremely slowly and simply doesn't have time to read everything his instructors assign. What advice would you give Philip?

Write your answer in paragraph form. Address it to Philip and be specific in your advice.

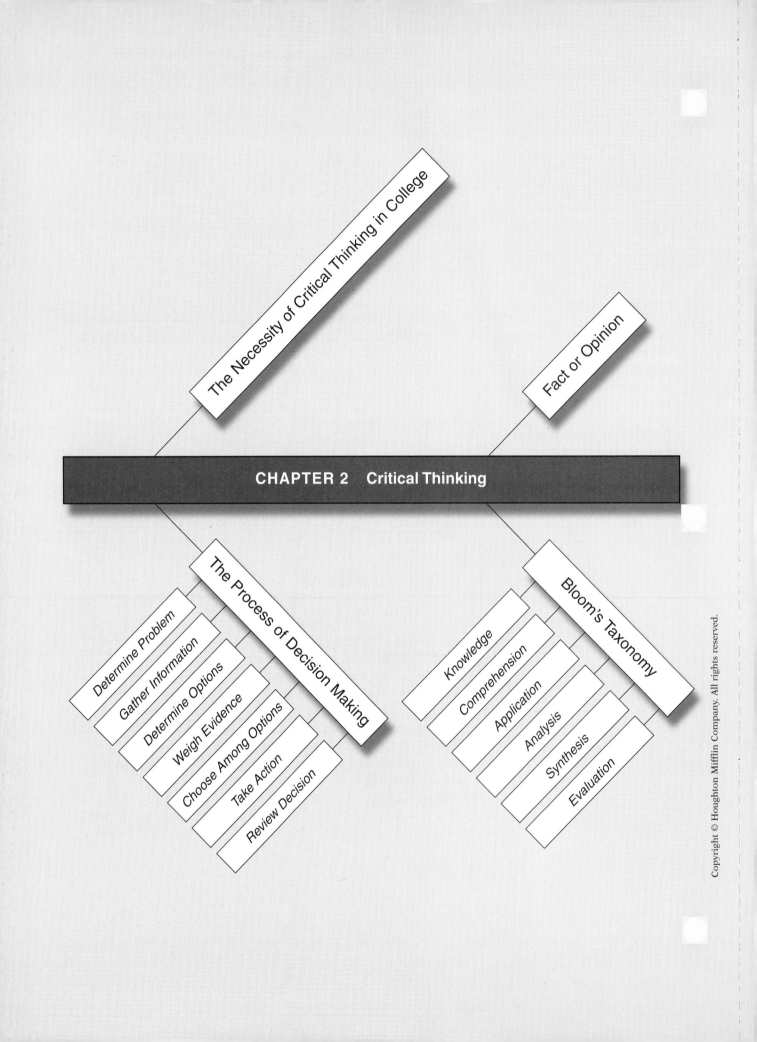

The Necessity of Critical Thinking in College

Fact or Opinion

CHAPTER 2   Critical Thinking

The Process of Decision Making

Determine Problem

Gather Information

Determine Options

Weigh Evidence

Choose Among Options

Take Action

Review Decision

Bloom's Taxonomy

Knowledge

Comprehension

Application

Analysis

Synthesis

Evaluation

CHAPTER 2

Critical Thinking

The Survival Kit has given you some concrete things to do until you can begin to learn and practice in depth the essential skills you need to be successful in college and, indeed, beyond college. You have begun to be in control of your time. Your primary job as a college student is to process information. In order to do your job well, you need to understand how your brain processes information. It will be necessary for you to take information from lectures and make that information yours. You want to grasp what you read and process it so that you own it. A good place to begin learning how to do this is with a brief discussion of critical thinking. The thinking demanded of college students goes far beyond the memorization of facts. You will meet some concepts of critical thinking here and then encounter them throughout the text. While you are developing basic skills in taking notes, reading textbooks, and taking tests, you will be simultaneously developing critical thinking skills that form the core of higher education and educated thinking.

The Necessity of Critical Thinking

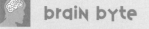 brain byte

Nobel Laureate Herbert Simon states that the meaning of "knowing" has shifted from being able to remember and repeat information to being able to find and use it.

There is a great deal of difference in learning the answer to a question and analyzing the implications of the answer, synthesizing and evaluating what you have learned, and applying what you have learned. Problem solving, critically analyzing a situation for the best solution, and creatively finding an answer to the problem are skills that involve *thinking*. Thinking is a skill, and like other skills, it is learned and improved with practice. In thinking, the focus is not on the final answer but on the process of getting the answer. In a previous history class you may have learned the dates of the Spanish-American War and the causes of that war. A *thinking* problem, however, is to analyze how our country might be different if the war had not occurred. Most of the courses you will take in college involve not just learning but the development of keen thinking skills. A critical thinker is constantly asking questions, trying to distinguish between fact and opinion. A critical thinker analyzes all sides of an issue to find more in the situation than the obvious. And a critical thinker makes assertions built on sound logic and solid evidence.

37

It is important to use critical thinking when learning and processing new information, but it is also necessary to use critical thinking in making decisions about when, where, and how to study, managing your time, and setting goals. You will use critical thinking when you take notes in class, read textbooks, and take tests. You will use critical thinking in determining the validity of an Internet or library source, the best way to complete assignments, or how to get along with your professor or classmates. You will need to use critical thinking to determine what you believe and what's important to you. And although not a part of this study skills text but certainly a major factor in your success at college, you will need to use critical thinking in your decisions about partying, drinking, taking drugs, and entering and maintaining relationships. Students seldom fail because they aren't smart enough; they more often fail because they make poor decisions or fail to seek solutions to problems. The critical thinking skills you develop will not only make you a better student; they will make you a better employee or employer, a better spouse or parent. Critical thinking is a life skill. The important decisions you make in your life will not be based on memorizing the "right answer." Each new situation demands questioning, analyzing, and evaluating. This is not some revolutionary new idea to you. But, you can use the opportunities this course provides to practice and fine-tune your critical thinking.

The Process of Decision Making

By thinking critically, you will find that your decisions are not made randomly. Rather they follow a pattern. You will first determine exactly what the problem is. Second, you will gather any information necessary for you to make an informed decision. The third step is to determine what your options are. A major decision seldom has one solution. There's always another way. Fourth, you will weigh the evidence. Ask all the "what ifs." You will then—fifth—make a choice among your options. The sixth step is to take action. Your action will be based on informed critical thinking . After you have taken action, you will review your decision and examine the consequences. Many times you may begin the process all over when your decision creates a consequence that requires a decision!

Walk yourself through the decision-making process by reflecting on your decision to come to this college at this time.

What were some of the problems?

Where did you gather information? What types of information did you gather?

What options became apparent?

What was some of the evidence you weighed?

What were some of your options?

What specific action did you take?

What have the consequences of that action been?

So now, what is the problem?

Your critical thinking about a decision may look something like this:

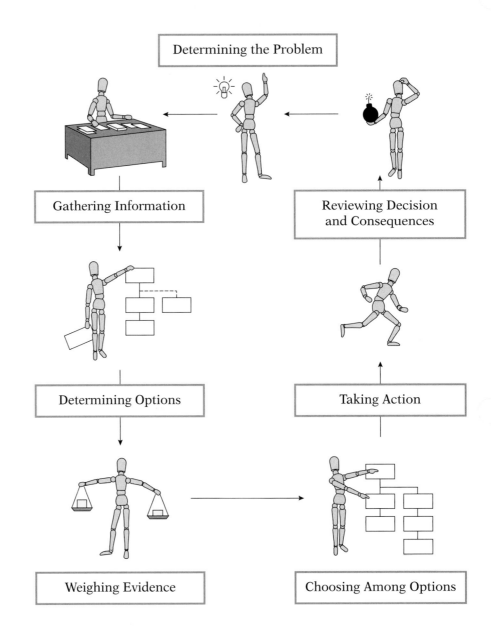

Begin with this problem.

You want to earn an A in this class.
Gather the information. List specific things you must do to earn an A.
What are your options?
What evidence is there that they will earn an A?
What options do you choose?
Set goals for those options and take action.

Thinking About Thinking

1. Describe the process of your thinking in both choosing to come to college and choosing this college over other colleges. You may want to include among other things: What facts did you gather? What opinions did you weigh? What issues were important to you?

 brain byte

In *Human Brain and Human Learning,* Leslie Hart suggests that if we are to expand our knowledge, we should seek alternative methods, multiple answers, critical thinking, and creative insights. The process is often more important than the end result.

2. You are an employer (set up your own situation). Give some examples of why you would want your employees to have developed good thinking skills.

3. Name four specific decisions you will have to make in the next several years that will require the use of critical thinking skills.

4. Name two problems you now have that you might solve using critical thinking skills.

5. Write a short paragraph in which you describe a past situation in which you wish your thinking skills had been better.

Fact and Opinion

A crucial part of critical thinking is distinguishing between fact and opinion. A fact is something that is true no matter what we think about it. A fact can be verified. Opinions, on the other hand, are personal prejudices. Our opinions should be based on fact and supported by fact, but should not be confused with fact.

Fact	18,000 students attend this university.
Opinion	The campus is too crowded.
Fact	Teenage pregnancies are at an all-time high.
Opinion	Sex education should begin in elementary school.

Exercise.   Read the following statements. Are they fact or opinion? In the blank to the left mark F for fact and O for opinion. If the statement is opinion, decide what kind of facts are needed to support that opinion.

_____ 1. Fair play is a thing of the past.

_____ 2. Mickey Mantle was the strongest switch hitter in baseball history.

_____ 3. During his career, Mantle hit 536 home runs.

_____ 4. Grades do not encourage learning.

_____ 5. Human life is not valued in a technological society.

_____ 6. The average car traveling at 57 miles per hour gets only two-thirds the gas mileage of a car moving at 50 miles per hour.

_____ 7. It is impossible to commit suicide by holding one's breath.

_____ 8. The society in the United States is violent.

_____ 9. A giraffe can go without water longer than a camel can.

_____ 10. The attention that the news media gives to criminals contributes to crime.

_____ 11. The visitation rules in the dorm are unfair.

_____ 12. We should drink less cola.

_____ 13. Eighteen ounces of an average cola drink contain as much caffeine as a cup of coffee.

_____ 14. We should ban smoking in public places.

_____ 15. In San Salvador, drunk drivers are punished with death before a firing squad.

_____ 16. The amount of nicotine the average pack-a-day smoker inhales a week—400 milligrams—would kill a person instantly if it were taken all at once.

_____ 17. The need to develop alternative energy sources is critical.

_____ 18. Television is a positive cultural force in the United States.

_____ 19. If the current rate of inflation continues, a worker making $7 an hour in 2000 will make $4,799 an hour in the year 2090.

_____ 20. There is an overemphasis on sports on college campuses.

A critical thinker, when trying to determine whether something is fact or opinion, asks questions. What was the source of information? Was the source of information an authority? Was the information accurate? Can it be substantiated? Where? Is the information current? Look back over the twenty statements on page 42. Do any that you marked as facts need more evidence? Place a question mark beside any that you think must be verified further. Be sure to explain what verification each needs.

Levels of Learning: Bloom's Taxonomy

When discussing critical thinking, learning experts usually categorize levels of thinking. One of the most influential models is *Bloom's Taxonomy of Higher Thinking.** The level or depth of your learning will probably depend on several factors. Your interest in learning the material and the urgency of your need to use or master it are two important factors. Bloom asserts that you must master one level before you can move on to the next. You can use Bloom's taxonomy as a road map of sorts to see where you are going with your thinking. In the next chapter you will consider ten memory principles and study habits. These memory principles are the core of learning strategies, and if you are going to be a successful college student, you should master these principles. You will experience the levels of learning of Bloom's taxonomy as you learn what the memory principles are and then use them to develop new study habits. According to Bloom:

1. The first level of learning is **knowledge.** You can know something without fully understanding it. The knowledge level is being able to make a list of something or to recognize it on a multiple-choice test, knowing it as fact. When you encounter the ten memory principles, the first thing you will do is memorize them so that you know the name and definition of each principle. You will see that you can easily do this without ever actually using the principles.
2. The second level of learning is **comprehension.** You understand the fact to the degree that you can explain it in your own words. You can translate or interpret it. Once you are able to list the memory principles, you will be able to explain them to someone. You will see that they are more than definitions. You will see that the principles explain how you personally can use your brain more efficiently.
3. The third level is **application.** With application, you find some practical use for the information and use it to solve problems. You will discover that you can use the memory principles to study faster and

brain byte

Brain Researcher Eric Jensen presents three factors that are critical for the learner to construct meaning.

Relevance:
activating an existing neural network
Emotion:
triggering chemical that strengthens learning
Context/Pattern:
recognizing patterns

*Bloom, B. S. (Ed.). (1959). Taxonomy of educational objectives: *The classification of educational goals. Handbook 1: Cognitive domain.* New York: David McKay Company.

better. You will be able to process information in less time and retain the information longer.

4. The fourth level is **analysis.** When you analyze, you break complex ideas into parts and see how the parts work together. With the memory principles, you will discover relationships between the various principles. You will see that there is a time and place to use certain principles, that some principles are best used in combination with other principles, and that some principles work better for you than others. You will see that different information and learning situations call for different combinations of memory principles. You can take the memory principles and develop a note-taking system or a textbook-reading system that uses a combination of memory principles that work for you. You will use analysis of the memory principles to determine the best time, place, and way for you to study.

5. The fifth level of Bloom's taxonomy is **synthesis.** When you synthesize, you make connections with things you already know. You are able to draw conclusions and make predictions. You will be able to take a specific learning situation and use the memory principles to make a plan for learning that is best suited for you and the information you need to learn. Summarizing a unit or predicting test questions are forms of synthesis. Using a note-taking system built on the memory principles in all of your classes is a way of using synthesis.

6. The sixth level of learning is **evaluation.** When you evaluate, you judge something's worth. Did the note-taking system work for you in history class or do you need to make adjustments? Did you use the right combination of memory principles to study for your psychology test or do you need to try a different combination?

When you first learn something, you can't be expected to jump to the sixth level. In order to master it, you have to know it, understand it, and apply it. This is why when you wait until the last minute to study for a test, you can do little more than memorize the information and then you are often caught short when the answer requires more depth.

You will continue to look at other aspects of critical thinking when you learn about taking notes, reading textbooks, studying for and taking tests, and doing research both in the library and on the Internet.

For a quick check of your understanding of levels of learning, list the level of learning that you think each of the following tasks involves.

Knowledge, Comprehension, Application, Analysis, Synthesis, Evaluation

_____ Changing a flat tire

_____ Finding the main idea of a paragraph

_____ Explaining a class lecture to a friend who was absent

_____ Summarizing an article

_____ Reducing a fraction to the lowest common denominator

_____ Finding the correct answer in a multiple-choice question

_____ Creating a webpage

_____ Appraising the damage on your wrecked car

_____ Listing the states and capitals

_____ Making an apple pie

_____ Comparison shopping for the best buy

_____ Writing an essay for English class

_____ Computing your grade point average

Virtual Field Trip:
Bloom's Taxonomy

Visit http://collegesurvival.college.hmco.com/students and select "Hopper," or go to http://www.mtsu.edu/~studskl/3evirtual-fieldtrips.html.

▪ Summary

To check to see if you grasped the major points of the chapter on critical thinking, do the following or answer the following questions:

List three characteristics of a critical thinker.

1.

2.

3.

What is the difference between fact and opinion?

▶

What are some important questions you should ask in trying to determine fact or opinion?

▶

List and explain the six levels of Bloom's taxonomy.

1.

2.

3.

4.

5.

6.

■ What's Your Advice?

Nenia is taking her first required history course at her university. She did very well in her history courses in high school and therefore was not worried about the first test. As she read each chapter, she made flash cards of dates, people, terms, and places. She even drew a time line so that she knew the sequence of events. She prepared a study plan and studied for several days before the test, including studying the night before. However, when she began her test, she found that she didn't know what to do. Instead of asking for dates, people, terms, and places, the questions were as follows:

- Compare and contrast the ways in which the Market Revolution affected middle-class white women and slave women.

- Describe the role that railroads played in sectional conflicts between 1850 and 1870.

- Trace the changes in Americans' expectations of government that occurred during the "Age of Anxiety," and explain what caused those changes.

- Compare and contrast the responses of Eisenhower, Kennedy, and Johnson to the Civil Rights movement.

- In your opinion, what was the true birthday of the United States: 1776, 1789, or 1812? Justify your answer.

What advice can you give to Nenia to prepare for her next test?

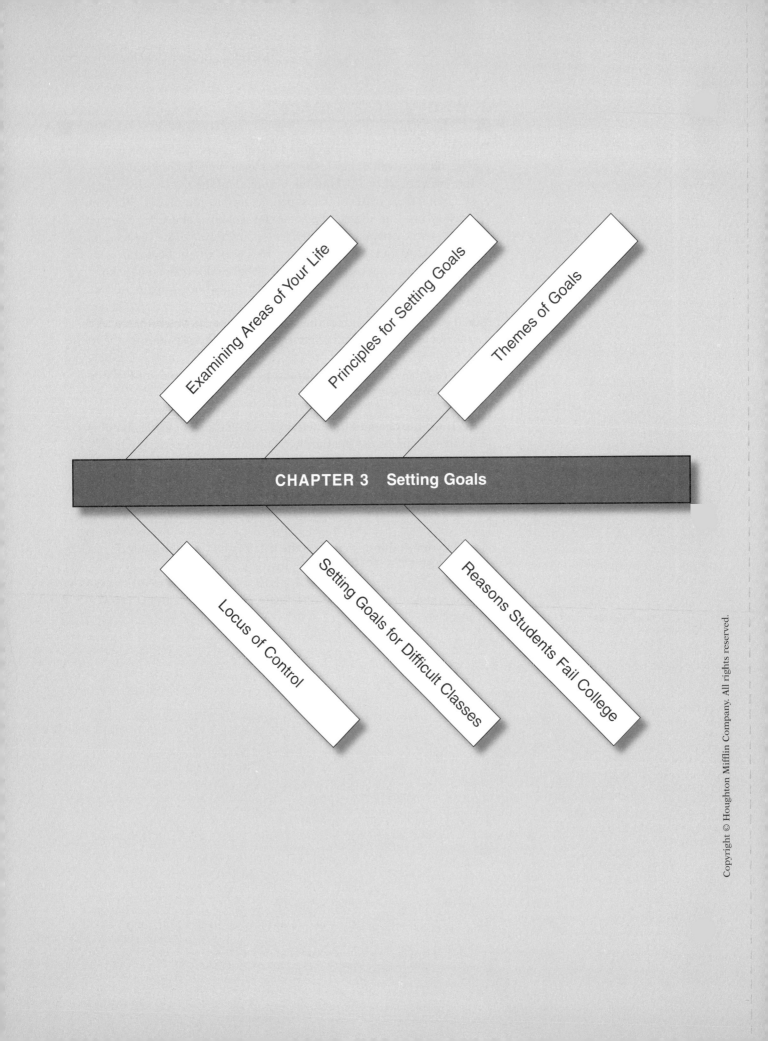

Examining Areas of Your Life

Principles for Setting Goals

Themes of Goals

CHAPTER 3   Setting Goals

Locus of Control

Setting Goals for Difficult Classes

Reasons Students Fail College

CHAPTER 3

Setting Goals

When you think about the skills you need to be successful in college, you probably think of skills in test taking, note taking, getting the main idea from textbooks, research, writing, memory, concentration, time management, or thinking. However, the driving force behind achieving all these skills is one we seldom think of as a skill at all. It is the skill used to set goals and priorities. If we are to become proficient at goal setting, we need to look at why we set goals, when we should set goals, and some ways to set useful goals.

Few of us really know specifically what we want out of life. And most of us don't spend time setting goals. We are too busy. We go with the flow and just let things happen to us. The truth is, however, we *can* make things happen. We have choices. The things that we spend our time, money, and emotional energy on are the things we make happen. This exercise was designed to make you think about you.

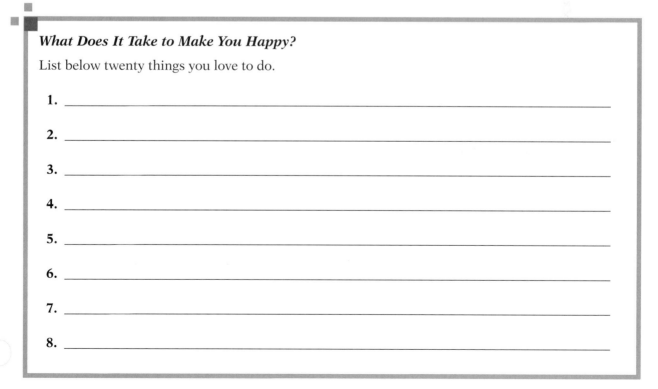

What Does It Take to Make You Happy?

List below twenty things you love to do.

1. _____

2. _____

3. _____

4. _____

5. _____

6. _____

7. _____

8. _____

9. _____

10. _____

11. _____

12. _____

13. _____

14. _____

15. _____

16. _____

17. _____

18. _____

19. _____

20. _____

Go back down your list and use the following codes for each item:

$	If it costs more than $10
A	For an activity that you prefer to do alone
P	For an activity that you prefer to do with people
AP	For an activity that can be done alone or with people
2	If this would not have been on your list two years ago
10	If you think this will make you happy ten years from now
M	If you think this might have been on your mother's list when she was your age
F	If you think this might have been on your father's list when he was your age

Personal analysis: Use another sheet of paper and write down what you have discovered about yourself.

Critical analysis: Explain why this exercise is relevant in a goal-setting chapter.

Why Have Goals?

Setting goals may be compared to target practice. You are attempting to hit the bull's-eye, and there is one way to ensure hitting the bull's-eye every time: shoot an arrow into the sky and just let it land anywhere, then locate the arrow and draw a bull's-eye around it. You will, of course, be successful. Life is much the same. You will always arrive at some destination or target whether you aim or not. However, if you focus your aim with a specific destination in mind, you might miss more often, but you significantly increase your chances of hitting something you intend to hit—something you actually want out of life. Like shooting arrows, when you set goals, you are essentially organizing a plan to hit a specific target. Few good things just *happen;* rather, they come with planning and hard work. Not planning leaves us drifting through life.

Locus of Control

 braiN byte

Brain research shows that students achieve more when they feel they are in control and have set specific goals for learning. There is a definite connection between being in control and setting goals.

The way you feel about being able to make changes in your life affects your ability to change. John Roueche and Oscar Mink in *Improving Student Motivation* say that students who feel powerless to change the direction of their lives are unlikely to try.[1] They say a person's locus of control is paramount for change and therefore a very important part of setting goals. The locus of control represents an individual's feelings of personal control over the events in his life, specifically his ability to derive positive reinforcement from his environment. A person who has an internal locus of control believes his actions, abilities, characteristics, and so on, are effective in controlling reinforcements received from the environment. In other words, a person with an internal locus of control believes in setting goals because he believes he has the power to reach them. A person who has an external locus of control believes that such factors as fate, chance, luck, or powerful others are more important than personal efforts in controlling what he can achieve. A person with an internal locus of control responds as a CREATOR. A person with an external locus responds as a VICTIM.

Examine the following statements made by students with either a strong internal or external locus of control. Supply an example for each blank.

External (Victim)   "They made me take this learning strategies class."
Internal (Creator)   "I should be able to gain skills in this class to make me a more successful student."

External (Victim)   "That teacher hates me, he'll never give me a good grade."
Internal (Creator)   "I can meet with my instructor to see how I can do better."

External (Victim)   "What's the answer to number 5?"
Internal (Creator)   "How do I find the answer to number 5?"

[1]J. Roueche and O. Mink, *Improving Student Motivation* (Austin, Tex.: College Associates, 1976).

External (Victim)	"The instructor assigns too much reading in history class."
Internal (Creator)	_____
External (Victim)	"My children won't let me study."
Internal (Creator)	_____
External (Victim)	"My boss makes me work too many hours."
Internal (Creator)	_____
External (Victim)	"I have never been good in math."
Internal (Creator)	_____
External (Victim)	"Other people in my class are smarter."
Internal (Creator)	_____
External (Victim)	"I always get the hard questions."
Internal (Creator)	_____
External (Victim)	"Just my luck to be externally motivated. There's nothing I can do."
Internal (Creator)	_____

brain byte

Dr. Ralph Hillman asserts that one of the benefits of using The **BREATHE** System described in the Survival Kit is that it helps you feel the confidence you need to be a creator rather than a victim.

Virtual Field Trip:
Locus of Control

Visit http://collegesurvival.college.hmco.com/students and select "Hopper," or go to http://www.mtsu.edu/~studskl/3evirtual-fieldtrips.html.

Students who are internally motivated are better adjusted, more independent, more realistic in aspirations, more creative, more flexible, more self-reliant, more open to new learning, more interested in intellectual achievement, and less anxious. They make higher grades than those who are externally motivated. It's your choice. However, when beginning to set goals later on in this chapter, if you measured a high degree of external motivation of your locus of control, you may want to begin with very specific short-term goals before venturing too far into your future. Mastering short-term goals is a sure-fire way of beginning to change your locus of control to internal.

Why Are You Here?

You have chosen to be a college student, but not everyone in college is here for the same reason. Why are you here? What are your goals? Stop for a minute and examine these reasons for going to college.

Rate your reasons from 1 (most influential in your decision) to 16 (least influential in your decision). Please use a different number for each item.

_____ To be exposed to new ideas or experiences

_____ To prepare for a job or profession

_____ To gain problem-solving skills

_____ To gain prestige or status

_____ To prepare for good citizenship

_____ To raise your economic status

_____ To gain maturity

_____ To become a productive member of society

_____ To get a degree

_____ To please your parents or family members

_____ To assimilate knowledge

_____ To have something to do

_____ To learn how to learn

_____ To find a spouse or mate

_____ To make friends

_____ To have fun

Dreaming

If you already had all the time and money you needed what would you be doing?

What would you drive?
Where would you live?
What kind of vacations or hobbies would you enjoy?
What kind of education would you provide for your children?
What type of charities or volunteer work would you be involved in?
What would your purpose in life be?

When Should You Set Goals?

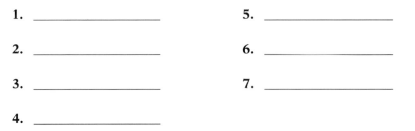

brain byte

Martin Ford says the goal-pursuing process will only be effective if learners have (1) enough feedback to make corrections; (2) enough belief in one's capability in the face of negative feedback; (3) enough actual skills to complete the task; and (4) an environment conducive to success.

You are constantly setting and reaching small or short-term goals. You probably should not begin any day without setting some goal to accomplish. This is a relatively simple task, requiring enough discipline to make it habit. However, anytime there is a major change in your life, you owe it to yourself to reevaluate. Some of these times are graduation, starting college, beginning a new job, moving to a new place, getting married, or getting divorced. A birth, death, promotion, illness, accident, or major change that may have altered previous goals is also a time to reevaluate your goals. Most of us dream of things we would like to do. The difference between dreams and goals is that goals are written down. You need to do more than simply scribble some ideas on a piece of paper. Our goals need to be complete and focused, but first you need to brainstorm. To guide you in a brainstorming activity, let's examine different areas of your life.

Examining Areas of Your Life

Beginning college is a major change for you. It's time to do some goal setting. Begin by thinking of different areas of your life.

At different times in our lives, one or more of these areas takes priority over the others. After you have completed the Brainstorming Exercise on page 55, list the seven areas in order of importance to you at this time.

1. _____   5. _____

2. _____   6. _____

3. _____   7. _____

4. _____

35-Minute Brainstorming Activity

You will need seven sheets of paper. Each paper should be labeled with one area of your life: (1) *Family/Home,* (2) *Mental/Education,* (3) *Financial/Career,* (4) *Social/Cultural,* (5) *Spiritual/Ethical,* (6) *Physical Health,* (7) *Fun/Recreation.*

Now spend five minutes on each area, listing anything you would like to happen or do in that particular area for the rest of your life. Be as specific as possible. In some areas you will write nonstop for the full five minutes and perhaps need more time. Other areas may be more difficult for you to develop ideas.

Themes of Goals

Just as goals can be categorized by areas of our lives, they can also follow certain themes. We may want to cut back on something such as smoking, or we may want to expand something such as the amount of time spent on studying. We may want to improve a situation in an area of our life or to solve a problem. Sometimes our goals involve maintaining our present situation. And sometimes we want to dream and become innovative.

To help you focus your thinking further, you may want to consider themes that goals might have. At the bottom of each of your seven sheets that you used to brainstorm ideas, list the following themes. (1) *Expansion or Cutting Back,* (2) *Improvement,* (3) *Problem Solving,* (4) *Maintenance,* and (5) *Innovation.* Continue your brainstorming by thinking of things you need to expand or cut back on in your family and home. Then think of things that you could improve in your family and home. Is there a problem in your family that you would like to solve? Are there good things about your family or home that you would like to maintain? And are there things you would like to try that are totally different from anything you've ever done? Continue this with each area of your life. When you finish, you will have a wealth of information to help you begin to set some concrete goals. You will probably want to develop goals in all areas of your life; however, you cannot be an expert in all areas. Again, it is a matter of what you value. If you aren't sure, look at where you spend your time, money, and effort. The areas that were easiest for you to brainstorm are probably the most important to you.

Some Guidelines

Make sure that the goal you are working for is something that you really want, not just something that sounds good. Be certain they are your goals and not someone else's. Be sure that your goal is positive instead of negative. You should also have as much control as possible—setting *performance* goals rather than *outcome* goals gives you this control. For example, in a race, a performance goal may be achieving a certain time or personal best. An outcome goal would be to finish in the top three. You might achieve a personal best time in a race and still be disqualified as a result of a poor judging decision or injury. If you had set an outcome goal of being in the top three, then this will be a defeat. If you set a performance goal of achieving a particular time, then you will have accomplished this goal and can draw satisfaction and self-confidence from the achievement.

Elements of a Useful Goal

brain byte

Two researchers, Locke and Latham, surveyed nearly 400 studies on goals, and the results were definitive. They found that specific, difficult goals lead to better performance than easy, vague ones.

You've begun to think about things that are important to you and things you would like to see happen in your life. Now let's talk about writing goals in such a way that you are likely to accomplish them. If a goal is vague or nonspecific or if you just think that *someday* it might be nice to do or have it, you are not likely to accomplish that goal. According to Claire Weinstein, in "Executive Control Processes in Learning," in order to be *useful,* a goal should be stated in terms that are:[2]

Specific	Describe what you want to accomplish with as much detail as possible.
Measurable	Describe your goal in terms that can be evaluated clearly.
Challenging	Take energy and discipline to accomplish.
Realistic	You know you are capable of doing or obtaining.
Inclusive of a completion time	Clearly specify target completion times; longer-term goals are broken into shorter pieces.

[2]"Executive Control Process in Learning," *Journal of College Reading and Learning* 21, p. 49.

Practice Writing Useful Goals

Using the elements explained on the previous page, examine the following sample goals and determine if they are written in a way that will be useful. For each of the goals below, put a check mark if the goal contains the elements of a useful goal: (S) Specific, (C) Challenging, (M) Measurable, (R) Realistic, and (D) Completion Date. If any elements are missing from the sample goal, rewrite it to include all the elements. Then evaluate your rewritten goals to be sure all the elements are present.

Sample Goal	S	C	M	R	D
1. I want a good grade in this class.					
2. I want to have a good career before I get old.					
3. I want to be happy.					
4. I want to go skiing in Vail, Colorado, during Christmas break.					
5. I want to graduate from this college in one year.					
6. I want to travel.					
7. I want a better relationship with my parents.					
8. I want to study more each day.					
9. I want to get up earlier.					
10. I want to buy a BMW before I'm thirty.					
11. I want to be successful.					
12. I want to obtain my degree in five years.					
13. In ten years, I want to be making $50,000 a year.					

Writing Your Goals in a Way They Are Likely to Be Accomplished

Review all the brainstorming you did on your seven sheets. Write three long-term goals—things you want to accomplish anytime in the future. You will need to analyze your long-term goals to determine what short-term goals you need to set in order to get closer to reaching your long-term ones. You will also need to prioritize. Trying to accomplish too much at once can be self-defeating. You are more likely to accomplish these goals if they contain all five elements necessary for a goal to be useful.

1. _____

   _____

2. _____

   _____

3. _____

   _____

Now write three short-term goals—things you want to accomplish this year or next. Make sure your goals contain all five elements necessary for a goal to be useful.

1. _____

   _____

2. _____

   _____

3. _____

   _____

Review what you learned about time management and write a goal for today, dealing with your management of time. Be sure it has all five elements.

Critical Thinking About **Follow-Up**

Let's use what you learned about critical thinking and decision making with one of the goals that you set. List one goal that you wrote and then think it through.

- What skills do I need to achieve this?

- What information and knowledge do I need?

- What assistance or collaboration do I need?

- What resources do I need?

- What can block progress?

- Am I making any assumptions?

- Is there a better way of doing things?

If in the last chapter your decision was to earn an A, use what you know about goal setting to write at least four specific goals for this class.

Educator Skip Downing suggests that it is useful to draw your goals so you can actually see them. He suggests framing your picture and putting it where you see it often.

Setting Goals for Difficult Classes

Think about the classes you are taking now. Choose a class in which you would like to do better. What specifically is your goal in this class?

Do you want an A?
Would you be satisfied with just passing?
Do you need to do better on tests?
Do you want to understand the professor better?
Do you wish you weren't so far behind?
Do you wish you understood better what was going on?

Now let's use some critical-thinking skills we have learned. Look at all sides of the issue. Ask the right questions. Determine what your options are and carefully weigh them. Choose among your options. Take control. Take action. Review your decisions and consequences. What can you specifically do to improve the situation?

As an example of what you can do, examine Gina's problem class, American History 221. Here is her brainstorm of what is specifically wrong:

> There is too much to read. I am behind three chapters and an outside reading book. He goes so fast, I can't take notes. I study, but his questions ask more than I know.

We should look at these problems one at a time. **"There is too much to read. I am behind."** If Gina is to be successful in the class, she must read all the material. Is there really too much to read so that there is no possible way to read it all within her current time schedule? If so, what can she **give up** in order to make time to read it? Does she need to drop the course until she is able to make time? If she chooses to stick with it, here are a couple of goals that will help her.

Gina's Goals I

1. Immediately find and set a time to catch up and set a time for keeping up with reading—a specific time, amount of time, and place.
2. Take notes while reading so that she won't have to reread. ("I will read and take notes on Chapter 3 today at 3 o'clock, Chapters 4 and 5 tomorrow at 10 o'clock.")

"He goes so fast, I can't take notes." Of course we know that if Gina had kept up with her reading, it would be easier to take notes. Where do the notes come from? Do they supplement or follow the reading assignments? Gina needs to analyze her note-taking system. (Taking good notes takes practice.) She needs to check her listening attitude and where she sits in class. She needs to discuss her problem with her professor. Probably, most of all, she needs a partner or two in the class. Immediately after class, her partner or group needs to meet and compare notes or nonnotes, as the case may be, and maybe even check with the professor to fill in spots.

Gina's Goals II

1. Analyze her note-taking system. Is she trying to write too much? Does she give up too easily? What specifically can she do to get more out of the lecture?
2. Find a partner or group willing to meet consistently after class and make the effort to get notes. Do it now! Don't wait until just before a test.
3. Make an appointment with the professor. Plan the conference before she goes. Tell what efforts she has made and ask for help with problems she has not yet solved. Be specific in what she asks for. (Just complaining or talking to the professor is not going to take the place of reading assignments and taking notes.) If the professor offers a suggestion, try it.

"I study, but his questions ask more than I know." One reason Gina has had trouble is that she wasn't keeping up with the assignments. When test time came, she had time to learn only on the first level of Bloom's taxonomy. She recalled facts only. Setting a daily time to study and process information improves the possibility of mastery at deeper levels. When Gina begins to synthesize the information, she can begin to predict what the test questions will be.

Gina's Goals III

1. Take time after each class to understand the information presented and prepare for the next class as if there were going to be a pop quiz on that material.
2. Read the assignment and try to predict what questions would come from each section. Write down the questions in the margin.
3. Analyze old tests from the professor.
4. In a study group, try to predict what the questions on the test will be.
5. Meet with the professor and test the predicted test questions by asking if she is on the right track with the kinds of questions that will be on the exam.

There is a real difference between saying you want to do well in class and actually giving your best effort. Often students fool themselves into thinking that they can treat the courses they are taking in college like those in high school. You have learned that you can count on at least two hours of outside work for every hour you are in class to earn a C. If you have been out of school for a time, it will take more time in the beginning. It takes time to become a good note taker and an efficient reader. Now, what is your goal? Do you want to master the material in each class or just take the class? If you are serious about learning, re-evaluate your master schedule. Are you sticking with your plan? Practicing time management will help you accomplish your goals.

Critical Thinking About **What's Your Problem Class?**

Brainstorm about your specific problems. Then write at least two goals that address these problems that you will tackle today. (Remember to write your goals in terms that are specific, measurable, challenging, realistic, and stated in terms of a completion time.)

Class _____

Brainstorm

Goal 1

Goal 2

Much of the time in a study session, students fail to have specific goals; they feel they just get homework. Having specific goals for each study session helps you get more from your time. You may want to use something like this:

Session 1
Date _____ Time _____ Amount of time scheduled _____
Goals for session:

Session 2
Date _____ Time _____ Amount of time scheduled _____
Goals for session:

 ## Reasons Students Fail College

Below are some of the primary reasons students fail. Critically examine each to see if it describes you. Determining the problem and being aware of the causes is a first step in seeking a workable solution. If you recognize yourself, set goals for overcoming the difficulty described. Students fail because they:

1. Have an inadequate concept of the amount and quality of work required.
2. Place too much importance on other activities.
3. Have vague or no long-term goals.
4. Fail to assume responsibility.
5. Choose an inappropriate major.
6. Have not mastered the language.
7. Experience interference from psychological problems.
8. Make little effort to overcome poor background.
9. Have chosen the wrong college.

Summary

Why have goals?	▶
Explain the locus of control.	▶
When is the best time to reevaluate goals?	▶

What are seven areas of your life described in the goal-setting exercise?

1.
2.
3.
4.
5.
6.
7.

What are five themes of goals examined in the goal-setting exercise?

1.
2.
3.
4.
5.

What is the difference between performance and outcome goals? ▶

What are the five elements of a useful goal?

1.
2.
3.
4.
5.

What are two specific goals you have set for your problem class?

1. _____

2. _____

Of the primary reasons for failing, which have you witnessed?

▶ _____

Is there one that might affect you?

▶ _____

What's Your Advice?

Bob has just graduated from high school. He has decided to go to a community college in his hometown because he can continue to work at Blockbuster, live at home, and still take classes. College is not something he's really excited about because he doesn't know what he wants to do. He knows his parents want him to continue his education, so he is really going to college to please them. There is plenty of time to see what comes up. Bob is working on his time management, and most of the time he is able to get everything done at work and at school without having too much free time left. He thinks that it's just his luck that he has instructors who give so much homework and that his boss is always changing his schedule. Given what you have learned about goal setting, what advice would you give Bob?

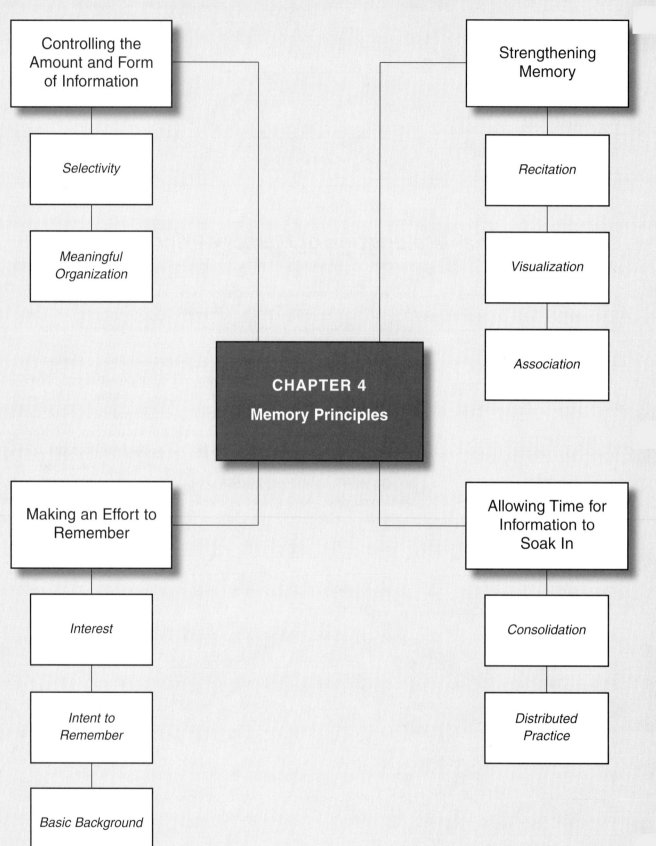

Controlling the Amount and Form of Information

Selectivity

Meaningful Organization

Strengthening Memory

Recitation

Visualization

Association

CHAPTER 4
Memory Principles

Making an Effort to Remember

Interest

Intent to Remember

Basic Background

Allowing Time for Information to Soak In

Consolidation

Distributed Practice

CHAPTER **4**

Memory Principles

A Brief Explanation of Memory Principles

To remember what you are studying (that is, to make it your own), you first have to understand the material. You must also have a desire to learn it. Sometimes you understand the material and truly want to learn it, but just don't know how to process the information in such a way that you are likely to remember it.

Your short-term memory holds only five to seven bits of information. When you receive more than that load of information, you must either push it out of your memory to make room for more or transfer it to long-term memory. This is why you sometimes understand everything that went on in class but do not remember it later: Your short-term memory has dumped that information in order to make room for more. The ten memory principles explained in this chapter are not ways to memorize. Memory is evidence that learning has taken place. Memory is learning that can be retrieved from your brain, not from your notes, or your text. The memory principles are ways to process or transfer information into long-term memory. The more familiar you are with these principles, the better you are able to manipulate information so as to learn it.

I own a computer and can make it do all sorts of amazing things. I use it to word process, make PowerPoint® presentations, send e-mail, surf the Internet, and make webpages. However, it is capable of doing much more than I personally make it do. I could learn how to do more by reading and studying the owner's manual. Your brain, like my computer, will do much more than you make it do. You need to read your owner's manual!

Owner's manuals begin with a quick look at features. They have a use-and-care guide and chapters detailing specific functions. At the back there is usually a troubleshooting section. I like it best when there is a chart or card that contains a quick-reference guide. The memory principles in this chapter are your quick-reference guide. As a college student, you have a limited amount of time to learn volumes of information in your classes. The memory principle reference guide will help you get the most out of the time you have to study. The strategies you develop to use the principles become your troubleshooting section. The

67

Brain Bytes scattered throughout the text margins are excerpts from the detailed chapters to help you understand why certain strategies work or act as tips for use and care of your brain.

I know you don't have time to read the entire manual. In fact, you've used your brain for a long time without ever owning a manual. On a sheet of paper, list how you remember things that are important to you. Try to list at lease five ways.

It is only in the last decade that scholars from separate disciplines like biology, chemistry, psychology, information science, philosophy, anthropology, and linguistics came together to discover the information contained in the manual. These neuroscientists have learned more about the brain in the last decade than in the entire preceding century. Research by neuroscientists has given us the reason why many strategies used by successful students are so efficient. They are able to "see" how the brain processes information using positron emission tomography (PET) scans and other neuroimaging devices. They are able to determine the chemical and electrical reactions taking place and have mapped exactly what part of the brain is used in various functions. The benefit for you is that the more you understand how your brain processes memory, the more empowered you are.

In analyzing what neuroscience is discovering about the brain and memory, Eric Jensen suggests that there are many pieces of the puzzle that make for efficient and long-term learning. Each piece of the puzzle is necessary for optimal learning. Too often, you concentrate on the content of what you need to learn and not on what you need to do to learn it. Each component plays a role in our learning. Jensen states that 1) our personal history; 2) present circumstances; 3) how information is input (sensory modes); 4) how information is processed (learning preferences); 5) what meaning you bring; and 6) how you respond (multiple intelligence) must be meshed for us to learn best. This is often referred to as brain-based or brain-compatible learning, using what you know about the brain to develop strategies for learning that work for you. The six components Jensen says must be considered for optimal learning are all incorporated in the ten memory principles. After you have begun to understand and use the memory principle, you will want to go back and look at the chart (page 12) to see where the pieces all fit. In the learning styles lesson in Chapter 7 you will examine the components of sensory modes (input), hemispheric dominance (processing preferences), and multiple intelligence (responses) in more detail.

Let's begin with a quick look at the features of your brain. Your brain works on electrochemical energy and weighs approximately three pounds. If you make a fist with your hands and put your fists together at the knuckles, you have a fairly accurate picture of the brain's size. Your brain has more than 100 billion brain cells called neurons. However, **it is not the number of neurons that is significant, it is the connections they make with each other that determine learning.**

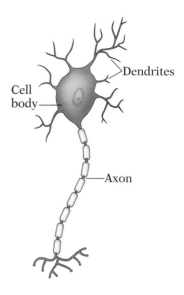

A typical neuron is made up of a cell body containing a nucleus and two branches, one sending and the other receiving information from other neurons. The axon is a long single fiber that sends information. Dendrites are minute twigs or web-like branches that receive information. The action inside the cell is electrical and the action between cells is chemical. Both the axon and dendrites have many connector points so that a neuron receives and sends many messages at a time. The electrical stimulation between cells results in the growth of new dendrites stretching from the neuron. As learning takes place, the branches spread and thicken, making more connections possible. No actual contact is made between axons and dendrites; rather, communication occurs through the release of chemical molecules in the space between the axon and dendrite called the synapse. In his article, "A Computer in Your Head?" Dr. Eric Chudler says, "When information is transferred from one neuron to another, molecules of chemicals ("neurotransmitters") are released from the end of one neuron. The neurotransmitters travel across the gap to reach a receiving neuron where they attach to special structures called receptors. This results in a small electrical response within the receiving neuron. However, this small response does not mean that the message will continue. Remember, the receiving neuron may be getting thousands of small signals at many synapses. Only when the total signal from all of these synapses exceeds a certain level will a large signal (an "action potential") be generated and the message continue." (From "A Computer in Your Head?" by Eric Chudler, as appeared in ODYSSEY MAGAZINE, March 2001. Reprinted by permission of the author.)

Synapse

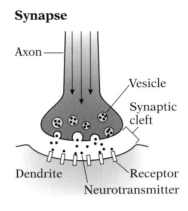

In *The Great Memory Book,* Karen Markowitz and Eric Jensen summarize other important brain facts:

- Stimulus enters the brain through senses

- This information is promptly processed by a complex network of neurons, protein, and electrical impulses.

- They are prioritized by value, meaning, and usefulness, as well as how it relates to prior learning.

- Memory is not stored in one place in the brain like a snapshot; bits and pieces of memory are stored in various functional areas. Neuroscientists are beginning to map the different parts of the brain where memory resides.

- When information is recalled, it is instantaneously retrieved from storage areas in many parts of the brain to form an integrated composition.

- Memory is continually changing and evolving as new information is added to it. (We speak of this as the brain's plasticity.)

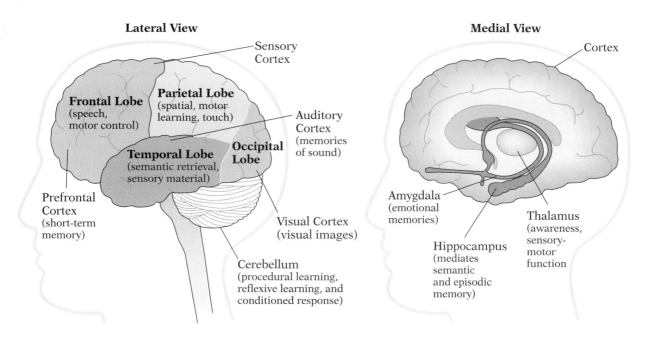

Lateral View

Sensory
Cortex

Frontal Lobe
(speech,
motor control)

Parietal Lobe
(spatial, motor
learning, touch)

Auditory
Cortex
(memories
of sound)

Temporal Lobe
(semantic retrieval,
sensory material)

**Occipital
Lobe**

Prefrontal
Cortex
(short-term
memory)

Visual Cortex
(visual images)

Cerebellum
(procedural learning,
reflexive learning, and
conditioned response)

Medial View

Cortex

Amygdala
(emotional
memories)

Hippocampus
(mediates
semantic
and episodic
memory)

Thalamus
(awareness,
sensory-
motor
function)

Reprinted with permission from WHERE MEMORY RESIDES by
Karen Markowitz and Eric Jensen. Copyright © 1999.

In this discussion, **it is not really important where memory is stored**
(our brain takes care of that automatically), **but, rather, that bits and
pieces of the same information or experience are stored in various
areas of the brain.**

On the next page is a list of ten memory principles with a short
explanation of each. After you have read these principles, make
some pocket work so that you can begin to learn them. Make a
flash card for each principle by writing the name of the principle
on the front of an index card and the explanation of the principle
on the back of the card. Then carry the cards around with you so
that you can study the principles while waiting in line, and so on.

Memory Principles

Making an Effort

Interest. In order to remember something thoroughly, you must be interested in it. You must have a reason to learn it.

Intent to Remember. Your attitude has much to do with whether you remember something or not. A key factor to remembering is having a positive attitude that you will get it right the first time.

Basic Background. Your understanding of new materials depends to a great degree on how much you already know about the subject. The more you increase your basic knowledge, the easier it is to build new knowledge on this background.

Controlling the Amount and Form

Selectivity. You must determine what is most important and select those parts to study and learn.

Meaningful Organization. You can learn and remember better if you group ideas into some sort of meaningful categories or groups.

Strengthening

Recitation. Speaking ideas aloud in your own words is probably the most powerful tool you have to transfer information from short-term to long-term memory.

Visualization. Another powerful memory principle is making a mental picture of what needs to be remembered. By visualizing, you use an entirely different part of the brain than you did by reading or listening.

Association. Memory is increased when facts to be learned are associated with something familiar to you. Memory is essentially formed by making neural connections.

Allowing Time to Soak In

Consolidation. Your brain must have time for new information to soak in. When you make a list or review your notes right after class, you are using the principle of consolidation.

Distributed Practice. A series of shorter study sessions distributed over several days is preferable to fewer but longer study sessions.

■■ Applying the Memory Principles

In the classroom, the most difficult part of your job is not understanding new concepts but, rather, *making those concepts your own,* so that you *don't forget them.* An understanding of how memory works will help you devise techniques to avoid forgetting what you have learned. The first three principles involve your making an effort to remember.

■■ Making an Effort to Remember

brain byte

Anytime a person's emotions are engaged, they are more likely to form a deeper imprint of the event. Excitement, humor, celebration, suspense, fear, surprise, or other strong emotions stimulate the production of adrenaline while also activating the amygdala (part of the brain that controls emotions).

1. The first memory principle is called **interest.** The plain and simple truth is that, in order to remember something thoroughly, you must be interested in it. Brain research has discovered that the brain is really poorly designed for textbook memory. Obviously, you can't just say, "My brain isn't designed this way." You need to find ways to make information relevant. The brain prioritizes by value, meaning, and usefulness. Because of your college's requirements for graduation, it's almost a sure thing that you will have to take some courses that you don't think you are interested in. So, in these classes you must devise some way to get interested. You must go beyond "textbook memory." You may create interest by having a study partner, getting to know the professor better, or doing some extra practice or research. (We tend to be uninterested in things we are not good at.) You might try teaching an assignment to someone else, seeking a way to make the information personal, or finding a way to make it kinesthetic (make something) and do something with it. We tend to be interested in things that we are good at, know a great deal about, are affected by personally, or enjoy doing; so sometimes developing an interest may be as simple as doing a bit of extra research or practice, trying to make the information personal, or approaching the material in a fun way. In addition, finding a study partner who is interested in the subject or getting to know the professor better often provides interest.

2. In addition to interest, attitude has much to do with whether you remember something. When you are positive that the speaker has nothing to say or that the lecture will be boring, you are ensuring that you will not remember it, if it even enters your brain at all. Being positive that you will remember is a key factor in remembering. We call this attitude the principle of **intent to remember.** Suppose that before you come into class today, your instructor pulls you aside and says, "I'm going to cover ten major points in my lecture today. Don't tell anyone, but at the end of class, I'll give you $20 for every major idea you can explain to the class." Would this make a difference in how well you listen? Would it make a difference in how many questions you ask or how many notes you take? It's this attitude of getting it right the first time and making sure you understand, this turning on of the *intent-to-remember switch,* that you

brain byte

Researchers Markowitz and Jensen have found that positive attitude (optimism—believing you can learn it) relaxes the body and directs its full energy to the task at hand. Positive attitude can change the brain in at least three ways: (1) It alters the chemistry of the brain with the production of dopamine, the feel-good transmitter. (2) It increases noradrenaline flow, which provides physical energy. (3) Constructive thinking activates the frontal lobes that are most responsible for long-term planning and judgment.

brain byte

In essence, the pattern of learning is as important as what is learned. Brain theorist Leslie Hart reminds us that what you perceive as a pattern depends upon prior knowledge, the existing neural networking of the brain used to process the input, and the context in which the learning takes place.

should begin each class with. You are seeking ways to learn faster and better, so this principle is one that needs constant practice.

According to Eric Jensen, brain research shows that as stimuli enter your brain through your senses, if the information does not get enough attention or if it is "not deemed necessary for long-term memory, it will be encoded in short-term memory only and ultimately discarded and reclassified." (Markowitz/Jensen, p. 9). He further suggests that although you can probably retrieve almost all of what you pay close attention to, the accuracy of the memory is very dependent on state, time, and context. (Jensen, 1997, p. 52). You can then increase the probability that you get it right the first time by getting enough sleep, eating a high-protein breakfast, limiting your caffeine intake, and eliminating as many distractions as possible. You can increase the oxygen supply to your brain by paying attention to your posture and breathing. Remember the Breathe System reference to Hillman from the Survival Kit. The big three: paying attention to posture, relaxing shoulder and neck muscles, and taking deep, cleansing breaths realigns your focus and gets more oxygen to the brain. When you become restless and inattentive, practicing the Breathe System may be the conscious switch you need to turn on the intent to remember. Physical activity can also increase the blood flow and the brain's oxygen supply.

3. Your understanding of new material depends to a great degree on how much you already know about the subject. Remember it is cellular connections building on one another that activate learning, consciousness, intelligence, and memory. The more learning, the more connections you make. The greater the number of connections in the brain, the greater the meaning derived from learning. If there is not a neural network for something, it simply doesn't exist in our brain. That is why totally new concepts are so difficult to grasp at first. Researchers have discovered that when you activate what you already know about a subject before learning something new, the brain actually makes more connections. Reviewing notes from the day before or surveying a chapter before you read it will increase your learning and comprehension. That's why taking basic courses that give you knowledge to build on is so important. The principle of **basic background** is at work here. If you find you do not have the background, you must make the effort to get it.

Controlling the Amount and Form of Information

Given the nature of short-term memory, you need to find ways to control the amount and form of the information you are trying to learn. These next two memory principles will help you do just that.

4. Brain researcher Eric Jensen notes that "most students are drowning in information and starved for meaning." I am sure you can relate to this. There is so much material covered in your classes that it

 **brain byte**

Because of the tremendous volume of information you encounter (millions of bits of random information per minute), it is crucial that you consciously cue into your memory system.

would be impossible to remember everything. You should therefore carefully determine what is most important and select this material to study and learn. In doing so, you are using the principle of **selectivity.** As you read a textbook, notice that the author has provided clues and guides as to what is important by dividing the chapter with major headings, using bold print and italics, and providing summaries and questions. Finding the important points in a lecture may be more difficult. But you can learn to concentrate on both verbal and nonverbal clues such as the numbering of items, the repetition of an idea, or things written on the board.

You have been assigned four chapters to read in your psychology course. How will you decide what is important to remember? _____

_____

Listen to a lecture and list the verbal and nonverbal clues the lecturer gives to indicate which ideas being conveyed are important. _____

_____

 **brain byte**

To form a sharp memory of something: The original information must be encoded accurately; maintained or strengthened over time; and triggered by association or cue. When information is poorly encoded there is no hope for data recovery.

5. Some scientists estimate that the average brain can hold as many as one quadrillion bits (that's 1 followed by 15 zeroes) in long-term memory. Neuroscientists assure us that our brains, however, are designed to retain meaningful rather than random bits of information. Since memory is stored in web-like fashion throughout the brain, depending on how we process it, it follows that you can improve your memory by learning to encode in a conscious and organized way.

How a person organizes their memory, much like they organize their office or their notebook, will determine how efficient their memory system is. Even though information is filed in your memory filing cabinet, your file needs a name to retrieve it. Because the conscious brain can process only five to seven bits of information at a time, you are able to learn and remember better if you group ideas into meaningful categories of fewer than seven items. This is the principle of **meaningful organization.** Note that it combines the principles of interest (making the group meaningful to *you*) and selectivity (cutting the job down to a manageable size) and that it also involves organization. For example, you might break down a list of twenty-five items into five groups of five (no more than seven) that have some organizational principle in common.

1. First look at the following list of items and try to remember them: *Car keys, a ribbon, a paper clip, a piece of peppermint, a pair of sunglasses, a birthday card, a stapler, a tea bag, a cookie, a windshield-wiper blade, a pencil, a flower, a spoon, a pair of scissors, a stamp, a scarf, a ballpoint pen, a computer disk,* and *a Kleenex.*

2. Study the list for one minute, and then cover it and see if you can list all the items.

3. Now group the items into meaningful categories on a separate sheet of paper; then cover them and see how many you can remember.

4. You are going to the grocery store and have forgotten your list. What are some ways to organize items you need to buy in ways that are meaningful so that you won't forget what you need?

_____

_____

_____

Mnemonic devices are a form of meaningful organization. When you can't find an obvious way to remember something difficult, you can organize it by using a mnemonic. While mnemonic devices do not replace the other techniques, sometimes they are the only way to remember something difficult for a short period of time. Mnemonic devices can be rhymes, phrases, or words arranged to help us remember. One familiar mnemonic rhyme is

i before *e*
except after *c*
or when sounded like *a*
as in *neighbor* or *weigh.*

A familiar mnemonic sentence is the device we use to remember the musical notes on the treble clef: **E**very **G**ood **B**oy **D**eserves **F**un. (In this case, the first letters of each of the words in the sentence remind us of the information we want to recall.)

A common mnemonic word is one used to remember the names of the Great Lakes (taking the first letters of each word or the most important word in a phrase and spelling a word): H O M E S. Can you name them?

_____   _____

_____   _____

_____

One important thing to remember in learning long lists is that it may be better to use several short mnemonics rather than one long one. As noted, your memory can usually handle no more than seven items at a time.

What other mnemonic devices do you know?

_____

_____

Now devise some of your own.

1. Devise a mnemonic (maybe two) to remember the ten memory principles just discussed.

    _____

    _____

    _____

2. Devise a mnemonic to help you remember the five elements necessary for a useful goal.

    _____

    _____

3. Make a mnemonic device for a biology class where you need to learn the seven major taxonomic categories, or taxa, used in classification: (1) kingdom, (2) phylum, (3) class, (4) order, (5) family, (6) genus, and (7) species. Remember, order is important here.

    _____

Strengthening Memory

Once you have manipulated what you wish to learn by selectivity or meaningful organization and have moved that material to long-term memory, you need to seek ways to strengthen and maintain that memory. The next three principles deal with this process. After all, what good is having something in your long-term memory if you can't get it back out?

6. **Recitation** is probably the most powerful tool you have for transferring information from short-term to long-term memory. Recitation involves saying something out loud in your own words. It is not the same as rereading. Recitation works because it triggers the intent-to-remember switch. If you know you're going to recite something, you tend to concentrate and pay more attention. Recitation gets you involved in the material. It makes you a participant, not an onlooker. Further, recitation gives you immediate feedback. You discover whether you know something well enough to say it in your own words or you need to go back and study it more. Remember, you are not just striving to understand; you are also struggling *not to forget*. You are trying to *own* the material you are learning. This is one reason why flash cards or study index cards are so effective. You now know that the more senses you use the stronger the neural trace. You need repetition and review and particularly the brain needs feedback in order to judge and correct its course. The more feedback you get, the faster and more accurate your learning. In fact, research says that you really need to know that you know something before learning really takes place. Recitation is where the difference in understanding something and knowing something becomes most apparent.

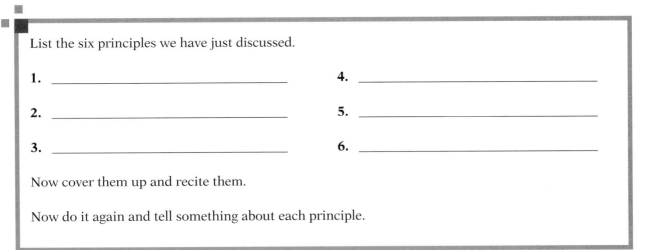

brain byte

Seeking feedback is a natural and essential learning tool that helps us minimize false impressions before inaccurate memories are formed.

List the six principles we have just discussed.

1. _____   4. _____

2. _____   5. _____

3. _____   6. _____

Now cover them up and recite them.

Now do it again and tell something about each principle.

brain byte

The brain has an attentional bias for high contrast and novelty. The brain has an immediate and primitive response to symbols, icons, and strong, simple images.

7. Another very powerful memory principle is **visualization,** which involves making a mental picture of what needs to be remembered. By visualizing, you use an entirely different part of the brain than you use for reading or listening. In addition, you remember pictures much longer than words. In fact, 90 percent of the brain's sensory input is visual. Researchers have found the brain's quickest response is to color, motion, form, and depth. Visualization can be a powerful part of preparing for a test. Experiments using new brain-imaging equipment show that the same brain patterns occur when someone visualizes himself doing something that happens when he actually engages in the task. Most memory experts say that short-term memory will hold more pictures than words. (Later, when learning styles are discussed, you will see that if you are a visual learner, making a mental video of things you want to remember is a must.) The following exercise illustrates the principle of mental visualization. It is important that you follow the directions carefully.

Follow directions carefully. Learn the following pairs of words by repeating the members of each pair several times to yourself. For example, if the pair is CAT–WINDOW, say over and over, "cat–window," "cat–window." Do not use any other memory method.

CUSTARD–LUMBER	MOTHER–IVY
JAIL–CLOWN	LIZARD–PAPER
HAMMER–STAR	BEAR–SCISSORS
APPLE–FRECKLES	CANDY–MOUNTAIN
SLIPPER–ENVELOPE	BOOK–PAINT
CANDLE–SHEEPSKIN	TREE–OCEAN

Now cover the list and try to remember as many pairs of words as you can.

ENVELOPE–_____   JAIL–_____

FRECKLES–_____   IVY–_____

TREE–_____   CANDLE–_____

CANDY–_____   BOOK–_____

SCISSORS–_____   LIZARD–_____

CUSTARD–_____   HAMMER–_____

Learn the following pairs by visualizing a mental picture in which the two objects in each pair are in some kind of vivid interaction. For example, if the pair were CAT–WINDOW, you might picture a cat jumping through a closed window with glass shattering all about. Just make up a picture and do not use any other memory technique. The more color and action your picture holds, the easier it will be to recall.

SOAP–MERMAID   MIRROR–RABBIT

LAKE–FOOTBALL   HOUSE–DIAMOND

PENCIL–LETTUCE   LAMB–MOON

CAR–HONEY   BREAD–GLASS

CANDLE–DANCER   LIPS–DONKEY

FLEA–DANDELION   DOLLAR–ELEPHANT

Now, cover the list and try to remember as many pairs as you can.

CANDLE–_____   DOLLAR–_____

FLEA–_____   CAR–_____

BREAD–_____   LIPS–_____

MIRROR–_____   PENCIL–_____

LAMB–_____   SOAP–_____

LAKE–_____   HOUSE–_____

Find something you need to learn for one of your classes. First list or explain exactly what you need to learn. Then explain *specifically* what you could do with the material visually to make yourself remember it.

brain byte

Researcher Eric Jensen reminds us that "Optimal learning occurs when the brain's multiple maps work in synchronization or network with each other. The more connected these neural networks are, the greater the meaning derived from learning."

8. Another way to strengthen your memory is to tie new information in with something you already have stored in your long-term memory. This is called the principle of **association.** By recalling something you already know about a subject and placing new information in the same brain file as the old information, you will find that the new information is easier to retrieve, easier to remember. For example, there are certain dates that you are sure of, such as the year Columbus discovered America, the year the Declaration of Independence was signed, your mother's birthday, and the year you graduated from high school. So, when you need to learn a new date, think of the new date as being, say, five years after or ten years before the one you already know.

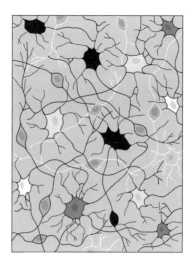

This is an illustration of the complex web of neurons. (Reprinted with permission from WHERE MEMORY RESIDES by Karen Markowitz and Eric Jensen. Copyright © 1999.) Remembering something requires activation of specific networks of neurons to trigger the exact memory. The darkened neurons are the ones activated. Others remain dormant unless stimulated. The activation of a memory can be triggered by any incoming stimuli on a random basis, or it can be consciously cued into your memory.

Allowing Time for Information to Soak In

As you are probably beginning to discover, the memory principles can be used together and, in fact, are more powerful when used in combination. For example, as you associate something new with something you already know, you will want to use visualization and perhaps recitation to strengthen your memory. The last two memory principles are important again, because of what we know about the nature of short-term memory. The brain can absorb only a certain amount of *new* information, and that information needs time to soak in. As you observe a PET scan or other neuroimaging devices, it becomes abundantly apparent that association is central to the process of encoding and retrieval. It is extremely important when you encode new information that you do so consciously.

9. An important factor to consider in terms of how your brain processes material is that it takes time for information to gel, soak in, or consolidate. Researchers Markowitz and Jensen remind us that the brain is not designed for nonstop learning. As the brain learns new information, new connections are formed. Learning is a biological process that literally changes the configuration of the brain. "Processing time is necessary to build the inner writing necessary for connectivity and recall." Repetition of information strengthens

brain byte

Richard Bandler, co-discover of neurolinguistic programming, says that for us to take ownership of new information, our brain needs to "know what it knows." Three criteria necessary for this are (1) Reinforcing in your preferred modality (visual, auditory, or kinesthetic); (2) Reinforcing the right number of times (for some once, for others it may be twenty times); (3) Reinforcing a sufficient length of time (a couple of seconds to several hours).

these new connections. We call this principle **consolidation.** You are usually bombarded with much more information than you can remember. You must, therefore, allow time to sort through it and for consolidation to take place. We have already discussed that the more ways new information is processed into the brain, the faster and deeper the connections. Encoding that is random is at best difficult to retrieve. The brain needs feedback and repetition. You must cause consolidation to take place. Here are a few ways to consolidate or allow new information time to soak in: taking notes in class, asking questions in class; reviewing notes; stopping after each paragraph you read and writing a jeopardy question; visualizing; reciting; making flash cards; and designing practice tests. You will notice that many of these activities give you a hard-copy backup of new information as well as strengthening connections in your brain.

List those memory principles that you think are most important in allowing memory to soak in.

_____

_____

Can you think of other activities that would promote consolidation?

_____

brain byte

Brain research suggests that breaks are needed for at least two reasons. First, new neural connections need time to fix and strengthen without interference of other new stimuli. Second, fatigue simply causes more errors.

10. You tend to remember better if you are not overly tired and are able to concentrate; therefore, a series of shorter study sessions (no longer than fifty minutes each) is usually better than hours and hours of straight studying. Using the principle of **distributed practice** is probably the most effective way to study. If the connections in your brain are strengthened by the number of times you use them, then several short sessions are better than long ones. The structure of your brain literally changes each time you add new information. When your study sessions are frequent and spread out, there is time for branches to form on dendrites and new chemical and electrical responses to occur. Each time you study, the brain will respond more quickly because there are more connections. If you wait until the last minute to cram for an exam, there are fewer dendrites and the connections are weaker. You tend to remember things at the beginning and the end, whereas things in the middle often get fuzzy or blurred. It stands to reason, then, that the more beginnings and endings you experience, the more you will remember. If you remember the first twenty minutes and the last twenty minutes of what you study in a fifty-minute study session, you are well on your way to _owning_ that material. However, what happens when you study for four hours straight? You remember the first twenty minutes and the last twenty minutes. Does that amount to three hours and twenty minutes of blur? Check your study schedule. Are you using distributed practice?

Putting Memory Principles to Use

Kelley has a history textbook assignment for her history class. Identify the memory principle she uses to complete the assignment. (A description may use more than one principle.)

Before she begins to read she reviews her notes from the class where the instructor introduced the material.

She reads the chapter summary, studies the review questions, and examines pictures and charts before she reads.

When she reads, she focuses on the bold print, topic sentences, and italicized words.

At the end of each paragraph she stops and chooses the important information and writes a question in the margin of her book. She then underlines as few words as possible to answer the question.

Before she goes to the next paragraph, she covers the text, asks herself the questions in the margin, and says the answer out loud in her own words.

In addition, she tries to picture what the people and events she is reading about look like. As she reads she tries to make connections with things they have already studied.

This chapter is about World War II, and she remembers hearing stories about her grandfather being in the war. She asks her parents exactly what he did and where he was at that time.

Kelley reads and marks a few pages right after history class, a few more when she has a break between classes, additional pages while she is waiting for her friend Marge, and finishes the chapter before she leaves school. Later that night she reviews the whole chapter.

When she is finished, she makes a chart that lists the role and major players of each country involved.

She also makes flash cards of terms, people, places, and dates.

Virtual Field Trip:

Memory Principles

Visit http://collegesurvival.college.hmco.com/students and select "Hopper," or go to http://www.mtsu.edu/~studskl/3evirtual-fieldtrips.html.

Virtual Field Trip:

Memory Principles Quiz

Visit http://collegesurvival.college.hmco.com/students and select "Hopper," or go to http://www.mtsu.edu/~studskl/3evirtual-fieldtrips.html.

How Memory Works: Putting Principles in Perspective

If you use Bloom's taxonomy to measure the depth of learning, you should be competent through three levels in your thinking about the ten memory principles. You have learned the names of the principles (knowledge); you understand how they help learn new material (comprehension); and you have begun to use them in developing strategies for learning (application). The deeper the level of our thinking, the stronger the neural traces or connections. Keeping the analogy of the brain owner's manual, let's dig deeper. You need to understand the relationships between the principles, to see how the principles fit into the overall pattern of information processing and learning, and to determine which combinations of principles work best for you in specific learning situations. When you analyze, synthesize, and evaluate, you have progressed from simply learning something for an exam to using it to become a better student. Neuroscientists may not know exactly how the brain processes information, but we know enough to see how the principles fit into the overall scheme for learning new material. We know that memory is not an object or file stored in one place in the brain; rather it is a "collection of complex electrochemical responses activated through multiple sensory channels and stored in unique and elaborate neuronal networks throughout the brain."

Memory can be described as an interactive process which takes place in three stages. First is **reception or encoding,** the gathering of information from your senses. This information enters your short-term memory. In **short-term memory,** information either fades away, is intentionally tossed away, or is processed for storage in **long-term memory,** stage two. Stage three is the tricky one. Once information enters the long-term memory, there must be a way to retrieve, or activate, the information so that you can use this information when you need it. Without a way to retrieve information from long-term memory, it may as well be lost. Information retrieved from long-term memory is temporarily placed in what we might call **active memory.**

The process will look something like this:

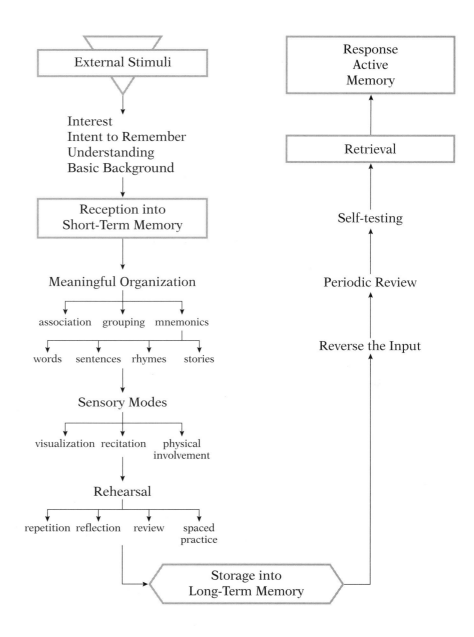

Stage One: Getting Information into the Brain—Reception into Short-Term Memory

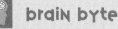

To form a sharp memory of something, the original information must be encoded accurately; maintained or strengthened over time; and triggered by an association or cue.

The first stage of the memory process involves information's entering the brain. We can call this gathering of information, this acquisition of knowledge, **reception.** The brain uses sensory receptors to gather information from things that you see, hear, smell, touch, or taste. Some of these simply pass on through—in one ear and out the other, so to speak—and others become part of the short-term memory. Obviously everything around you is not important; thus, you do not receive everything. In a classroom lecture, there is more happening in the room than just the lecture. There are other people in the room, each doing his or her own thing. Or there may be something going on outside the window, in the hall, or in your mind. You are feeling, smelling, seeing more than you can take in, but basically you are in control of what you select to receive. Some of the time you choose to receive nothing at all.

Factors That Influence Reception

When information is received from sensory input, it is encoded in various parts of the brain to form synaptic connections with cell bodies called neurons. The axon of the cell reaches out and connects to the newly formed dendrites on other cells. Sometimes, however, you discover that no connections are formed at all or the connections are very weak. There are four factors that influence whether information you need to learn is even received by your brain or whether new connections are formed. Three of these are the memory principles categorized earlier as Making an Effort. The first has to do with your attitude—your **intention to remember.** If you are not listening or reading as if there will be a pop quiz on the material, the information may not even get into your short-term memory. If there is no intent on your part to get it right the first time, you may hear or see the information but no synaptic connections are made and no dendrites are grown. A second influence is the principle of **interest.** If you are not interested, the information never makes it into short-term memory to even begin to make connections. A third factor influencing whether transmitted information is received or encoded into the brain is not a memory principle but deals with a more basic concept, **understanding.** Most of us have heard something said in a language that we do not speak or seen a sign written in a language we cannot read. That information simply does not enter the brain as meaningful information to be processed. This is also true of material presented either in lecture or print that we do not understand. If we do not understand it, it has little chance of being received into short-term memory. If the intent and interest are there, we may ask for a translation, but information must be understood in order to be processed. You can probably all think of times when you memorized terms for a test without understanding. In such situations no real learning or remembering takes place. A fourth influence on what you actually allow to go into short-term memory is **basic background.** Every-

Learning is different from attention. But if we are not attending, we are not learning.

thing you see, hear, smell, touch, or taste is affected by that which you already know. If there is no prior knowledge, there is nothing to connect it to. This is why the more you know about something, the easier it is to learn about it. Your lack of knowledge makes some concepts difficult for you to understand while for some of your classmates the concepts seem simple. For example, your classmate builds model airplanes. History lessons about World War II may be easier for her because she has built models of planes used in the war. They may also be easier for the classmate who has heard war stories from his grandfather. You may have noticed that when you learn a new vocabulary word one day, you begin to see or hear it everywhere.

If you are going to encode something in your brain, you must employ the strategies you developed for using the principles of intent to remember, interest, and basic background, in addition to making sure that you understand the information.

Critical Thinking About **Reception**

From the four factors that influence reception you can create strategies to ensure that what you want to remember is at least on its way:

- Make a conscious decision that you intend to remember. Concentrate and try to eliminate both internal and external distractions.

- Create interest in the information being transmitted; personalize it. Try to make it mean something to you.

- If you don't understand what is being transmitted, ask for a translation or explanation. Never just memorize it.

- If you lack basic background about the information, try to acquire it.

Your assignment for psychology class is to read Chapter 3 in your text. You read it, but the next day on the quiz, you find you can't remember anything you read. Using some of the strategies above, make a plan for studying your psychology assignment for tomorrow.

1. _____

2. _____

3. _____

The Nature of Short-Term Memory

Information that you *choose* to receive or encode (selectivity) goes into **short-term memory.** We have said that short-term memory is limited. Usually it can hold only five to seven bits of information at a time. When you are presented with more than seven bits, one of two things must happen. You must get rid of what's in the short-term bank by letting it escape, that is, forgetting it, or you must transfer it to long-term memory. This is the reason you can understand an entire lecture while you are listening to it but later cannot recall the major points. This becomes an important point in developing strategies for note taking and textbook reading, which are discussed in later chapters. You need to hold or record information until you can process it into long-term memory. You must be very careful when you process information for storage into long-term memory because the transferring of information to long-term memory is not enough. You must be able to retrieve this information after it is filed. Just as there are several factors influencing whether sensory information gets to short-term memory, there are instructions in your brain's owner's manual for processing information into long-term memory in such a way that you can later retrieve it. Once synaptic connections are made, if they are not strengthened, they may be lost.

Stage Two: Processing from Short-Term to Long-Term Memory

There are three broad categories that influence transference from short-term memory to storage in long-term memory, and each has several divisions. The first makes use of various forms of **organization** and **association.** The second way of transferring from short-term to long-term memory is by making use of various **sensory modes.** The third can be classified as **rehearsal.**

Organization

Organization is one method of ensuring that information you want to remember is properly stored. If you go into my office, you will usually see my desk piled with stacks of papers. If I wanted my desk cleared, I could randomly stack this information and shove it into a desk drawer. However, if I want to be able to find things again, they must be sorted and organized. Your memory is similar to my desk. If you just pile information in, you may not be able to find what you need when you need it. The strategies you developed when using meaningful organization such as color coding and mnemonics help process the information into long-term memory so that retrieval is possible. You now understand that the brain is a web-like network of neurons that can form memory only by association. Memory or facts are not stored in one place in the brain, but when you need to recall something, memory is re-created by the electrical/chemical connections from many parts of the brain by way of synaptic connections. The more associations you make when you process new information the stronger the connection. If associations are not consciously made, connections may be weak and information lost.

Explain strategies for using **meaningful organization** to remember information that seems overwhelming.

How could you use **mnemonics** to organize information you want to move from short-term to long-term memory?

Give an example of how **association** could be important in organizing information you need to remember.

Sensory Modes

Another way to ensure that information from short-term memory is properly transferred for storage in long-term memory and the neural traces are strengthened is to use various **sensory modes.** Most of us have a preferred mode of learning. Some of us are visual learners, others learn best by hearing, and still others learn best by doing. You will want to be sure that you process new information in your preferred mode; however, the more senses you involve, the more neurons are used in the connections, and the *more likely you are to remember.* This is where Visualization and Recitation fit in. You may also want to include what something smells like or tastes like.

Three ways of using your sensory modes for learning are to visualize, to recite, and to do something to become physically involved in your learning. You have a long list of history terms you will need to explain on an upcoming test. Devise specific strategies for learning these terms using each of the following. Include an explanation of why these strategies will work for you.

Visualization

Recitation

Physical involvement

Rehearsal

A final way to transfer information from short-term memory to long-term memory is **rehearsal,** or practice. You are familiar with the rehearsal used by actors to learn their lines. Rehearsal does something similar for us. One form of rehearsal is repetition. **Repetition** is saying or doing things over and over until you are familiar with the information. Repeating something over and over may temporarily transfer information to long-term memory at the knowledge level, but in order to make sure the information is permanent, you need to understand it. The second form of rehearsal is **reflection.** This involves a deeper level of learning and takes you to at least the comprehension level of Bloom's taxonomy. You quickly lose that which you don't understand. One way of promoting a deeper understanding of a concept is reflection, examining information and trying to discover how it relates to that which you already know and what meaning it has for you. The more meaning something has for you, the more likely you are to remember it.

A third form of rehearsal is **review.** Once a transfer has been made from short-term memory, review is necessary to make sure you can retrieve the information later. Good times to review are right before class, right after class, and thirty minutes before you go to bed. Reviewing before class strengthens your basic background and enables you to more easily store that which is presented in class. Review right after class catches material before short-term memory has time to completely dump it and while you still understand certain concepts and can identify concepts you need to ask about. And review before you go to bed gets your subconscious working while you sleep. Note that we said review, not study for the first time. Neurochemical and biochemical studies using imaging of the brain show that when something new is introduced, to be understood by the learner a sufficient review of this information *must* take place during the following twenty-four hours in order for long-term memory to retain the concept. This will be difficult for many students who are extremely pressed for time as it is. However, reviewing within twenty-four hours will actually save time later. Your master schedule becomes an essential tool.

A fourth important principle of rehearsal is that you tend to remember better with several spaced practices than with one long session. We called this principle **distributed practice.** Forty-five- to fifty-minute sessions with a five- to ten-minute break seems to be about right for most students. Don't fool yourself into thinking you can do it all at once. We tend to remember things at the beginning and end of the presentation or study time better than those things in the middle. If there are more beginnings and more ends and less middle, then we remember more! Cramming is one big middle! Instead of cramming, start studying several days before a test with spaced practices. This is the hardest thing for most students to do but the most effective way of learning material, and it will save you from having to pull an all-nighter. The more combinations of organization, sensory modes, and rehearsal you use, the more **consolidation** takes place. And the more powerful the transfer to long-term memory, the more likely you will be able to retrieve the information you need when you need it.

The Nature of Long-Term Memory

While short-term memory can hold only a limited amount of information for a very short time, long-term memory acts as storage for larger amounts for longer periods of time. Notice that the term is not *permanent* memory but *long-term*. Some things do become part of permanent memory through rehearsal, but more things decay with time and interference. It appears that the more we take things in and out of our long-term memory, the more interest we have in the information, and the more understanding we have of the concepts involved, the longer the information will stay in our long-term memory. Again, long-term memory is not a **place** but a **process** that takes place in many parts of the brain to reconstruct memory.

Stage Three: Retrieving from Long-Term Memory

You have cleared your cluttered desk and your information is either in the trash or in the file cabinet we call long-term memory. Now comes the real challenge, getting the information back out. When test time comes, do you know which drawer to open and how you filed the information? Obviously, the storage and retrieval processes are interactive. The more you use the information—activate connections—the more likely you are to remember where you filed it. There are basically three steps to retrieving information: **reversing the storage process, self-testing,** and **periodic review.** If you were systematic in your filing, to retrieve the information you **reverse the process of storage.** For example, if you grouped information in categories to remember it, recall the categories to retrieve it. If you used a mnemonic device to file the information, use the same mnemonic device to take the information out of the file. You can use meaningful grouping, association, and mnemonic devices to retrieve information as well as store it. If you stored information using sensory modes, you can use visualization, recitation, or physical involvement to retrieve that information. If you used the rehearsal process to ensure depth of storage, a similar rehearsal can be used to bring the material out of storage.

As we have said, long-term memory is not necessarily permanent memory. How long lasting long-term memory is depends on such things as your understanding, your interest, how you stored it, and how often you retrieve it. You can retrieve information by **self-testing.** Asking yourself questions about the information is important for several reasons. First of all it simulates test conditions; it gives you practice taking tests. Self-testing also gives you feedback so that you know if you remember what you need to know. Brain research shows that an essential part of learning is knowing that you know something. And self-testing is, after all, a form of rehearsal and will strengthen the retrieval process and add to the depth of storage in your memory. In addition, **periodic review** is necessary because information in long-term memory seems to decay or fade away without review. You should review at least once a week for each class you have. All the time you spend reading and studying is wasted if you can't remember what you have read or studied; therefore, an investment of a little extra time spent retrieving and reviewing filed material is worth it. The bottom line is connections must be strengthened or they fade.

What Happens When You Retrieve Information from Long-Term Memory?

When you retrieve information from long-term memory, you activate it, or transfer it to what we call active or working memory. You can compare active memory to your actual desktop or your computer desktop. This is the space where you gather information you need to solve a problem, answer a question, or draw a conclusion. There is a limited amount of work space in active memory, and when it becomes cluttered, you must refile the information in long-term memory or trash what information you no longer need. The more you activate information, take it out of long-term memory and refile it, the more permanent it becomes. Systematically retrieving and refiling material saves hours and hours of time in the long run. In fact, your aim is to make this filing and refiling a habit. The owner's manual is certainly a simplification of how your brain operates; however, you can now begin to use what you know about the memory principles and how they are used in your brain to devise strategies for processing information.

You studied five hours for your geology test. You remembered most of what you needed to know on the test. On the next test there are many of the same questions but you do not remember the answers. Explain what you think happened.

What could you have done to prevent this from happening?

Virtual Field Trip:
Learning More About the Brain

Visit http://collegesurvival.college.hmco.com/students and select "Hopper," or go to http://www.mtsu.edu/~studskl/3evirtual-fieldtrips.html.

Can you re-create the flow chart describing how memory works?

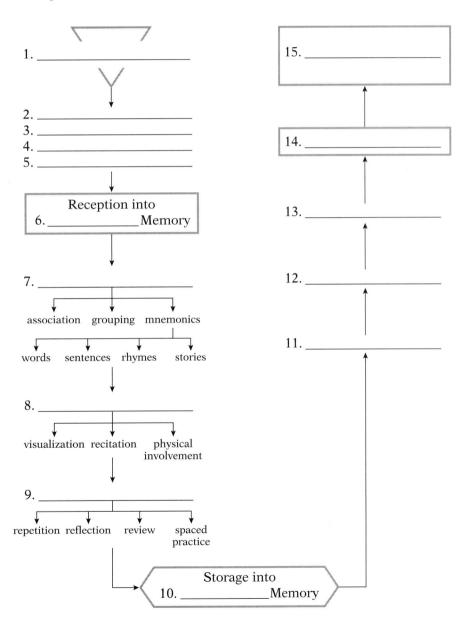

▪▪▪▪▪▪▪ Summary

To check to see if you have grasped the major points of this chapter on **memory principles,** answer the following questions:

What disciplines came together to discover more about the brain?

▶ _____

What is brain-compatible or brain-based learning?

▶ _____

Define the following:
- **Neuron**
- **Dendrite**
- **Axon**
- **Synapse**
- **Neurotransmitters**

▶ _____

Memory is not a snapshot stored in one place in the brain. Explain.

▶ _____

What three memory principles require that you make an effort to remember?

1. _____

2. _____

3. _____

What two memory principles control the amount and form of information to be remembered? Explain and give an example of each.

1. _____

2. _____

What is a mnemonic?

▶ _____

Name three kinds of mnemonic devices.

1. _____

2. _____

3. _____

What three memory principles strengthen the memory? Explain and give an example of each.

1.

2.

3.

What two memory principles allow time for information to soak in? Explain and give an example of each.

1.

2.

What are three factors that influence reception into short-term memory?

1.

2.

3.

What are three ways of organizing information for transfer to long-term memory?

1.

2.

3.

Name the three sensory modes used to transfer to long-term memory.

1.

2.

3.

What are three ways to rehearse?

1.

2.

3.

Once information is in long-term memory, what are three steps in retrieving it?

1.

2.

3.

■ What's Your Advice?

Marlene is a very conscientious and capable 30-year-old student who has quit her job as a receptionist in a doctor's office to work on her degree in nursing. She attends class every day. Marlene keeps up with her reading assignments and homework and listens carefully in class. She uses a planner to make sure she has plenty of time set aside for studying for tests. The night before a test Marlene re-reads the chapters in the text and looks over any review sheet the professors may give. She repeats definitions and facts she thinks will be on the test over and over. However, Marlene is very frustrated after failing her first history and psychology tests, and barely passing her biology test. She is beginning to think she may have made a mistake in her decision to attend college. Using what you know about how the memory works, what advice can you give Marlene?

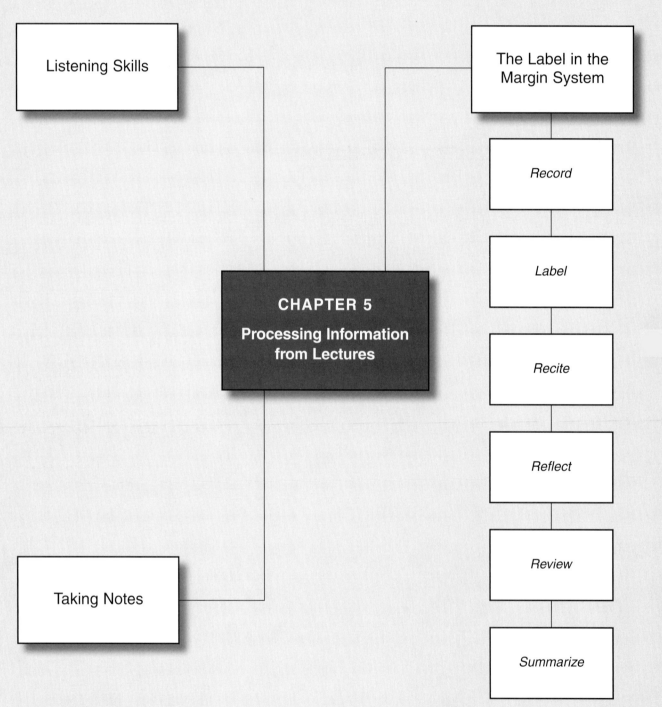

Listening Skills

The Label in the
Margin System

Record

Label

Recite

Reflect

Review

Summarize

CHAPTER 5

Processing Information
from Lectures

Taking Notes

CHAPTER 5

Processing Information from Lectures

Processing Information

Your primary job as a college student is to process information. You want to take information from lectures and make that information yours. You want to grasp what you read and process it so that you own it. Otherwise, you would spend a great deal of time going to class and even more time reading, yet benefit little in the long run. How, then, do you process information from lectures and textbooks so that you are in control of that information? You already have the answer: through systematic study in which you apply the memory principles. By examining these principles with your task in mind, you can devise a system that uses as many principles as possible and makes the best use of what you know about time management and how memory works. The result should be a system that processes information faster and better than any you have used before. Because most people gather information differently when they listen to a lecture than when they read a textbook, the gathering or input stage also differs. But by using the memory principles, you should be able to process both auditory and visual information into your long-term memory in much the same manner. Because the label in the margin system is based on the memory principles and incorporates various learning strategies, it works for most learning styles.

99

Before we get started, take the following inventory. Put a check beside the statements which you have under control.

_____ I am a really good listener.

_____ I am usually prepared for a pop quiz in any class.

_____ I have a good system for taking notes.

_____ After I take notes, I go over them before the next class.

_____ From my notes it is easy to predict what will be on a test.

_____ When I read a chapter in a textbook, I won't have to reread it before a test.

_____ From the markings in my textbook, I can easily predict what will be on a test.

_____ Once I understand a new concept, I immediately process it into long-term memory rather than waiting until test time to learn it.

_____ I understand how I learn best.

_____ I use a variety of strategies to learn something new.

If you have checked fewer than four of the above, you can benefit from this chapter.

Relating Information Processing to Memory Principles

In most college classrooms, the primary mode of teaching is lectures. However, according to Edgar Dale's research, people generally remember only 20 percent of what they hear.[1] Given that our short-term memory holds only five to seven bits of information, it is possible to understand everything that the lecturer says, yet remember only a few things. It is important, then, to use what we know about our memory to process information from lectures.

Let's review the memory principles so that you know what you are working with. Remember that they are divided into four categories:

1. **Making an effort to remember** involves *interest, intent to remember,* and *basic background.*
2. **Controlling the amount and form of information** involves *selectivity* and *meaningful organization.*
3. **Strengthening memory** involves *recitation, mental visualization,* and *association.*

[1]R. Winman and W. Meierhenry, *Educational Media* (Charles Merrill, 1969).

4. Allowing time for memory to soak in involves *consolidation* and *distributed practice.*

(You may need to go back and study each principle more carefully before you begin the exercise below.)

Critical Thinking About **Information Processing**

Let's do some critical thinking about your classroom lectures and reading textbooks. What could you do, using the following memory principles, to help process what you hear or read? List below things you might do either in class or after class that would employ these memory principles.

1. Interest, intent to remember, and basic background

_____

_____

_____

2. Selectivity and meaningful organization

_____

_____

_____

3. Recitation, mental visualization, and association

_____

_____

_____

4. Consolidation and distributed practice

_____

_____

_____

Listening Skills

A quick inventory on college campuses reveals that as much as 80 percent of what you need to learn is delivered through lectures. Sometimes the lectures are exciting and easy to follow. Others may be dry, or it may be difficult to grasp the main idea. No matter how entertaining, confusing, or boring the lecture may be, you are responsible for the information delivered. If you are having problems with your note taking, follow the steps of critical thinking and first determine what the problem is. One cause may be bad listening habits. Examine the exercise below to check your listening habits. One of the first things you probably concluded was that intent to remember and interest are triggered by listening carefully. You may be guilty of some sort of bad listening habits.

From the list below choose the five obstacles that most often get in the way of your listening in class. In the space following the obstacle, explain in detail how you can overcome this obstacle (not just, "I won't do it anymore!").

Obstacles to Listening

1. Talking instead of listening

2. Thinking of what you're going to say instead of listening

3. Mentally arguing with the speaker

4. Thinking about something else while the speaker is talking

5. Getting impatient with the speaker

6. Giving in to a poor environment—too noisy, too hot, too hungry!

7. Dividing your attention—getting homework, writing a letter, staring at someone cute!

8. Not listening actively—not taking notes, not asking questions, and so on.

9. Not being motivated to listen—the subject is boring!

10. Being distracted by the speaker's mannerisms, voice, or appearance

Improving Your Listening

There are some commonsense principles that will help you become a better listener in class. Study the list below and answer the questions which follow.

1. Come to class prepared. What does this involve? _____

_____

How will this make you a better listener? _____

_____

What memory principles does this involve? _____

2. Sit as close to the instructor as possible. Why? _____

_____

3. Come to class as early as possible. Why? _____

_____

4. Listen for verbal clues that something is important. What are some examples of things the instructor might say to let you know that a point is important?

_____

_____

_____

5. Watch for nonverbal clues that a point is important. What are some examples?

_____

_____

_____

_____

6. **Listen with a pen or pencil in your hand.** Why? _____

_____

_____

7. **Think of questions as you are listening.** Mentally ask questions such as "What is the main idea?" Or, "What point is she trying to make?" What other questions might you ask? How will this help?

_____

_____

_____

Virtual Field Trip:

Let's Go Improve Your Listening

Visit http://collegesurvival.college.hmco.com/students and select "Hopper," or go to http://www.mtsu.edu/~studskl/3evirtual-fieldtrips.html.

Why Take Notes?

Remember, you listen better if you understand the lecture. This involves being prepared, developing a basic background of the material if you don't already have one, and asking questions. You probably also noted that you pay more attention and become more interested if you take notes.

Below is a list of reasons for taking notes in class. Read them, decide which is the most important reason to you and number it 1. Number all the reasons in order of importance to you with number 1 being the most important and number 8 being the least important. If there are reasons you think of that are not listed, list and rate them.

_____   1. Taking notes makes me pay attention. It keeps my mind from wandering. I am more likely to remain conscious of what is important.

_____   2. Taking notes helps me concentrate. When I am trying to take good notes, I concentrate more on what the speaker is saying.

_____   3. Taking notes gives me a record of what was said in class. I know what was said on which days and also what was not covered in class.

_____   4. Taking notes forces me to select the main ideas. I can't write down everything.

_____   5. The simple act of writing something down helps me remember it longer.

_____   6. Taking notes gives me a place to write down assignments so that I will be able to find them later.

_____   7. Taking notes gives me information to use to study for tests and for class assignments.

_____   8. Taking notes reminds me of what the teacher has emphasized.

_____   9. _____

_____ 10. _____

Using the Label in the Margin System for Lectures

As noted in the Survival Kit, the label in the margin system is a system for processing information.

Controlling the Amount and Form of the Information

While you can't control the amount of information in and form of a lecture, you *can* control what you write down and how you write it down. The label in the margin system introduced in the Survival Kit is the best way I know to control both the amount and the form of your notes. The label in the margin system is more than a system for taking notes. It is a complete system for processing information from lectures that makes use of almost all of the memory principles. First of all, you use the principle of selectivity to choose what's most important to write down in your notes. Second, you organize your notes in question-and-answer form using the principle of meaningful organization.

The label in the margin system is based on the Cornell note-taking system developed at Cornell University in the 1950s. This system may take some getting used to, but in the long run you will find that it is energy efficient and saves you time. Note taking is a skill, and as with all new skills, it takes practice. The more you use it, the better at it you become!

> There are six basic steps in the label in the margin system.

Before You Begin

You will need a loose-leaf notebook with wide-ruled lines. If possible, take your notes in pen rather than in pencil.

First, draw a line down your paper about $2\frac{1}{2}$ inches from the left side. Disregard the red vertical line usually used for the margin. You will use the wide section on the right to record your notes in class. The section on the left becomes your label or question margin, where you will write key words, phrases, or questions.

The margin at the top of the page is used for indicating the date, class, and page number, and for writing assignments or other important information that you don't want to forget.

Six Steps

> **Step 1: *Record what is said.*** Use a telegraphic form of writing to *record* what is said. When you send a telegram, you are charged for each word. Pretend you are being charged for each word in your notes. Be stingy with your words. Never write a whole sentence when a word or two will do. The whole idea behind note taking is to write no more than you need in order to remember what was said. Use abbreviations whenever possible.

For example, if your instructor says: "Recitation is the most powerful way of transferring information from short-term memory to long-term memory," you might write:

Recite most pow'ful way to get s-t-mem to l-t-mem

Your instructor says:

Four reasons recitation is so powerful are that is makes you pay more attention because you know you are going to recite. It makes you participate in your learning. You must understand in order to explain in your own words. And it gives you feedback as to how much you actually know.

You might write:

1. Makes pay attent
2. Makes participate
3. Have to understnd
4. Feed bck

Label notes with a question here.	*Take telegraphic notes here.*
	Put name, date, class, and page number above here

Note-Taking Exercise

1. Your instructor says:

Because of Switzerland's strict neutrality, Geneva provides an impartial meeting ground for representatives of other nations.[2]

You write:

Switz neutral
so Geneva impartial meeting grnd
for other nations

---

2. Your instructor says:

The Olympic games were held in ancient times on the plain of Olympia in Greece every four years. It was a time for laying aside political and religious differences, as athletes from all Greek cities and districts competed.[3]

---

[2]E. D. Hirsch, Jr., J. F. Kett, and J. Trefl, *The Dictionary of Cultural Literacy* (2d ed.; Boston: Houghton Mifflin, 1993).
[3]Ibid.

Your turn to try. You write:

3. Your instructor says:

   Obsolescence is a decline in the value of equipment or of a product brought about by an introduction of new technology or by changes in demand.[4]

   You write:

Step 2: *Label.* Recording the information during the lecture is only the first step in using the label in the margin system. The next step is to *label* the recorded information with a key word, phrase, or question. This is done in the label or question margin, the 2½-inch margin on the left, and as soon after class as possible. The best way to label your information is to play *Jeopardy.* What question does this answer? If this information appears on a test, how will it be asked? This labeling makes you use your critical thinking skills. You have gone beyond just the facts you have written down. You understand the information enough to analyze how it might be asked on a test. For example, you might label what you had recorded on the right as shown on the following page.

[4]Ibid.

Copyright © Houghton Mifflin Company. All rights reserved.

Put name, date, class, and page number above here.

Label notes with a question here:

Take telegraphic notes here:

What principle is best for transferring from short-term to long-term memory?

Recite most pow'ful way to get s-t-mem to l-t-mem.

What are four reasons why recitation works?

1. makes pay attent
2. makes participate
3. have to understnd
4. feedbck

Go back to the three samples you just recorded and label them in the margin. The *Jeopardy* question for the first sample might be "Why is Geneva a good place for other nations to meet?"

Step 3: *Recite.* The third step in the label in the margin system is to test yourself. This is part of strengthening your memory and begins to process the information to your long-term memory. Cover up the wide column and use the key words, phrases, or questions in the left margin to *recite* the covered material. Repeat this until you are able to recite each section.

What memory principles do the first three steps of the label in the margin system follow? On a separate sheet of paper, discuss why this system should be effective.

Step 4: *Reflect.* Step 4 strengthens the memory as it further processes information into long-term memory. Step 4 is to *reflect*. Here you want to think about the ideas and how they fit in with other things you know. Try to get interested in them. Make them personal. Make use of association and mental visualization in your reflection.

Here is an example of how I might reflect about the notes you just wrote pertaining to obsolescence, sample 3 on page 108.

> Obsolescence—that's a tough word to spell, I need to figure out a way to spell it—maybe if I just break it up—ob-soles-cence. (it ends with the same letters as fence). So much for the spelling; what does it mean? Something not being worth anything because newer things have worn out. That's sure true of my computer. When I bought it three years ago, it was top of the line, now it won't do half of what I need it to do. How does this fit into what this chapter is talking about? Oh, I know. How can businesses make a profit if their equipment keeps becoming obsolete and they have to replace it every year. Now, how can I remember the word? It sounds sort of like *adolescence*. So let me picture an adolescent lobbing (**ob**) an old computer out a window. He could be saying, "**so** I have **less cents**" because he threw away the useless computer.

My train of thought may be a bit weird for you, but you get the idea. You are doing more than just memorizing; you are thinking about your notes when you reflect.

> **Step 5: *Review*.** Reflection begins the soaking-in or consolidation process. Reviewing continues it. Step 5 is to *review* your notes systematically. If your reviews are regular and routine, you can keep the level of recall high.

Tony Buzan in *Use Both Sides of Your Brain* makes the following suggestions:[5]

1. Use distributed practice to review. You should stop after about an hour of learning and take a ten-minute break. Your **first review** should come after this ten-minute break and should probably last about ten minutes. This should keep the recall high for approximately one day.
2. The **second review,** then, should take place within one day and should probably not take longer than three or four minutes. This should help you retain the information for about one week.
3. The **third review** should come before the week is up. It should require only a few minutes since you are reviewing, not relearning, the information.
4. A **fourth review** will probably be required if you have not used the material within a month. This should firmly place the information into long-term memory.

In the first review you should include bringing notes up to date by labeling them and reciting, reflecting, and so on. In other words, use the label in the margin system on the notes you took in class to process the information into your long-term memory.

[5]New York: Penguin Books, 1990.

In the second, third, and fourth review, you should make use of any consolidating method you know. Do anything necessary for the information to soak in. You could use the reciting part of the system again or write down everything you can remember about the question you wrote in the label or question column. Reviewing might include such things as making and using flash cards, creating mnemonics, making practice tests, and rerunning your mental videos. This activates your memory. You are taking information *from* your long-term memory. The more you activate information from your long-term memory, the easier it is to find that material when you need it. Make sure you are self-testing, not just mentally mumbling.

The times you set in your master schedule for routine study of a subject should be used for these reviews. Of course, immediately before and immediately after class are good review times. Right before you go to bed is also a good time to review.

One of the most significant aspects of reviewing is the cumulative effect it has on all aspects of learning, thinking, and remembering. You are building basic background. The more you know, the easier it is to learn. The person who does not review is, in effect, wasting the efforts he puts forth the first time. Your time is too valuable for that.

Step 6: *Summarize.* Either at the bottom of the page or at the end of your lecture notes, write a *summary*. You will want to do this after you review. Summarizing is a form of selectivity. If you understand your notes enough to make a concise version of them, you are probably well on your way to owning them. Your summary may be just one sentence; it may be a few sentences, a paragraph or even a page. It may even be a list or a chart. Mapping is also a form of summarizing that you may find useful if you rely heavily on visualization to remember. See the illustrations at the beginning of each chapter.

Lecture notes from the information presented about the label in the margin system might look something like the sample on the next page.

Sample Notes—Label in the Margin

Why use the label in the margin system?	L-M system based on mem principles Process info into long-term mem
What is step one?	Set up w/line 2½" Write important info on right—wide—telegrph **RECORD**
What is step two?	After class asap label infor w/ ?? here **LABEL**
What is step three?	After label, cover notes—ask question & say answer out loud in own wrds **RECITE**
What is step four?	After basic understand'ng of info, try to make personal, visualize, make connections **REFLECT**
What is step five?	B 4 put up notes, go back over all Also within day, week, and before test Use difrent techniques like flash cards, practice tests, etc. **REVIEW**
What is step six?	Condense info by writing summary at bottom of page or on sep page **SUMMARIZE**

The label in the margin system uses most of the memory principles and consists of six steps—Record, Label, Recite, Reflect, Review, and Summarize.

Probably the most difficult part of using the label in the margin system for many students is breaking the habit of writing too much or in complete sentences. Since you will be bringing your notes up to date very soon after class, you can get by with writing less. Remember that taking notes telegraphically is a skill that you must develop. Most likely, you won't be good at it for quite some time. If you have ever driven a car with a stick shift, remember when you first began to drive it? You had to really think yourself through it, and sometimes the ride was jerky. Now you shift without even thinking about it. The same is true with taking notes in shortened telegraphic form. At first you have to really think about what you are going to write. Sometimes it takes more time to think about what you are leaving out than it would to write it! Don't worry. You can think four times faster than most lecturers talk, so you have time to determine what you will write. With practice, this shortened form of note taking will become natural. You'll do it without much effort. Don't get me wrong. Taking notes is hard work. You have to become involved in class both physically and mentally. At the end of class, you will probably be exhausted. You don't learn by passively sitting. You process information only by becoming involved in what you are learning.

Although the lectures in your class certainly won't be this short, you need practice writing telegraphically. As a check to make sure you understand the system, **get someone to read you the following short lectures. Set your notebook paper up to use the system. When you have finished your notes, label your notes with questions in the margin.**

Where Memory Is Stored

The cerebral cortex can be divided down the middle, lengthwise, into two halves called the cerebral hemispheres. Each hemisphere of the cerebral cortex is divided into four lobes: The **frontal lobe** is concerned with reasoning, planning, parts of speech and movement (motor cortex), emotions, and problem solving. The **parietal lobe** deals with perception of stimuli related to touch, pressure, temperature, and pain. The **temporal lobe** is concerned with perception and recognition of auditory stimuli (hearing) and memory (hippocampus). The **occipital lobe** deals with many aspects of vision.[6]

Nicotine

Nicotine interrupts the flow of oxygen to the brain, particularly in the right hemisphere. The resulting oxygen deprivation is accompanied by depressed metabolism of glucose, which translates into sluggish and faulty memory, ineffective problem solving, and lower mental output in general. In addition, nicotine elevates levels of cortisol, the stress hormone. On a different note, nicotine appears to release a flood of beta-endorphins and dopamine which together serve to enhance mood.[7]

Sleep and Diet

Milk products stimulate melatonin production, which improves sleep. Simple sugars and fats decrease the oxygen supply to the brain, which decreases alertness and makes you sleepy. Alcohol consumption reduces the relative amount of time spent in REM sleep; therefore, sleep following alcohol consumption is not as restful as alcohol-free sleep. The more alcohol we consume, the less REM we get and the less rested we are in the morning. Food additives in general, and artificial sweeteners in particular, tend to increase alertness, which interferes with sleep. Eating a large meal in the evening also interferes with sleep.[8]

[6] http://faculty.washington.edu/chudler/lobe.html.
[7] From THE OWNER'S MANUAL FOR THE BRAIN by Pierce Howard. Copyright © 2000 by Pierce Howard. Reprinted by permission of the author.
[8] Ibid.

Have someone read this lecture to you as you practice taking notes using the label in the margin system.

Left Brain or Right Brain

There has been a lot of talk recently about left-brain, right-brain theory. The whole theory is somewhat confusing to students who want to know: "Am I left-brained or right-brained? How do I find out? Why should I care? Which is "good"? For a few minutes let's talk about some of these questions. To oversimplify things, the brain is primarily made up of two hemispheres. Although the right and left hemispheres work together, each side has a different function and processes information differently. Most people seem to have a dominant side. The catch is that we need to use both sides of the brain, so that left is not better than right; left is different from right. It appears that most classroom teaching is addressed to those who are predominantly left-brained, leaving those of us who are more right-brained feeling somewhat inadequate.

A closer look at the attributes of each side of the brain should clear up some of this confusion. The left brain processes material in a linear, sequential, logical way. The left brain is language oriented and also geared to mathematical reasoning. It responds to verbal instructions, sees things in parts that fit together neatly and logically into the whole. Learning rules, outlining, identifying and naming parts, sequencing events, arranging from part to whole, locating the main idea, and reading and following verbal instructions are all functions of the left brain. It is the left brain that pays attention to the mechanics of writing, such as spelling, punctuation, and agreement. Math, science, languages, writing, and logic are processed by the left brain.

The right brain, on the other hand, processes material in a more holistic, random, and intuitive way. The right brain is visual and creative. It responds by looking at a plan as a whole, not at the parts that make up the whole. Instead of memorizing vocabulary words, the right brain processes the words in context. Instead of sequencing events or numbering events in order, the right brain relates events to a whole theme. The right brain wants to see it, not be told about it. In writing, it is the right brain that pays attention to writing coherent sentences in meaningful sequence. Music appreciation, art appreciation, dance, perception, fantasy, and creativity are processed by the right brain.

If we are predominantly left-brained or predominantly right-brained, we should find ways to exercise the side of the brain that we use less. When learning new material, we should process the material in various ways, so as to use both sides of the brain. You may want to do some further research into your brain.

Exercise for Making Connections

Study the flow chart we constructed about how the memory works on page 93. Explain how the label in the margin system is built on this model.

■■■■■■■■■■■■■■■■

Summary Sheet for Label in the Margin: Lecture Notes

What you do	When to do it	Why you do it
INPUT OR GATHER INFORMATION		
RECORD *Listen carefully.* Write down *important information* from the lecture in the wide margin of your page. Don't write whole sentences; be *telegraphic.*	Get out your paper and pen as soon as you come to class. Take notes from beginning to end of class.	Short-term memory will not hold what you hear in class, so you need a record. Use *selectivity* and *write telegraphically* because you can't write down everything. Taking notes also helps you *pay attention.*
PROCESS INFORMATION GATHERED		
LABEL Read over your notes. *Determine the main ideas* of each section and label them in the form of a possible test question. *Underline*, number, or clean up notes so that they are clear and legible.	Most students think that when they have taken notes in class, their job is over. But forgetting begins immediately; therefore, as soon as possible after class, begin an immediate review of your notes.	Since you forget quickly, if you just take notes and do nothing, you'd end up relearning the material rather than remembering it. Reading over notes begins to *process the information. Labeling* them ensures that you *understood* what you wrote and *organizes* them in a meaningful way.
RECITE *Cover up* your notes. Use the labels as cues. *Say the main ideas out loud in your own words.*	This should be done as soon as you record and label your notes.	*Recitation* is the most powerful means we have of *transferring information from short-term memory to long-term memory.* You have begun to *learn* the material instead of merely recording it.

REFLECT
Think about the lecture. Make *connections* with things you already know. How does the lecture connect to the *textbook*? Make it *personal*. *Visualize*. Begin to *organize* your notes.

As soon as you recite or while you are reciting, begin to reflect. (You may want to reflect before you recite.)

Reflection makes the information *real* and *personal*. Therefore, you process information more deeply into your long-term memory.

ACTIVATE

REVIEW
Go over your notes. *Recite* by making use of the narrow margin. Make *flash cards, mnemonic devices,* or *practice tests,* or *map* the ideas found in the notes.

Review *ten minutes after you finish going over your notes,* keeping recall fresh for one day. Review again in *one day,* in *one week,* and then once more *before the test.*

Periodic review keeps you from forgetting what you already know. Before a test, you will just need to review, not relearn, the material.

SUMMARIZE
At the end of each section or each day's notes, write a short summary, or make a summary sheet such as this one.

Summarize *during* one of your *reviews.*

Summarizing allows for *consolidation* and promotes a deeper *understanding* of the material.

Questions about lecture notes:

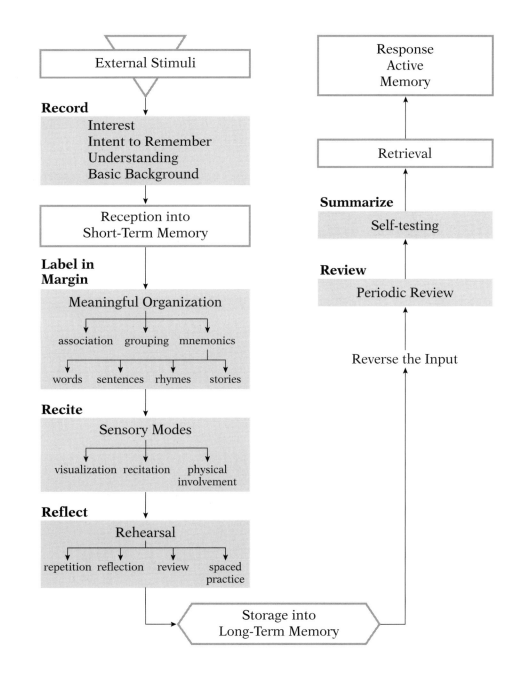

Virtual Field Trip:
Expanding What You Know About Note Taking

Visit http://collegesurvival.college.hmco.com/students and select "Hopper," or go to http://www.mtsu.edu/~studskl/3evirtual-fieldtrips.html.

Critical Thinking About **Taking Notes**

Critical thinkers are critical note takers. In the space below list what you think critical note takers do.

1. Critical note takers are willing to spend time reflecting on the ideas in their notes.

2. Critical note takers _____

3. Critical note takers _____

4. Critical note takers _____

5. Critical note takers _____

   _____

▪ Summary

To check to see if you have grasped the major ideas, answer the following questions:

What are the five obstacles that keep you from listening well?

1.

2.

3.

4.

5.

Name five things you can do to improve your listening.

1.

2.

3.

4.

5.

What do you consider the three most important reasons for taking notes during a lecture?

1.

2.

3.

List and explain the six steps of the label in the margin system for processing information from lectures.

Step 1:

Step 2:

Step 3:

Step 4:

Step 5:

Step 6:

What'ſ your Advice?

Sara is a freshman taking twelve credit-hours in college. She lives in the dorm, and it is her first time away from home. Sara was a very good student in high school and didn't have to study much to get As and Bs. Now she is doing exactly what she did in high school, and is struggling to even pass. She listens in class and reads her assignments unless the instructor is going to lecture on them anyway. Then she thinks it isn't necessary to read the assignment. Sara does her homework at night in her room and usually finishes it before visiting her friends or watching TV. Her roommate suggested that Sara needs to take notes in class. Although she never had to in high school, it was worth a try. Her history professor talked so fast that when she tried to write down what he was saying, she couldn't write fast enough. Fifteen minutes into the class she was so frustrated that she quit writing. She started to take notes in her psychology class, but got so interested in the discussion that she forgot about taking notes. Sara was unable to read what notes she did manage to take in her biology class when she got ready to study for a test. Although she reads all the assignments her English professor assigns, she has yet to pass the daily reading quiz. You are sitting at Sara's table at the grill. She is almost in tears and ready to give up and go home. Using what you have learned in this and previous chapters, can you help Sara? Help Sara make a list of things she might do. She has not had the benefit of taking this class and needs more instruction than a list. In addition to your list of what to do, you should suggest to her how to do it.

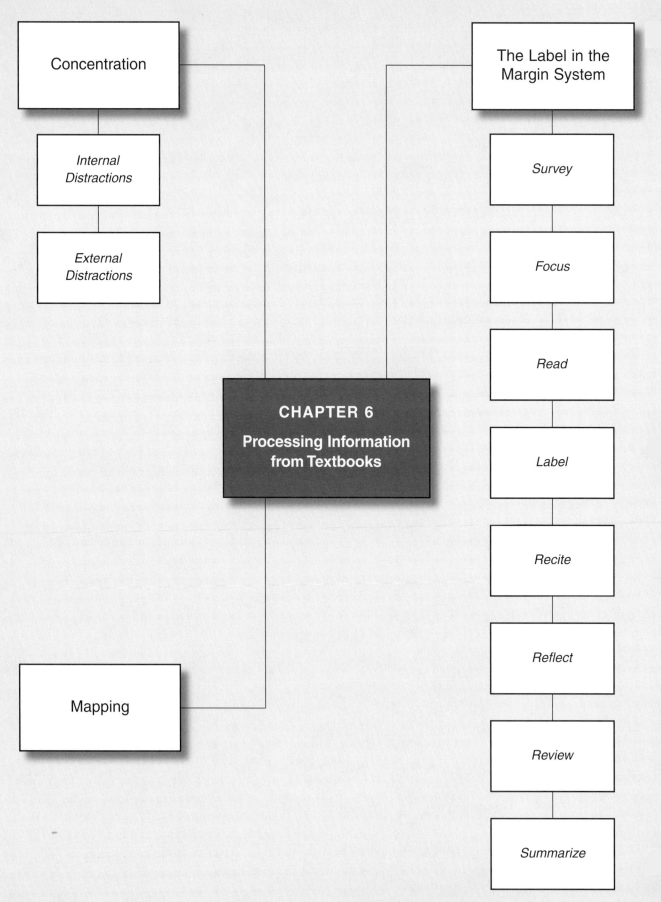

Concentration

Internal Distractions

External Distractions

Mapping

CHAPTER 6

Processing Information from Textbooks

The Label in the Margin System

Survey

Focus

Read

Label

Recite

Reflect

Review

Summarize

CHAPTER 6

Processing Information from Textbooks

Using the Label in the Margin System for Textbooks

Now that you have the basics of the system down, let's look at how it will work when reading a textbook. Remember that the first thing you want to do is to use as many memory principles as possible to gather the information. Now name several differences in gathering information from lectures and from textbooks.

Lectures	Textbooks

Making an Effort to Remember

Like listening to lectures, reading textbooks involves making an effort to remember. The three memory principles in this category are *interest, intent to remember,* and *basic background.* You want to make a conscious effort to use the memory principles before you begin to read. One of the best ways to do this is to **survey** the material before you begin. Look at the title, major and minor topics discussed, and the bold print; look at the pictures, study the graphs and charts, read the summary, and examine the review questions *before* you do any reading. As you are doing this, try to recall everything you already know about the subject. Surveying often builds interest, but most of all it gives you a basic background about the material you are going to read. Knowing something about the subject makes it easier to pay attention and easier to remember. By knowing where the reading is going, you can make connections as you read the material for the first time.

Think for a moment about your concentration when you read. If someone gave you a page and said, "Read this," would you read it in the same way as if he or she said, "Read this page to find three ways to process information or five ways to save time"? If you know why you are reading something, you will probably get more out of it. An obvious study strategy to use when reading a textbook, then, is to note the headings or the topic sentence of each paragraph and try to determine what you are looking for as you continue through the paragraph. This **focusing** should be done after you survey and before you begin to read.

Controlling the Amount and Form of Information

As you begin to read, you can control the amount and form of the information you gather by reading not more than one paragraph at a time before you process that information. Remember that your short-term memory can hold only five to seven bits of information at a time. Each paragraph will likely hold about that amount. If you read the entire chapter without processing bits of information into long-term memory, you would probably have to go back and reread most of the chapter in order to process it. Instead, why not use distributed practice, by processing information along the way?

Once you have read a paragraph, you want to process that information before you go on to the next one. The system works the same here as it did with taking notes. After you read a paragraph, to ensure you got the main idea and have selected the important points, write a question in the margin that labels those important points. Next, underline the answer to your question. Just as you were stingy with what you wrote while taking notes, you want to underline only the main words. You don't want to have to go back and reread the whole paragraph to find your answer. Underlining should be done *after* you read, *not while* you are reading, and the underlined words should answer the question you have written in the margin. This labeling and underlining is time-consuming, but you are going to have to process the information at some time before a test, so why not do it the first time? The result of your efforts is that each paragraph is labeled with a possible test question or two, and you can quickly review the main points without having to reread the chapter.

Review what you know about using the label in the margin system for reading textbooks.

In order to gather the information from your assignment, you first **survey** what you need to read.	What does this involve?
The second step of this gathering is to **focus.**	How is this accomplished?
The third step needed in gathering the information is to **read paragraph by paragraph.**	Why read only one paragraph at a time?
Then you **label the margin with a question.** The answer to the question should be the main ideas in the paragraph.	Explain why this is a good method to use.
Then you should **underline the answer to the question.**	

From here on, the system works the same as it did for lecture notes. You process the information by covering answers and asking yourself the question in the margin. You **recite** the answers until you are sure you have grasped the information. Before going on, **reflect.** Link the information to what you already know, relate it to the previous paragraph, and consider where the author may be going in the next paragraph. Make it personal. How will you use that information? How will you remember it for a test? If possible, make a mental video to help you *see* the information.

Once you are in control of the information in one paragraph, go on to the next and repeat the process. Because this system is demanding, you will probably want to do only several pages at a time. Make use of those minutes you used to waste. When the entire chapter is labeled, **review** the chapter to get the whole picture.

Go back to the section on reviewing lecture notes (pages 110–111) and apply this discussion to your textbook notes.

When should you review? _____

Why should you review? _____

Name some ways to review. _____

The last step in the label in the margin system is to **summarize.** Many students find it more useful to study from their notes than from their marked textbook. Making a summary sheet to study for each chapter will be helpful. In fact, many students prefer to write their notes from each chapter on paper, as with lecture notes, instead of writing in the textbook. Writing a summary is a good check to make sure you understand the information enough to condense it in your own words.

Practice Using the Label in the Margin System for Textbooks

Directions: Practice the Label in the Margin System on the selection entitled "Learning Styles: How a Person Learns Best," beginning on page 127. (Adapted from a presentation by A. Ducharme and L. Watford.)

1. **Survey.** Read the title, introduction, and each boldface term before you read the article.

2. **Focus.** Turn the headings into questions to help you determine what main ideas to look for. Also read the topic sentence of each paragraph.

3. **Read.** Now read each paragraph. Do not mark or underline while you are reading.

4. **Label.** Now determine what test question might come from that paragraph and write that question in the margin of this book. (I have modeled the first section paragraph for you. Now you can underline the answer to your question in as few words as possible.)

Read and label each paragraph of the passage before you go to the next paragraph.

5. **Recite** and **Reflect.**

Learning Styles: How a Person Learns Best

What senses do auditory learners use?

How do auditory learners learn?

Subjects good at?

Now it's your turn. Write questions in the margin, then underline the answers. Complete this reading through p. 129.

Everyone does not learn material in the same manner. And although we often have no control over how the instructor presents material in class, if as students we can analyze how we best learn, then we can make a conscious effort to reinforce what is taught in class by using our strengths.

Auditory learners use their <u>voices</u> and their <u>ears</u> as the primary mode of learning. If you are an auditory learner, you remember what you hear and what you yourself say. When something is hard to understand, you want to talk it out. When you're excited and enthusiastic about learning, you want to <u>verbally express</u> your <u>response</u>. And when an <u>assignment</u> is <u>given orally</u>, you probably remember it without writing it down. You <u>love class discussion</u>, you seem to <u>grow by</u> working and <u>talking with others</u>, and you <u>appreciate</u> a <u>teacher's</u> taking time to <u>explain</u> something to you. You are also easily distracted by sound because you attend to all of the noises around you, but ironically you may often interrupt a quiet moment by talking because you find silence itself disturbing. When you want to remember something, you should <u>say</u> it <u>aloud several times</u> because the oral repetition will set it in your mind. You find it difficult when a teacher asks you to work quietly at your desk for an extended period of time or when you try to study in a quiet room. For some auditory learners, their abilities serve them well in learning <u>music, foreign languages</u>, and in other areas that depend on good auditory discrimination.

Visual learners want to see the words written down, a picture of something being described, a time line to remember events in history, or the assignment written on the board. If you are a visual learner, you are very attuned to all the physical things in the classroom and appreciate a pleasant and orderly physical environment. You probably carefully organize your own materials and decorate your work space. You seek out illustrations, diagrams, and charts to help understand and remember information. You appreciate being able to follow what a teacher is presenting with material written on an overhead transparency or in a handout. You should review and study material by reading over your notes and by recopying and reorganizing in outline form.

Kinesthetic learners prefer it and learn better when they touch and are physically involved in what they are studying. If you are a kinesthetic learner, you want to act out a situation, make a product, do a project, and in general be busy with your learning. You find that when you physically do something, you understand it and remember it. You may take lots of notes to keep your hands busy, but you probably never reread the notes! You learn to use the computer by trying it, experimenting, and practicing. You learn concepts in social studies by simulating experiences in the classroom. You may become interested in poetry by becoming physically involved in the thoughts expressed. You want to be as active as possible during the learning experience. You usually express your enthusiasm by jumping up and getting excited when something is going well. And when asked to sit still for long periods, you fidget and may have been labeled as a behavior problem.

Mixed modality learners are able to function in more than one modality. In terms of achievement, students with mixed modality strengths often have a better chance of success than do those with a single modality strength, because they can process information in whatever way it is presented.[9]

To be successful, learners need to understand how they learn best and how to use their modality strengths to transfer learning from the weaker areas.

Finding an Effective Way To Study Through Your Modality Strengths

Auditory

If you learn best by hearing, you should listen carefully in class. You should ask your teacher's permission to tape-record the lesson. Listen to the tape several times if the material is new or difficult. Keep the tape to review for tests. Another study technique is to discuss the material with another student. If no one is available, turn on the tape recorder and discuss the information as if you were explaining it to someone else. Then listen to the recording. Once you have listened to the lesson tape and your discussion tape, you should do some reading about the subject. Remember to write down notes concerning important items to remember. Listening, reading, and writing will help strengthen your understanding of the material. If the teacher announces the new subject ahead of time, ask if there are any tapes, sound films, or filmstrips available on the new material. If so, use the available material before the material is taught in class.

Visual

If you learn best by seeing the material, you should read the material to be discussed in class before you get to class. When you are reading, remember not only to read the words but also to look at pictures, charts, maps, or graphs. You should take notes about the information while you are reading. You will probably benefit from mapping, clustering, outlining, or even using flash cards. Writing and placing information into maps, graphs, or the margin of your book will help you remember what you have read. Be sure to take notes while you are listening to class lectures and discussions.

[9]Pat B. Guild and Stephen Garger, *Marching to Different Drummers* (Alexandria, Va.: Association for Supervision and Curriculum Development, 1986).

Kinesthetic

If you learn best by doing something, you should write notes about what you are to learn. As you read, underline the important ideas *after* you have read a section, or write notes in the margin. It may also help you to make flash cards or maps, or to make charts, crossword puzzles, word bingo, picture puzzles, or mnemonic devices. Another effective way is to make a practice test about the material to be learned. Making a sample test will help point you to areas that are important and need to be studied more. You will learn best by using as many activities as possible.[10]

As a **review** take the quiz below.

(When we discuss mapping in the next few pages, I will ask you to come back and map the **Summary** of this article.)

Practice Quiz

If you have followed the system carefully, you should be able to pass the following quiz without looking back at the selection. Match the type of learning style to the characteristics, subjects, and effective ways of studying by putting the correct letter in the blank. You may use more than one style per question.

a. Auditory   b. Visual   c. Kinesthetic

_____   **1.** Learn better when they touch or are physically involved in what they are studying.

_____   **2.** Should recite information they want to learn.

_____   **3.** Want assignments written on the board.

_____   **4.** Should try to explain material to someone else.

_____   **5.** Are good at learning music and foreign languages.

_____   **6.** Would prefer to make a model or do a project.

_____   **7.** Would benefit from flash cards.

_____   **8.** Might want to tape a lecture and listen to it while commuting.

_____   **9.** Like material presented on overhead transparencies or in handouts.

_____   **10.** Don't like silence.

[10]Adapted from J. L. Sanders, *How to Do Homework Through Your Own Perceptual Strengths* (Jamaica, N.Y.: School of Education and Human Services, St. John's University, 1985).

brain byte

Pierce Howard says in the *Owner's Manual for the Brain* that if learning is made too simple in the classroom, it will be more difficult to actually use that information in the "street, home, or workplace." He says we should have to work and dig out our understanding. Isn't this what the label in the margin system asks you to do?

Summary Sheet for Label in the Margin: Textbooks

What you do	When to do it	Why you do it
INPUT OR GATHER INFORMATION		
SURVEY Skim the *title, major headings, bold print,* and *charts,* and read the *summary* and *review questions.*	Don't begin reading with the first page of the chapter. *Survey before you read.*	Surveying helps develop *interest* in what you are about to read. It gives you a *basic background.* Your subconscious begins to work.
FOCUS Turn each *major heading* into a *general question,* or use some other method of determining what you are looking for in the paragraph.	*Before you begin* reading each paragraph, determine what you will look for when you read.	Looking for the answer to a question rather than just reading promotes better *concentration* and *understanding.* In addition, you use the principle of selectivity.
READ Read each section *paragraph* by *paragraph* to find the answer to the question you have formulated. Look up any unfamiliar words. Read the section out loud if necessary.	*Do not go on to the next paragraph until you understand the one you are reading.* Do not underline or highlight at this time.	Reading paragraph by paragraph puts *small bits of information* into your memory so you needn't try to remember the whole chapter at once. It ensures *understanding.*
PROCESS INFORMATION GATHERED		
LABEL *Label* the *main idea* by writing a *question* or brief statement *in the margin.* Then *underline* the answer to your label. Be stingy with your underlining.	*After you read* each paragraph, determine the main idea and label it. Then *underline* what you labeled. Do not underline while reading.	This step ensures that you *understand* the main ideas in each paragraph. *Selectivity* eliminates the need to reread the chapter and organizes it in a way that allows you to *process* it into *long-term memory.*
RECITE *Cover* the underlined text and *recite* in your own words the answer to your margin question.	*Recite as soon as you complete the labeling and underlining.* Do not go on to the next paragraph until you can recite the main idea of this paragraph.	*Recitation* is the most powerful means you have of moving information from short-term to long-term memory.
REFLECT *Think about* what you have read. Make *connections* with things you already know. Make it *personal. Visualize.* Begin to *organize* your notes.	*As soon as you recite,* or while you are reciting, begin to reflect.	*Reflection* makes the information *real,* by processing it more deeply into your long-term memory. It is the difference between memorizing something and learning it.

ACTIVATE

REVIEW
Go over what you have read. *Recite* margin labels. Make *summary sheets, flash cards, mnemonic devices,* and *practice tests,* or *map* the ideas found in the chapter.

Review ten minutes after you finish the whole chapter, keeping recall fresh for one day. Review again in *one day, one week,* and then once more *before the test.*

Periodic review keeps you from forgetting what you already know. Before a test, you will need to just *review, not relearn,* the material.

SUMMARIZE
Make a summary sheet or notes on paper to condense main ideas.

Do this during one of your reviews.

Summarizing promotes the consolidation and understanding needed to use material that you have learned.

Learning Activity	When Listening to Lectures	When Reading Textbooks
Input or Gather Information	1. **Listen** carefully. 2. Write down important information telegraphically.	1. **Survey** the title, major headings, pictures, graphs, bold print, and summary. 2. **Focus** your attention on what you will read by turning each major heading into a question. 3. Read each section **paragraph by paragraph,** looking for the answer to the question.
Process Information Gathered	1. **Read** over notes and **label** them. 2. Cover notes and **recite** them. 3. Make the information personal by **reflecting.**	1. After completing each paragraph, label what the paragraph is about by writing a question in the margin. **Underline** the answer to the question. (Be stingy with your underlining!) 2. Cover your underlining in the text and **recite.** 3. Make the information **personal** by **reflecting.**

| Activate | 1. **Review** ten minutes after going over entire lecture. Review again in one day, in one week, and before a test. Use other methods such as flash cards, practice tests, and mnemonic devices.
2. **Summarize** at the end of each section of notes. | 1. **Review** ten minutes after finishing the chapter. Review again in one day, in one week, and before a test. Use other methods such as flash cards, practice tests, and mnemonic devices.
2. Make a **summary sheet** for each chapter. |

Do You Understand How the Label in the Margin System Works?

Label the following situations with the correct *source* (classroom lecture or textbook reading) and the correct *stage* (input or gather, process information gathered, or activate). Use the chart on pages 131–132.

1. When he was finished reading, José went back through the entire chapter and tried to recite the answers to the questions he had written in the margin.

   Source _____ Stage _____

2. After class, Jean read over her lecture notes and wrote the key words and phrases on the left side of her paper.

   Source _____ Stage _____

3. Sally wrote a question beside each paragraph in Chapter 3 of her History 201 textbook and then underlined the answer to each question.

   Source _____ Stage _____

4. In order to study for his upcoming exam, Bobby covered up his lecture notes and recited the importance of the key words he had written.

   Source _____ Stage _____

5. When the instructor had concluded her lecture series on the different breeds of beef cattle, David wrote a summary at the end of that section in his notes, putting it into his own words.

   Source _____ Stage _____

6. To make sure he retained the information from his chapters, Mark regularly went over the labels he had written in his textbook.

   Source _____ Stage _____

7. Jeff made summary sheets and flash cards and used mnemonics in order to refresh rather than to relearn the information from his German 210 class.

   Source _____ Stage _____

8. When class began, Curtis listened carefully to everything that the instructor said.

   Source _____ Stage _____

9. To begin her Psychology 141 reading assignment, Jane read the title, checked out the bold headings, and surveyed the graphs and the chapter summary.

   Source _____ Stage _____

10. While reading, Joe turned each major heading into a question, and then read each paragraph to answer the question.

    Source _____ Stage _____

11. When Beth's instructor said, "There are seven stages in Chickering's student development theory called vectors," Beth wrote "7 stages (vectors)—Chickering s.d. theory."

    Source _____ Stage _____

12. JoEllen took a few minutes to think about all of the information she had been reciting from Chapter 10 in her Sociology 310 textbook.

    Source _____ Stage _____

Questions I need to ask about the system:

Virtual Field Trip:
Let's Learn More About Critical Reading and Mapping

Visit http://collegesurvival.college.hmco.com/students and select "Hopper," or go to http://www.mtsu.edu/~studskl/3evirtual-fieldtrips.html.

Mapping

brain byte

The human brain is not organized or designed for linear, one-path thought. Many brain researchers confirm that graphic organizers like mapping help learners understand and recall information better. Maps that are revised and color-coded boost learning and retention.

If you find some information particularly difficult, you may want to use the memory principle of visualization to process it. A method called mapping is useful for students who learn well visually. A map of any reading selection or lecture is simply a **visual representation** of important information selected from the text. It's like a picture outline. The central focus of the map is the focus of the material, such as the topic or the main idea of the piece. It is represented as the center of attention. A map is usually hierarchical and shows the relationships among pieces of the whole.

Mapping can be used to organize information from sections of a chapter or even an entire chapter, depending on the complexity of the material. It serves best as a study aid by organizing information into manageable parts with observable relationships that can be easily understood and remembered.

Below is a paragraph given to students with the instruction to map the paragraph so that they could remember the material better. Following the paragraph are several examples of their mapping.

Four Kinds of Art

Each art form puts different demands on artists. Drama requires training of the voice and an ability to re-create life on stage. To excel in ballet, one must have great strength and endurance. A career in opera requires unique natural gifts and a willingness to spend years in training. Unlike these other arts, sculpture requires a talent for composing in three dimensions and a liking for manual labor. It is interesting how different countries bring a particular art form to mind. Because of Shakespeare, England comes to mind when one thinks of great drama. Russia recalls the performances of its spectacular ballet companies. Italy is synonymous with drama set to lush melodies of opera and with sculpture by the greatest artists who ever lived.

Before looking at examples of other students' work, try this exercise. In the space below, illustrate how you might visually depict the information given in the paragraph above in order to learn it for a test.

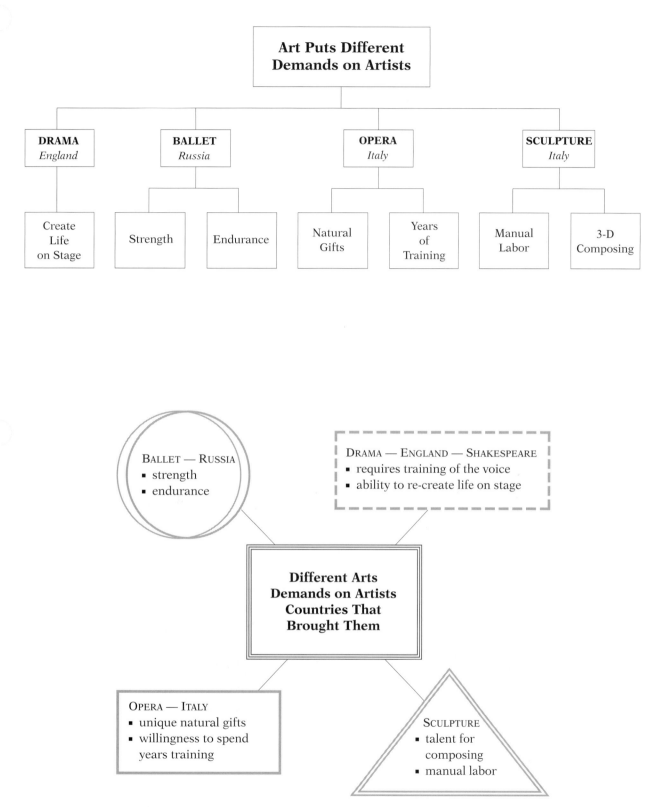

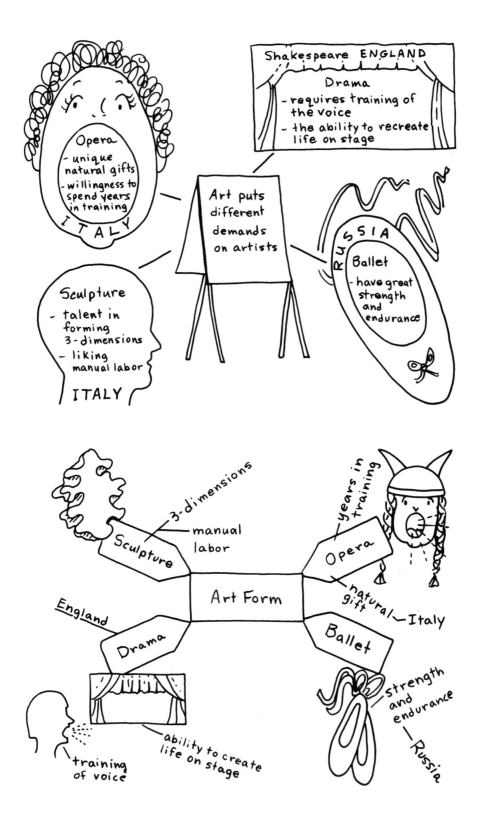

On page 137 is a short article about things homeowners can do to save energy. On the next page you will find a student's study notes on the first paragraph. The first example is how the information looked in her notes when her instructor was lecturing. The second is her version of the label in the margin system from this textbook. The third is her attempt at mapping.

Your job is to examine the second paragraph below and map it. Because the goals of the label in the margin system and mapping are the same, the strategies used to process the information into long-term memory will also overlap. When mapping, I find it easier to label in the margin before I map. Remember, you are mapping not to be artistic but to help you remember the details you might need for a test.

Practice with Mapping

Read the article below. First label in the margin. Then use another sheet of paper to map it.

All homeowners can take action if they are serious about saving on energy costs. Those with more than a hundred dollars to spend should consider any of the following steps. First, sidewalls and especially the ceiling of a home should be fully insulated. Proper insulation can save thirty percent or more of a heating or cooling bill. Next, storm windows should be installed throughout the house. They provide an insulating area of still air that may reduce energy loss by ten percent or more. Finally, a homeowner might consider installing a solar hot-water heating system. Four key factors in such a decision are geographical location, the amount of sunlight available, energy costs in the area, and the construction of the house.

Homeowners with less than a hundred dollars to spend can take many energy-saving steps as well. To begin with, two kinds of inexpensive sealers can be used to reduce energy leaks around the house. Caulking will seal cracks around the outside windows, door frames and at the corners of the house. Weather stripping can be applied to provide a weathertight seal between the frame and moving parts of doors and windows. Another inexpensive step is to check that a home-heating or cooling system is clean. A dirty or clogged filter, for example, can make a furnace or air conditioner work much harder to heat or cool a house. In addition, a "low-flow" shower head can either be purchased separately or a small plastic insert available at the hardware store can be added to a regular head to limit water flow. Blinds and drapes can be used to advantage throughout the year. In winter, they can be closed at night to reduce heat loss. In summer, they can be closed during the day to keep the house cooler. Finally, a ceiling fan can be turned on in the summer to distribute cool air. When the thermostat is set at 78 degrees, the fan will make it seem like 72 degrees. If one reverses the blades to go clockwise in the winter, the fan will force heat down and circulate it throughout the room. A ceiling fan uses no more electricity than a 100-watt light bulb. These and other relatively inexpensive steps can be used to produce large savings.

Sample Notes if This Had Been a Lecture

What are three actions a homeowner with more than $100 can take to save energy?

Save energy cost > $100
1. Insulate sidewalls and ceilings, 30% sav
2. Install storm windows
3. Solar hot-water heater. Factors to consider:
   Geo location
   Amt sunlght avail
   Energy costs
   Construction of house

Sample of the Label in the Margin System for Textbooks

What are three actions a homeowner with more than $100 can take to save energy?

All homeowners can take action if they are serious about saving on energy costs. Those with more than a hundred dollars to spend should consider any of the following steps. First,[1] sidewalls and especially the ceiling of a home should be fully insulated. Proper insulation can save thirty percent or more of a heating or cooling bill. Next,[2] storm windows should be installed throughout the house. They provide an insulating area of still air that may reduce energy loss by ten percent or more. Finally,[3] a homeowner might consider installing a solar hot-water heating system. Four key factors in such a decision are geographical location, the amount of sunlight available, energy costs in the area, and the construction of the house.

Sample Mapping

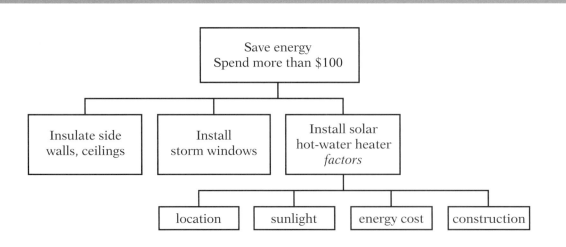

In order to study for your test on which you know you will be asked to name and explain the steps of the label in the margin system, **construct a map of the label in the margin system as a summary sheet.**

Promoting Concentration

Have you ever finished a chapter in a book and realized that you had no idea what you just read? Or sat in class and realized that fifteen minutes had passed and, although your body was there, your mind had taken a vacation or dealt with something that was bothering you? These are examples of lapses in *concentration*. Many times stress is the cause of these lapses in concentration, and lack of concentration can cause a great deal of stress. If concentration is improved and efficient studying accomplished, there will be less stress. You already know some strategies for promoting concentration. The memory principles provide the basis for strategies that promote concentration. In order to develop the best plan for concentration, you need to determine which kinds of distractions prevent you from concentrating.

Internal Distractions

Many times the causes of your stress are the same things that cause a lack of concentration. These are usually referred to as internal distractions. There are so many things going on in your life that the balancing act you are performing may also bring about anxiety and other internal distractions that are detrimental to concentration. Internal distractions come from some source outside, but you have internalized the problem—your financial-aid check is lost, your mother is ill, your best friend has been in a car wreck.

List some things that are going on in your life that prevent you from concentrating.

_____

_____

_____

You can't always eliminate internal distractions, but you do want to be able to control them when you need to concentrate. Here are a few hints that will help you now.

1. **Keep an attention list.** When you are trying to concentrate and you keep thinking of something else, stop and make a note on your attention list. That way, you won't forget that something needs your attention, even though you have physically put it aside for the time being.

2. **Check your concentration.** Physically addressing breaks in concentration will help you get back on track. Try this technique in programming your mind to concentrate. In class or when reading an assignment, have a sheet of paper handy. When you note that you are not paying attention, put a check on the paper and immediately return to your task. The first time you check your concentration, you may fill up an entire sheet. But each subsequent time you use this technique, you will have fewer and fewer checks. (Popping a rubber band on your wrist when your attention strays would have a similar effect, but it's so much more painful!)

3. **Review the time management and memory principles.** In particular, look for techniques that might be particularly effective for you—taking breaks, visualizing, reciting, and so on.

After reviewing the concentration, time-management, and memory principles discussed thus far, name three things that you will try this week, each time you are in class and each time you study, that you think will help promote your concentration.

1. _____

2. _____

3. _____

External Distractions

Often, there are external or physical distractions in your study environment. We know that studying every day at the same time and at the same place programs the mind and promotes concentration. Your time-management analysis should have helped you determine the best time for you to study each subject. Now, let's develop a plan for analyzing your place to study. Your regular place should be one that you use exclusively for studying. If you studied in the chair where you normally watch TV, your mind would automatically want to know what's on TV. If you studied at the kitchen table, you would get hungry. If you studied in bed, even if you weren't sleepy before, you would become sleepy. Your regular study place should have a desk, a comfortable chair, the necessary supplies, good lighting, and so on. Obviously, your senses are involved. Examine each of them to determine the factors that might affect your concentration when you study.

Visualize yourself studying and list the factors concerning each sense that would either promote or hinder your concentration.

	Promote	*Hinder*
Sight		
Hearing		
Smell		
Taste		
Touch		

Now, write a short paragraph in which you describe your ideal study place.

Discovering the Best Place for You to Study

Directions: This week choose two different study times and places to do your regular studying that you think will promote concentration. Use the chart on page 142 to analyze the time and place for its effectiveness as a regular study time and place for you.

Time and Place 1

Place

_____

Time

_____

Visual Distractions	*Auditory Distractions*
_____	_____
_____	_____
_____	_____
_____	_____
Other Distractions	*Features That Make This a Good Place to Study*
_____	_____
_____	_____
_____	_____
_____	_____

Overall analysis of time and place for use as a regular study place (RSP):

_____

Time and Place 2

Place

_____

Time

_____

Visual Distractions	*Auditory Distractions*
_____	_____
_____	_____
_____	_____
_____	_____
Other Distractions	*Features That Make This a Good Place to Study*
_____	_____
_____	_____
_____	_____
_____	_____

Overall analysis of time and place for use as a regular study place (RSP):

_____

Study Habits Analysis

Are you using all that you've learned so far about studying to learn things faster and better? We are creatures of habit, and often we don't realize that our habits are keeping us from being successful. Choose assignments from three different classes this week and use them to analyze your study habits. One check sheet is provided below. You will need to make copies of the check sheet for the other assignments, and several extra to use at a later time. Remember to use the time-management and memory principles.

Assignment Check Sheet

Name _____   **Class Chosen for Assignment**

Analysis _____

1. Describe in detail the assignment you chose.

2. When did you begin working on the assignment in relation to when it was due?

3. Was this a good time to work on the assignment? Why?

4. Where did you work on the assignment?

5. Was this a good place? Why?

6. Did you
    _____ Take breaks?
    _____ Take notes even though it was not required?
    _____ Visualize as you were learning new concepts?
    _____ Give your full attention to studying?
    _____ Try to determine when you might be tested on this assignment?
    _____ Try your best?

Virtual Field Trip:
Searching for Concentration Tips

Visit http://collegesurvival.college.hmco.com/students and select "Hopper," or go to http://www.mtsu.edu/~studskl/3evirtual-fieldtrips.html.

▪▪▪ Summary

To check to see if you have grasped the major points of this chapter on **processing information from textbooks,** answer the following questions.

_____

How does gathering information from lectures differ from gathering information from textbooks?

▶ _____

What are the three steps of gathering information from textbooks?

1. _____

2. _____

3. _____

How does the labeling system in textbooks differ from the labeling step in lecture notes?

▶ _____

Why should you survey before you read a chapter?

Survey _____

How do you focus on the paragraph you are reading?

Focus _____

Why should you process a paragragh before you go on to the next one?

▶ _____

Explain the rest of the label in the margin system for textbooks.

Recite _____

Reflect _____

Review _____

Summarize _____

▶ _____

What is the goal of mapping?

**Explain how to check
your concentration.**

▶ _____

**How can you eliminate or
at least minimize physical
or external distractions?**

▶ _____

**Describe what would be
an ideal study place for
you.**

▶ _____

▪ What's Your Advice?

This is KaToya's third semester at her university. She has done
well, but this semester she is having a difficult time. Four of her
classes require a great deal of reading. So far she has managed to
get all the reading done, but she rarely remembers what she has
read. She has set aside every weeknight from 7:00 PM to 11:00 PM
for reading assignments. As she reads, she uses a highlighter and
often finds that she has highlighted an entire page. One professor
gives pop quizzes based on the reading, so KaToya saves that assignment for last, thinking she'll remember it more easily. She
even reads it in bed where it is nice and quiet. She has yet to pass
a quiz and her exam scores are not much better. What advice can
you give KaToya?

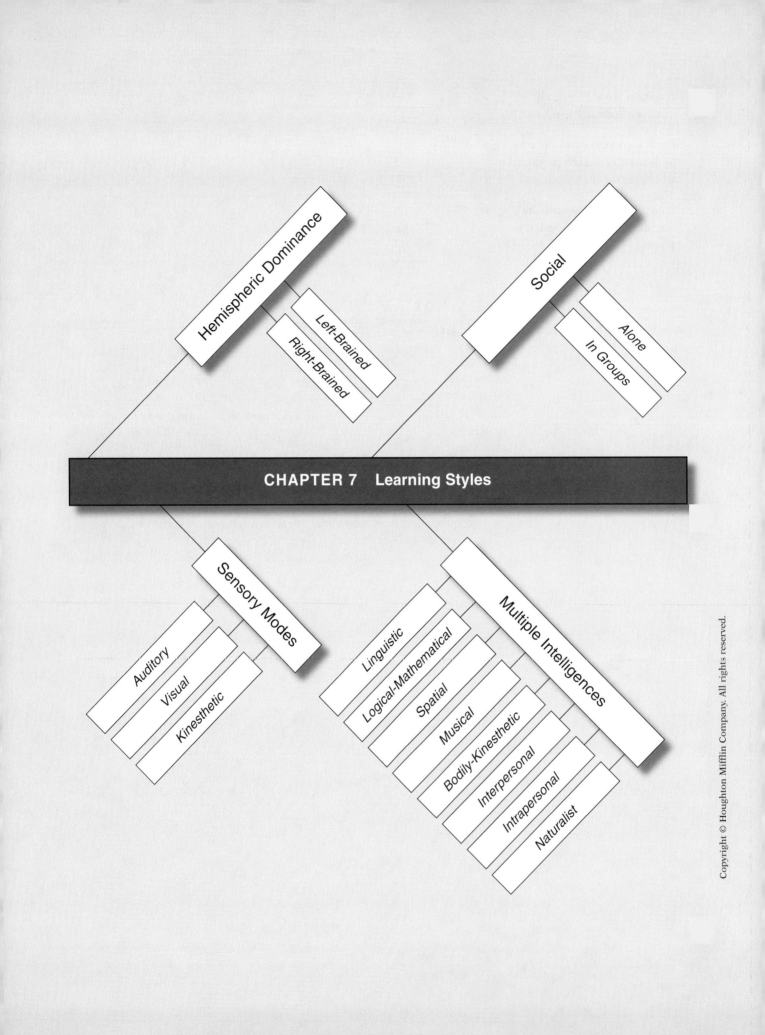

CHAPTER 7   Learning Styles

Hemispheric Dominance
- Left-Brained
- Right-Brained

Social
- Alone
- In Groups

Sensory Modes
- Auditory
- Visual
- Kinesthetic

Multiple Intelligences
- Linguistic
- Logical-Mathematical
- Spatial
- Musical
- Bodily-Kinesthetic
- Interpersonal
- Intrapersonal
- Naturalist

CHAPTER 7

Learning Styles

Why Determine Learning Style?

In previous chapters you have been briefly introduced to the idea of learning styles. You took practice notes about left-brain and right-brain theory on page 114, and you worked a label in the margin exercise from a textbook selection about modality strengths, pages 127 to 129. The way you process information is unique. Because the label in the margin system is based on the memory principles and incorporates various learning strategies, it works for most learning styles. You may have found that you need to modify it slightly to better fit your learning style, or to rely heavily on one aspect of it because of your learning style. No one else processes information in exactly the same way you do. If you discover how you process information best, you can learn things both more efficiently and in less time. By applying strategies that address your learning style, you can study faster and better.

You can expand the strategies you use for learning and studying and customize some of the strategies already discussed in this book. When learning something new or difficult, you naturally tend to use the learning style you prefer. It is good to know what your learning style is so that you can process information in the most efficient way. Even when material is not presented in the way you prefer, you can use your knowledge of learning styles to adjust and be flexible. No matter who your instructor is or what the subject matter is, you need to know how to convert what you need to learn to the way you learn best. However, it is also good to reinforce learning in as many different ways as possible. So, while knowing your style preference is good, you also need to expand your ways of learning. Knowing your learning style and being able to recognize and understand the learning style of others who play a role in your learning—your professors, roommate or spouse, and those in your study group—is useful in getting the most out of any situation.

Hemispheric Dominance

Differences Between Left and Right Hemispheres

One way of looking at learning styles is to determine your hemispheric dominance. Are you more right-brained or left-brained? We know that the cerebral cortex is the part of the brain that houses rational functions. It is divided into two hemispheres connected by a thick band of nerve fibers (the corpus callosum) which sends messages back and forth between the hemispheres. And while brain research confirms that both sides of the brain are involved in nearly every human activity, we also know that the left side of the brain is the seat of language and processes in a logical and sequential order. The right side is more visual and processes intuitively, holistically, and randomly. Most people seem to have a dominant side. Our dominance is a preference, not an absolute. When learning is new, difficult, or stressful, we *prefer* to learn in a certain way. It seems that our brain goes on autopilot to the preferred side. While nothing is entirely isolated on one side of the brain or the other, the characteristics commonly attributed to each side of the brain serve as an appropriate guide for ways of learning things more efficiently and ways of reinforcing learning. Just as it was more important for our purposes to determine that memory is stored in many parts of the brain rather than learn the exact lobe for each part, likewise it is not so much that we are biologically right-brain or left-brain dominant, but that we are more comfortable with the learning strategies characteristic of one over the other. What you are doing is lengthening your list of strategies for learning how to learn and trying to determine what works best for you. You can and must use and develop both sides of the brain. But because the seat of our preferences probably has more neural connections, learning may occur faster. This section will look at some differences between left- and right-brain preferences. Be on the lookout for practical strategies that work for you. Following is an inventory to help you determine the balance of your hemispheres. It might be a good idea to take this inventory before you read the subsequent explanations. This section will examine some differences between the left and right hemispheres and provide a few suggestions for both left- and right-dominant students.

How Does Your Brain Process Information?

Check the answers that most closely describe your preferences.

1. Are you usually running late for class or other appointments?

    _____ a. Yes

    _____ b. No

2. When taking a test do you prefer that questions be

    _____ a. Objective (true-false, multiple-choice, matching)

    _____ b. Subjective (discussion or essay questions)

3. When making decisions

    _____ a. You go with your gut feeling—what I feel is right

    _____ b. You carefully weigh each option

4. When relating an event

    _____ a. You go straight to the main point and then fill in details

    _____ b. You tell many details before telling the conclusion

5. Do you have a place for everything and everything in a place?

    _____ a. Yes

    _____ b. No

6. When faced with a major change in life, you are

    _____ a. Excited

    _____ b. Terrified

7. Your work style is like this

    _____ a. You concentrate on one task at a time until it is complete.

    _____ b. You usually juggle several things at once.

8. Can you tell approximately how much time has passed with a watch?

    _____ a. Yes

    _____ b. No

9. Which is easier for you to understand?

    _____ a. Algebra

    _____ b. Geometry

10. Is it easier for you to remember people's names or to remember people's faces?

_____ a. Names

_____ b. Faces

11. When learning a new piece of equipment

_____ a. You jump in and wing it. (A manual is the last resort.)

_____ b. You carefully read the instruction manual before beginning.

12. When someone is speaking, do you respond to

_____ a. What is being said (words)

_____ b. How it is being said (tone, tempo, volume, emotion)

13. When speaking, do you use few or many gestures? (Do you use your hands when you talk)?

_____ a. Few (very seldom use hands when you talk)

_____ b. Many (couldn't talk with hands tied)

14. What is your desk, work area, or laundry area like?

_____ a. Neat and organized

_____ b. Cluttered with stuff I might need

15. When asked your opinion

_____ a. You immediately say what's on your mind (often foot-in-mouth)

_____ b. You think before you speak

16. Do you do your best thinking sitting at your desk, walking around, or lying down?

_____ a. Sitting

_____ b. Walking around or lying down

17. When reading a magazine do you

_____ a. Jump in at whatever article looks most interesting

_____ b. Start at page one and read in sequential order

18. When you're shopping and see something you want to buy

_____ a. You save up until you have the money

_____ b. You charge it

19. In math, can you explain how you got the answer?

_____ a. Yes

_____ b. No

Adapted from "Learning Style Preferences" by Adele Ducharme and Luck Watford, Valdosta State University, National Association for Developmental Educational Conference, Orlando, 1987.

Now, using the diagram of the brain below, color in the sections that correspond to your answers on the questionnaire. For example, if your answer for question 1 is a, you will find 1a on the right side of the brain. Color in this section; then continue with the remaining questions. When you are finished, you will have a better sense of whether you are predominantly left- or right-brained or whether you use both sides equally.

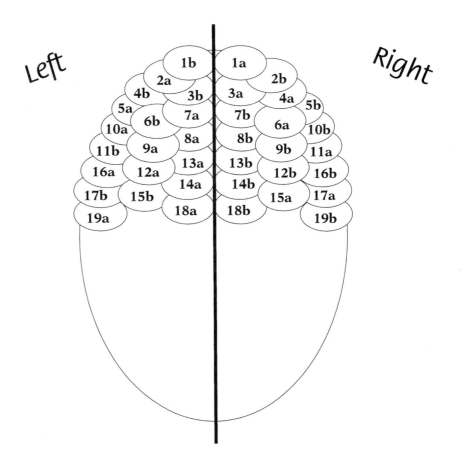

Linear Versus Holistic Processing

The left side of the brain processes information in a linear manner. It processes from part to whole. It takes pieces, lines them up, and arranges them in a logical order; then it draws conclusions. The right brain, however, processes from whole to parts, holistically. It starts with the answer. It sees the big picture first, not the details. You can understand, then, why some of the strategies you have learned work well for right-brained students. If you are right-brained, you may have difficulty following a lecture unless you get the big picture first. Do you now see why it is absolutely necessary for a right-brained person to read an assigned chapter or background information before a lecture or to survey a chapter before reading? If an instructor doesn't consistently give an overview before he or she begins a lecture, you may need to ask at the end of class what the next lecture will be and how you can prepare for it. If you are predominantly right-brained, you may also have trouble outlining. (You've probably written many papers first and outlined them later because an outline was required.) The mind maps that begin each chapter in this book may be a better brainstorming and organizing method for you to use. You're the student who needs to know *why* you are doing something. Left-brained students would do well to exercise their right brain in such a manner!

List some specific strategies described in the paragraph above that would use the right side of the brain.

_____

_____

Let's carry this beyond study strategies. When you are dealing with right-brained professors, classmates, spouses, children, or bosses, it is important to give the big picture before you begin details. Describe a situation where this might have been helpful to you.

_____

_____

Sequential Versus Random Processing

In addition to thinking in a linear manner, the left brain processes in sequence, that is, in order. The left-brained person is a list maker. If you are left-brained, you were in your element when master schedules and daily planning were discussed. You complete tasks in order and take pleasure in checking them off when they are accomplished. Likewise, learning things in sequence is relatively easy for you. For example, the steps of the label in the margin system make sense to you, since they are a logical sequence for processing information from lectures and textbooks. Spelling involves sequence as well. If you are left-brained, you are probably a good speller. The left brain is also at work in the linear and sequential processing of math and in following directions.

By contrast, the approach of the right-brained student is random. If you are right-brained, you may flit from one task to another. You will get just as much done, but perhaps without having addressed priorities. An assignment may be late or incomplete, not because you weren't working but because you were working on something else. You were ready to rebel when I suggested making a schedule and lists. But because of the random nature of your dominant side, you must make lists and you must make schedules. This may be your only hope for survival in college. You should also make a special effort to read directions. Oh yes, the mention of spelling makes you cringe. Use the dictionary, carry a Franklin speller, use the spell checker on your computer. Never turn in an assignment without proofing for spelling. Because the right side of the brain is color-sensitive, you might try using colors to learn sequence, making the first step green, the second blue, the last red. Or you may want to walk a sequence, either by physically going from place to place or by imagining it. For the first step of the sequence, you might walk to the front door; for the second, to the kitchen; for the third, to the den; and so on. Or make step one a certain place or thing in your dorm room or study place, and step two another. If you consistently use the same sequence, you will find that this strategy is transferable to many tasks involving sequence.

 braiN byte

Researchers have discovered that musicians process music more on the left side, while non-musicians process it on the right side. Musicians tend to analyze the music more, changing the function of the task.

Time management and stress management can be improved by noting the random nature of the right side of the brain, making a plan, and taking action. What are two specific things you can do to combat the random nature of the right brain?

_____

_____

List some specific strategies students can use when trying to process something that involves sequence.

_____

_____

Symbolic Versus Concrete Processing

The left brain has no trouble processing symbols. Many academic pursuits deal with symbols such as letters, words, and mathematical notations. The left-brained person tends to be comfortable with linguistic and mathematical endeavors. Left-brained students will probably just memorize vocabulary words or math formulas. The right brain, on the other hand, wants things to be concrete. The right-brained person wants to see, touch, or interact with the real object. Right-brained students may have had trouble learning to read using phonics. They prefer to see words in context, to see how the formula works. To use your right brain, create opportunities for hands-on activities. Use something real whenever possible. You may also want to draw a math problem or illustrate your notes. Mapping is another strategy you will definitely want to try.

Think of a class you are taking. List some specific strategies you can use in that class to make things more concrete.

Class _____

_____

_____

_____

Logical Versus Intuitive Processing

The left brain processes in a linear, sequential, logical manner. When you process on the left side, you use information piece by piece to solve a math problem or work out a science experiment. When you read and listen, you look for the pieces so that you can draw logical conclusions. If you process primarily on the right side of the brain, you use intuition. You may know the right answer to a math problem but not be sure how you got it. You may have to start with the answer and work backward. On a quiz, you have a gut feeling as to which answers are correct, and you are usually right. In writing, it is the left brain that pays attention to mechanics such as spelling, agreement, and punctuation. But the right side pays attention to coherence and meaning; that is, your right brain tells you it feels right.

How can you use the left side of your brain to proofread your papers?

_____

How can you use the right side of your brain to proofread your papers?

_____

Why would a right-brained student be more likely to fall for trick test questions? What strategies can a student use to ensure that he identifies the trick questions?

_____

Verbal Versus Nonverbal Processing

Left-brained students have little trouble expressing themselves in words. Right-brained students may know what they mean but often have trouble finding the right words. The best illustration of this is to listen to people giving directions. The left-brained person will say something like, "From here, go west three blocks and turn north on Vine Street. Go three or four miles and then turn east onto Broad Street." The right-brained person will sound something like, "Turn right [*pointing right*] by the church over there [*pointing again*]. Then you will pass a McDonald's and a Walmart. At the next light, turn right toward the BP station." So how is this relevant to planning study strategies? Right-brained students need to back up everything visually. If it's not written down, they probably won't remember it. And it would be even better for right-brained students to illustrate it. They need to get into the habit of making a mental video of things as they hear or read them. Right-brained students need to know that it may take them longer to write a paper, and the paper may need more revision before it says what they want it to say. This means allowing extra time when a writing assignment is due.

What are some ways to visually back up things you need to learn?

_____

_____

_____

Reality-Based Versus Fantasy-Oriented Processing

The left side of the brain deals with things the way they are in reality. When left-brained students are affected by the environment, they usually adjust to it. Not so with right-brained students: They try to change the environment! Left-brained people want to know the rules and follow them. In fact, if there are no rules for situations, they will probably make up rules to follow! Left-brained students know the consequences of not turning in papers on time or of failing a test. But right-brained students are sometimes not aware that there is anything wrong. So, if you are right-brained, make sure you constantly ask for feedback and reality checks. It's too late in the day just before finals to ask if you can do extra credit. Keep a careful record of your assignments and tests. Visit with your professor routinely. While this fantasy orientation may seem a disadvantage, in some cases it is an advantage. The right-brained student is creative. In order to learn about the digestive system, you may decide to become a piece of food! And since emotion is processed on the right side of the brain, you will probably remember anything you become emotionally involved in as you are trying to learn.

Critical Thinking About **Reality Checks**

List some ways to create reality checks for yourself throughout the semester.

_____

_____

_____

These are just some of the differences that exist between the functioning of the left and right hemispheres, but you can see a pattern. Because left-brained strategies are the ones used most often in the classroom, right-brained students sometimes feel inadequate. However, you now know that you can be flexible and adapt material to the right side of your brain. Likewise, those of you who are predominantly left-brained know that it would be wise to use both sides of the brain and employ some right-brained strategies. One last word to right-brained students: Being right-brained is a reason you do things the way you do, not an excuse!!

Sensory Modes of Learning

braiN byte

A fire breaks out in the room. Your immediate, first reaction will be one of the following: (1) **visual** (quickly you size up the situation, looking for exits, others in need, etc.); (2) **auditory** (start yelling "Fire" or giving directions or screaming); (3) **kinesthetic** (start running for the exits or assisting others to exit). While you may do all three, one will be an instinctual first reaction. That's your learning style.

Intrinsic to the theory of hemispheric dominance is sensory modality. In order for your analysis of information to be more balanced, you need to use both sides of the brain. You can probably see that the right side of the brain is more visual and kinesthetic, two modes that are often ignored in lecture-centered classes. The left side tends to favor an auditory mode of learning. Just as you are not totally left- or right-brained, you also do not learn in one mode exclusively. The inventory on the next few pages will help you determine the mode in which you learn best. You will want to take this inventory before you read about each mode; however, you probably already know which one you prefer. A brief example may be in order. If you were learning how to use a new computer program, would you want to read the directions and study examples (visual)? Would you want someone to tell you how it works or read the directions out loud (auditory)? Or would you want to do it yourself, perhaps with someone showing you (kinesthetic)? As noted, you probably prefer to learn new or difficult material within your mode; but in order to get the full impact, you need to reinforce that learning with other modes.

According to research done by Edgar Dale, people generally remember only 10 percent of what they read.[1] (Do you see why the label in the margin system is necessary?) They remember 20 percent of what they hear and 30 percent of what they see. Retention is increased to 50 percent if they hear *and* see something, as when watching a movie or a demonstration. People generally remember 70 percent of what they say or write and 90 percent of what they say as they do something. However, they remember 95 percent of what they teach to someone else.

[1]Cited in Winman and Meierhenry, Educational Media.

Sensory Modality Inventory

There are twelve incomplete sentences and three choices for each. Score the three choices by rating:

> 3 The answer most typical of you
> 2 Your second choice
> 1 The one least like you

1. When I have to learn something new, I usually

   _____ a. want someone to explain it to me.

   _____ b. want to read about it in a book or magazine.

   _____ c. want to try it out, take notes, or make a model of it.

2. At a party, most of the time I like to

   _____ a. listen and talk to two or three people at once.

   _____ b. see how everyone looks and watch the people.

   _____ c. dance, play games, or take part in some activities.

3. If I were helping with a musical show, I would most likely

   _____ a. write the music, sing the songs, or play the accompaniment.

   _____ b. design the costumes, paint the scenery, or work the lighting effects.

   _____ c. make the costumes, build the sets, or take an acting role.

4. When I am angry, my first reaction is to

   _____ a. tell people off, laugh, joke, or talk it over with someone.

   _____ b. blame myself or someone else, daydream about taking revenge, or keep it inside.

   _____ c. make a fist or tense my muscles, take it out on something else, or hit or throw things.

5. A happy experience I would like to have is to

   _____ a. hear thunderous applause for my speech or music.

   _____ b. photograph the prize-winning picture for a newspaper story.

   _____ c. achieve the fame of being first in a physical activity such as dancing, acting, surfing, or a sports event.

6. I prefer a teacher to

_____ a. use the lecture method with informative explanations and discussions.

_____ b. write on the chalkboard, use visual aids, and assign readings.

_____ c. require posters, models, in-service practice, and some activities in class.

7. I know that I talk with

_____ a. different tones of voice.

_____ b. my eyes and facial expressions.

_____ c. my hands and gestures.

8. If I had to remember an event so that I could record it later, I would choose to

_____ a. tell it to someone or hear an audiotape recording or song about it.

_____ b. see pictures of it or read a description.

_____ c. replay it in some practice rehearsal using movements such as dance, playacting, or drill.

9. When I cook something new, I like to

_____ a. have someone tell me the directions (a friend or TV show).

_____ b. read the recipe and judge by how it looks.

_____ c. use many pots and dishes, stir often, and taste-test.

10. In my free time, I like to

_____ a. listen to the radio, talk on the telephone, or attend a musical event.

_____ b. go to the movies, watch TV, or read a magazine or book.

_____ c. get some exercise, go for a walk, play games, or make things.

11. If I am using equipment such as a VCR, camcorder, or computer for the first time,

_____ a. I want someone to tell me how to use it.

_____ b. I want to read the directions or watch someone else do it.

_____ c. I want to jump right in and do it. I'll figure it out sooner or later.

12. I like the classroom to be arranged

_____ a. in a circle so I can interact with other students.

_____ b. in neat rows facing the instructor.

_____ c. in random order in case there are activities.

To interpret your sense modality, add your rating for each letter.

Total rating for

a. _____ Auditory

b. _____ Visual

c. _____ Kinesthetic

If your highest category was

a. You learn best through listening.

b. You learn best by seeing it in print or other visual modes.

c. You learn best by getting physically involved.

The Auditory Learner

If you learn best by hearing, you should, of course, listen carefully in class. However, just because you learn well auditorily doesn't mean you don't need to take notes; remember the nature of short-term memory? You need to keep a record. You may want to tape-record a difficult class. But remember that taping a lecture is not a time saver. A better strategy is to tape-record a recitation of the questions in the margins from your class notes and textbook reading. Leave time for answers; then record the answers. If you commute, this is a great way to maximize your time. The recitation portion of the label in the margin system reinforces your auditory learning. It gets you involved, provides feedback, and supplies motivation. This is especially true for the auditory learner. The auditory learner likes discussion and usually learns well in a study group or with a study partner. Auditory learners often need to hear what a difficult passage sounds like or to talk out a difficult concept. As an auditory learner, you should proofread your assignments out loud. Your ears seldom fail you. You may even want to try setting a long or difficult idea to music and singing it. (Remember how you learned the alphabet?) Your recall is best when you teach something to someone. And you will probably learn best by explaining something out loud to someone else.

What specific study strategies do you use that involve auditory learning?

_____

_____

What are some that you can try?

_____

_____

The Visual Learner

Visual learners need to see something in order to remember it. If you are a visual learner, you want to see the words written down, a picture of something being described, a time line to remember events in history, or the assignment written on the board. You need to read the material being discussed in class. You also need to study the pictures, charts, maps, or graphs. You should take notes in class in order to see what you are hearing. Of all the memory principles, visualization works best for you. You need to consistently make mental videos of things you want to understand and remember. You benefit from mapping, clustering, outlining, and flash cards. You should make use of color as much as possible. Most students, regardless of their preference, will benefit from this type of learning. A picture usually lasts longer than words for most of us. Those who are visual learners will find that when they learn something in their preferred mode, it is easier to remember. Because visual learning uses primarily the right side of the brain, this is a way for the left-brained student to involve both sides of the brain.

What specific study strategies do you use that involve visual learning?

_____

_____

What are some that you can try?

_____

_____

The Kinesthetic Learner

Kinesthetic learners prefer the sense of touch and learn better when they interact with what they are studying. The mapping strategies explained in the previous chapter are not only visual but also kinesthetic. As a kinesthetic learner, you find that when you are physically involved, you understand and remember. The simple act of doing it helps you understand. The label in the margin system will work for you as a kinesthetic learner because it requires physical involvement. You may find that during the recitation step you want to walk around. Making flash cards is a great strategy for kinesthetic learners. You will find that by making and using flash cards, you employ all ten memory principles. No wonder they work so well. And as you learned in the time-management chapter, flash cards are also easy to carry as pocket work to make use of those bits of time that are normally wasted. The visual learner may want to add color to the flash cards. In addition to maps, note taking, and flash cards, you may want to make charts, games, or mnemonic devices. As you will discover in the test-taking unit, making sample tests will help you physically select the main idea and an added bonus is that taking these tests will cut test anxiety. Yet learners with kinesthetic preference are not alone in benefiting from *doing* it. All learners seem to benefit. Remember that (as Edgar Dale noted), the highest level of remembering comes when you teach someone else. It appears that with all learners, the more actively involved in learning you are, the more you learn. If your instructors do not provide opportunities for active involvement with your learning, you will have to create these opportunities yourself.

List some ways you could create hands-on opportunities in a history class in which your professor always lectures.

_____

_____

_____

Social Learning Preference: Alone or In Groups

To reinforce what you have already learned about students' learning styles, let's examine your social learning style. Do you learn best alone or with others? Again, you will want to apply the principle of learning in your strengths and reinforcing your learning with as many other methods as possible. If the following inventory indicates you learn best alone, you will need to make sure you understand the concept you are striving to learn before you study with others. You need to customize your study environment for minimum distractions. Reciting by writing questions and answers or in the traditional manner of saying it out loud is a good strategy for you to use alone. If the social inventory on page 164 indicates that you learn best with a group, you want to be careful that your study group or study partner shares your study goals. A few guidelines may be helpful. Pay attention in class to who the dedicated students are. Who takes good notes? Who asks logical questions? Who turns in completed assignments on time? Who makes good grades on tests? Although studying with friends is nice, it can lead to visiting instead of studying. For each class you are taking, find three or four people you think would make up a good study group. Set a time and place to meet.

At the study session, you may want to do the following:

1. Make sure your goals are the same.

2. Determine what the test will cover. Comparing notes is a good way to do this.

3. Divide up your assignments so that each person is responsible for certain material. (Teaching material to others is a very effective way of making sure you know it.)

4. Predict test questions. Come up with a test that is similar to the one you will take.

5. Ask others in the group to help with material that is confusing or difficult for you.

6. Drill out loud on possible test questions.

7. Decide if another session would be profitable, and set a time. Make assignments for the next session. For example, ask each member to create a practice test for the next time.

We have now examined two ways to view your learning style: in terms of whether you process predominantly with the left or right side of your brain and in terms of which sense you prefer. The social inventory that follows is an indication of how you study best socially. Do you function best alone or with others?

Social Inventory: Learning Styles

Check a or b in the following questions:

1. When shopping, running errands, or working, I

    _____ a.   usually try to go with friends.

    _____ b.   seldom go with friends.

2. When something is very important to me,

    _____ a.   I seek the advice of others.

    _____ b.   I do it myself.

3. For a grade in chemistry class, I would prefer to

    _____ a.   work with a lab partner.

    _____ b.   work alone.

4. When working with groups in class, I would rather

    _____ a.   work with the group on the whole task.

    _____ b.   divide the task up so that each individual does one part.

5. I prefer instructors who

    _____ a.   include discussion and group activities as part of the class.

    _____ b.   allow students to work on their own.

6. When listening to a speaker, I respond more to

    _____ a.   the person speaking.

    _____ b.   the ideas themselves.

7. When faced with difficult personal problems,

    _____ a.   I discuss them with others.

    _____ b.   I try to solve them myself.

8. For a summer job, I would prefer

    _____ a.   working in a busy office.

    _____ b.   working alone.

Add the numbers of a's and of b's.
If you checked more a's than b's, you would rather work with someone.
If you checked more b's than a's, you would rather work independently.

You now want to use what you have learned about your learning style to develop more effective ways to study. Don't, however, lock yourself into one way. *Be flexible.*

Multiple Intelligences

Howard Gardner and other Harvard researchers speak of intelligence in terms of multiplicity.[2] They say that instead of thinking about intelligence in terms of what IQ tests measure, people should be aware that there are many kinds of intelligences. Gardner lists eight kinds of intelligences and says that everyone possesses all eight kinds. Individuals will have some of the intelligences more developed than others, but they can develop all the intelligences to a certain degree of proficiency.

While these intelligences are not usually referred to as learning styles, they are certainly related to the ways we learn and process information. An examination of these intelligences may be useful for several reasons. First, as a student, you are seeking ways to process information so that you own it. Second, you are seeking ways to learn things faster and more efficiently. Third, the theory of multiple intelligence gives you opportunities to look at your abilities in a different way. What you thought was simply a talent may, in fact, be an intelligence and a way to learn something. Fourth, recognizing your strongest intelligences may be of help in choosing a major and, ultimately, a career that is satisfying. Just as you examined your hemispheric dominance, sensory learning style, and social learning style, you also need to check your multiple intelligences. The idea is to find your strengths. It is easier to learn something new within your strengths and then to reinforce that learning in as many ways as possible. The more ways you learn something, the more likely you are to remember it.

Thomas Armstrong defines intelligence in this way: "Intelligence is the ability to respond successfully to new situations and the capacity to learn from one's past experiences."[3] In short, intelligence is about solving problems. Basic background becomes especially important here, and drawing on the particular intelligence(s) needed in a real-life situation is essential. Let's very briefly examine the eight kinds of intelligence you possess.

[2]Howard Gardner, *Frames of Mind: The Theory of Multiple Intelligences* (10th anniversary ed.; New York: HarperCollins, 1993).
[3]Thomas Armstrong, *Seven Kinds of Smart: Identifying and Developing Your Many Intelligences* (New York: Penguin Books, 1993).

Eight Kinds of Intelligences

- **Linguistic intelligence** involves your verbal skills. Will you learn something best by using words or playing with the verbal structure? Do you need to create a mnemonic to remember something?

- **Logical-mathematical intelligence** deals with your ability to reason. Can you determine the cause? Can you follow the logic in order to learn something?

- **Spatial intelligence** uses pictures and images to learn. Do you benefit from drawing or mapping something?

- **Musical intelligence,** of course, deals with rhythms and melodies. Can you set what you are trying to learn to music—give it a beat?

- **Bodily-kinesthetic intelligence** is where hands-on activity is required. Do you need to do something in order to learn it? Intuition or "gut feeling" is associated with this intelligence.

- **Interpersonal intelligence** involves working with and understanding others.

- **Intrapersonal intelligence** determines how well you are attuned to your inner self.

(The last two mentioned above determine your social learning style.)

- **Naturalist intelligence** involves your ability to discriminate among living things (plants, animals) as well as your sensitivity to other features of the natural world (clouds, rock configurations).

You possess all eight intelligences in varying degrees.

Multiple Intelligences Exercise 1

To say that there is a test to determine what your strongest intelligences are would be to limit the scope of the theory. However, the more you understand about what each intelligence involves the more you can determine your strengths. Use the following exercise to determine which intelligences you use. More than one intelligence may be involved. In the space before the situation described, list the intelligences you used:

Linguistic   Bodily-kinesthetic
Logical-mathematical   Interpersonal
Spatial   Intrapersonal
Musical   Naturalist

_____ **1.** Singing in the choir at church

_____ **2.** Working a jigsaw puzzle

_____ **3.** Working a crossword puzzle

_____ **4.** Solving "who done it" in a mystery

_____ **5.** Giving advice to people at work

_____ **6.** Writing poetry

_____ **7.** Knowing the words to many popular songs

_____ **8.** Enjoying having time for yourself

_____ **9.** Humming a jingle you've heard on TV

_____ **10.** Doodling while talking on the phone or taking notes

_____ **11.** Computing numbers in your head

_____ **12.** Reading for pleasure as often as possible

_____ **13.** Playing a sport

_____ **14.** Sewing

_____ **15.** Framing a house

_____ **16.** Writing an essay

_____ **17.** Keeping a personal journal or diary

_____ **18.** Taking photographs

_____ **19.** Meditating

_____ **20.** Arguing

_____ **21.** Appreciating the color and balance of a picture

_____ **22.** Creating mnemonics

_____ **23.** Rearranging a room

_____ **24.** Categorizing objects

_____ **25.** Perceiving the moods of others

_____ **26.** Working alone on a problem

_____ **27.** Keeping rhythm to a song

_____ **28.** Studying in a group

_____ **29.** Using concept maps, graphs, or pictures to learn

_____ **30.** Organizing collections

_____ **31.** Finding a rational explanation for an occurrence

_____ **32.** Having trouble sitting still

_____ **33.** Noticing changes in the environment

_____ **34.** Showing someone how to do something

_____ **35.** Visiting with friends

_____ **36.** Spending a weekend alone

Multiple Intelligences Exercise 2

Using the list for exercise, circle the twelve items that you do most often. How many did you circle for each of the following intelligences? The higher the number the stronger the intelligence.

_____ Linguistic	_____ Bodily-kinesthetic
_____ Logical-mathematical	_____ Interpersonal
_____ Spatial	_____ Intrapersonal
_____ Musical	_____ Naturalist

Virtual Field Trip:
Learning More About Multiple Intelligence

Visit http://collegesurvival.college.hmco.com/students and select "Hopper," or go to http://www.mtsu.edu/~studskl/3evirtual-fieldtrips.html.

Applying Strategies That Use Multiple Intelligences

If for a biology test you needed to learn the seven major taxonomic categories, or taxa, used in classification—(1) kingdom, (2) phylum, (3) class, (4) order, (5) family, (6) genus, and (7) species—you might use each of the intelligences to learn them. (Remember to learn new material in your strength but reinforce it in as many ways as possible.) Below is a list of the multiple intelligences. Describe how you might use each intelligence to learn the classification system for your biology test. Then put into practice what you suggested. For example, if you suggested singing, the classification musical intelligence, think of a specific tune and try it.

Linguistic _____

_____

Logical-mathematical _____

_____

Spatial _____

_____

Musical _____

_____

Bodily-kinesthetic _____

_____

Interpersonal _____

_____

Intrapersonal _____

_____

Naturalist _____

_____

Using Multiple Intelligences to Make Decisions

Not only can you use the assessment of your learning style and multiple intelligences to develop study strategies, but you will also find there is a parallel in multiple intelligence strengths and job skills and preference. Below is a brief list of job skills and sample professions for each of the eight intelligences. Can you add to the list? Do your goals parallel your strongest intelligence? Can you add college majors you would suggest for each intelligence? Knowing your strongest multiple intelligence may be useful in choosing a major in college and ultimately a career. We usually find that performing tasks that employ our strengths provide the most satisfaction . Study the job skills and sample professions that are suggested for your strongest intelligences.

brain byte

Although we possess all eight intelligences, high performance in one is not necessarily a predictor of high performance in another domain. Outstanding performance by people in two or more domains is rare. Pierce Howard asserts that employers should not expect high performance in all domains. Asking a human resources expert (interpersonal) to be a financial expert (logical-mathematical) is like asking a starting quarterback (bodily-kinesthetic) to be a best-selling writer (linguistic).

Linguistic

- **Jobs skills:** talking, telling, informing, giving instructions, writing, verbalizing, speaking a foreign language, interpreting, translating, teaching, lecturing, discussing, debating, researching, listening (to words), copying, proofreading, editing, word processing, filing, reporting

- **Sample professions:** librarian, archivist, curator, editor, translator, speaker, writer, radio/TV announcer, journalist, legal assistant, lawyer, secretary, typist, proofreader, English teacher

Logical-mathematical

- **Job skills:** financing, budgeting, doing economic research, accounting, hypothesizing, estimating, counting, calculating, using statistics, auditing, reasoning, analyzing, systemizing, classifying, sequencing

- **Sample professions:** auditor, accountant, purchasing agent, mathematician, scientist, statistician, actuary, computer analyst, economist, technician, bookkeeper, science teacher

Spatial

- **Job skills:** drawing, painting, visualizing, creating visual presentation, designing, imagining, inventing, illustrating, coloring, drafting, graphing, mapping, photographing, decorating, filming

- **Sample professions:** engineer, surveyor, architect, urban planner, graphic artist, interior decorator, photographer, art teacher, inventor, cartographer, pilot, fine artist, sculptor

Musical

- **Job skills:** singing, playing an instrument, recording, conducting, improvising, composing, transcribing, arranging, listening, distinguishing (tones), tuning, orchestrating, analyzing, and criticizing (musical styles)

- **Sample professions:** disc jockey, musician, instrument maker, piano tuner, music therapist, instrument salesperson, songwriter, studio engineer, choral director, conductor, singer, music teacher, musical copyist

Bodily-kinesthetic

- **Job skills:** sorting, balancing, lifting, carrying, walking, crafting, restoring, cleaning, shipping, delivering, manufacturing, repairing, assembling, installing, operating, adjusting, salvaging, performing, signing, miming, dramatizing, modeling (clothes), dancing, playing sports, organizing outdoor activities, traveling

- **Sample professions:** physical therapist, recreational worker, dancer, actor, model, farmer, mechanic, carpenter, craftsperson, physical education teacher, factory worker, choreographer, professional athlete, forest ranger, jeweler

Interpersonal

- **Job skills:** serving, hosting, communicating, empathizing, trading, tutoring, coaching, counseling, mentoring, assessing others, persuading, motivating, selling, recruiting, inspiring, publicizing, encouraging, supervising, coordinating, delegating, negotiating, mediating, collaborating, confronting, interviewing

- **Sample professions:** administrator, manager, school principal, personnel worker, arbitrator, sociologist, anthropologist, counselor, psychologist, nurse, public relations person, salesperson, travel agent, social director

Intrapersonal

- **Job skills:** carrying out decisions, working alone, self-promotion, setting goals, attaining objectives, initiating, evaluating, appraising, planning, organizing, discerning opportunities, looking inward, understanding self

- **Sample professions:** psychologist, cleric, psychology teacher, therapist, counselor, theologian, program planner, entrepreneur

Naturalist

- **Job skills:** observing, understanding, organizing various types of environments, classifying, collecting, diagnosing

- **Sample professions:** molecular biologist, herbalist, chef, criminologist, mechanic, historian

Virtual Field Trip:
Career Guide

Visit http://collegesurvival.college.hmco.com/students and select "Hopper," or go to http://www.mtsu.edu/~studskl/3evirtual-fieldtrips.html.

Careers and Majors

Do you think the information you either learned or confirmed about your learning style and multiple intelligences is significant when it comes to your choice of major or career? Discuss your reasons.

_____

_____

_____

A college advisor recently told me that she finds many college students choose a major and set career goals without ever talking to anyone who has majored in that subject at their college. She added that many students set career goals without talking to someone in that career. For example, because June was good at drawing, she decided to become an architect without ever knowing an architect. Discuss some of the dangers inherent in this. What plan of action do you need to make to ensure that you have done all you can to be prepared?

_____

_____

_____

▦ Your Learning Profile

Beginning with your strongest, list in order what you think your multiple intelligences are:

1. _____

2. _____

3. _____

4. _____

5. _____

6. _____

7. _____

8. _____

Do you process information primarily in the left or right hemisphere or equally? _____

List the sensory modes you use in order of preference (auditory, visual, kinesthetic).

1. _____

2. _____

3. _____

Do you prefer to work alone or with others? _____

Given the information above, list **specific learning strategies** in the order that you should be using them to process new material.

1. _____

2. _____

3. _____

4. _____

5. _____

Summary

Why is it important to determine your learning style?

▶

What are some characteristics of left-brain processing?

▶

What are some characteristics of right-brain processing?

▶

What did Edgar Dale discover about how much people generally remember?

▶

Explain some study strategies that a visual learner should use.

▶

Explain some study strategies that an auditory learner should use.

▶

Explain some study strategies that a kinesthetic learner should use.

▶

What are good strategies for those students who learn best alone?

▶

Name several ways to determine who might potentially be a good member for your study group.

▶

Name several guidelines for group study.

▶

List and briefly explain the eight kinds of intelligences.

1.

2.

3.

4.

5.

6.

7.

8.

■ What's Your Advice?

Jon and Mandy are having a difficult time studying for their psychology test, so they formed a study group with two other classmates. From inventories they had taken in a previous class, Jon discovered that his left hemisphere is dominant. He prefers auditory input and his multiple-intelligence strengths are logical, linguistic, and intrapersonal. Mandy on the other hand is right-brained, prefers visual and kinesthetic input, and her strengths are interpersonal, musical, and kinesthetic. They had memorized what their learning styles were for the final exam, but really didn't understand what those meant. The preferences and strengths of the other students (Marc and Amanda) were not known. The upcoming test is about how the brain learns.

1. List some strategies that the group could use to study.

2. Assign specific tasks to each group member to complete before the study session.

3. Make specific suggestions for strategies to use during the session.

4. Make specific suggestions for strategies each should use after the session.

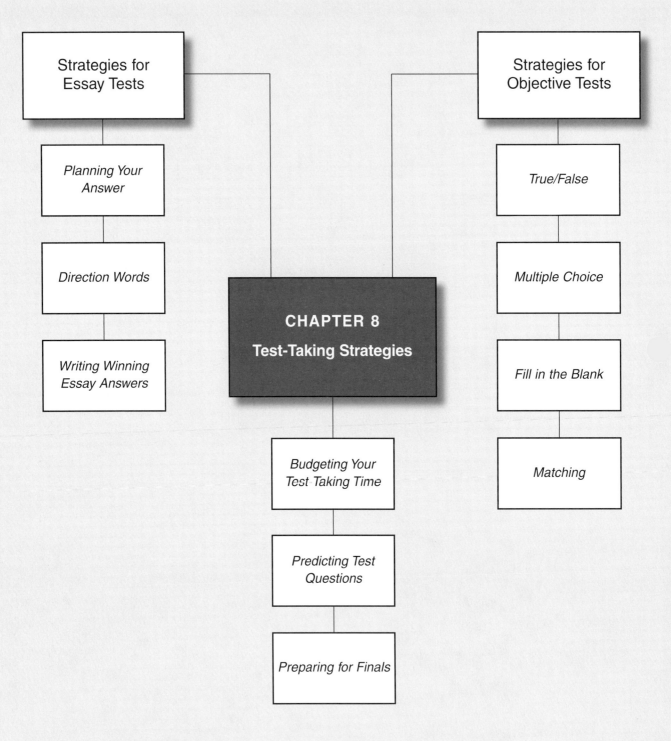

Strategies for Essay Tests

Planning Your Answer

Direction Words

Writing Winning Essay Answers

CHAPTER 8

Test-Taking Strategies

Budgeting Your Test Taking Time

Predicting Test Questions

Preparing for Finals

Strategies for Objective Tests

True/False

Multiple Choice

Fill in the Blank

Matching

CHAPTER **8**

Test-Taking Strategies

In previous chapters, you have discovered the importance of critical thinking; you have learned how to use your owner's manual for the brain to develop wise study strategies; and you have acquired a system for processing information from both lectures and texts. In other words, you know the fundamentals for preparing for a test. Now you need to address some strategies for taking tests. There are two basic categories of tests. The first is objective. For each item in an objective test, there is one correct answer. This kind of test usually depends on recognition to get the answer out of your long-term memory. In other words, there are clues within the question to jog your memory. Objective tests contain true/false, multiple-choice, matching, and fill-in-the-blank questions. The other category of tests is subjective. There is a correct answer for each question on a subjective test but also a range of possible ways to give this answer. Discussion questions, essay questions, and many short-answer questions fall into this category. They depend on recall, not just recognition. Recall requires that you bring the information out of your long-term memory and organize it in a way that effectively answers what has been asked. Left-brained students usually prefer objective tests, whereas right-brained students respond better to the whole picture and thus usually prefer subjective tests. There is no substitute for having studied thoroughly and knowing the answers. However, certain strategies can be used with each kind of test so that you get the most out of your effort.

Before you begin practicing specific test-taking strategies, let's make sure you are effectively preparing for tests. Below is a list of ways that successful students used to prepare for tests. Rate yourself on how well you practice each of them. A 5 means that you almost always do it; 4, that you usually do it; 3, that you sometimes do it; 2, that you rarely do it; and 1, that you never do it. Be totally honest in your evaluation.

_____ **1.** Keep up to date with assignments.

_____ **2.** Take notes in *every* class *every* day. This includes asking questions when you don't understand.

_____ 3. Process information as you come to it. Learning information is very different from becoming acquainted with it.

_____ 4. Process information systematically. The label in the margin system works well for most people. Adapt it to suit your learning styles. Capitalize on the discipline the label in the margin system requires and make it a habit to process information from texts and lectures, not just go over it.

_____ 5. Have a study place that is free of distractions.

_____ 6. Have a specific time for the initial study of each subject. You may need more than this time, but having a set time will save you time.

_____ 7. Make up summary sheets, flash cards, and practice tests.

_____ 8. Always carry some kind of pocket work and make use of what would otherwise be wasted spare minutes by reciting and thinking about what you are learning.

_____ 9. Learn something new or difficult in your strongest intelligence or sense or in your dominant hemisphere. Reinforce it in as many different ways as possible.

_____ 10. Find a study partner or two in each class and routinely take turns teaching each other the material.

_____ 11. Prepare for each class as if there will be a pop quiz.

_____ Total your score.

When you have totaled your score, choose the appropriate writing assignment from the list below.

Writing Assignment

■ If your score is from 44 to 55, write a paragraph or two in which you describe the results of using the study strategies listed. Be specific. A comparison of the benefits of your old study habits and your new ones might be one approach.

■ If your score is from 33 to 43, write a paragraph or two in which you describe both your good and bad study habits. Discuss reasons for both and goals for incorporating more of the strategies listed.

■ If your score is below 33, write a paragraph or two in which you try to determine why you have not used the strategies listed to your advantage and which strategies you think you might be able to use effectively. Set some realistic goals and discuss how you might achieve them.

Critical Thinking About **Tests**

In the Critical Thinking chapter you learned that there are levels, or depths, of thinking and learning. We used Bloom's taxonomy as a model: **knowledge, comprehension, application, analysis, synthesis,** and **evaluation.** You may want to review each. When taking a test, it is important to know what *level* of learning will be tested. You can study all night memorizing definitions for a test; however, if the test asks for analysis, synthesis, or evaluation of those definitions, you are sunk!

Identify the level of learning being asked for in the following test questions:

_____ What evidence can you present to support that the Confederate army was unprepared in the Battle of Shiloh?

_____ Where were the first Olympic games held?

_____ Name and explain each step of the label in the margin system.

_____ What would happen if you combined sulfur with iodine?

_____ Demonstrate that you know how to take notes using the label in the margin system.

_____ What were the merits of Hannibal's plan to take Rome?

Strategies for Objective Tests

Self-Analysis: Preparing for Tests

Now that you know some strategies that will help you study for tests, let's discuss taking a test. Many students feel that one reason they are not top students is that they are poor test takers. The following diagnostic inventory is designed to help you rate your present test-taking skills and habits. It will also serve as an overview of the topics discussed in this test-taking unit. It is divided into three sections: strategies used to prepare for a test, general test-taking strategies, and strategies for specific types of tests. *Be totally honest. This is not a test!*

Test-Taking Skills: Diagnostic Inventory

Write the number in the column that best describes you.

Strategies Used to Prepare for a Test	1 Never	2 Infrequently	3 Generally	4 Frequently	5 Always
1. Do you find out as much about the test as possible?	____	____	____	____	____
2. As you review material, do you anticipate possible test questions?	____	____	____	____	____
3. Do you have notes to review?	____	____	____	____	____
4. Do you review your notes systematically?	____	____	____	____	____
5. Do you make summary sheets?	____	____	____	____	____
6. Do you recite and/or write down material in your own words?	____	____	____	____	____
7. Do you use mnemonic devices and other memory principles for lists, dates, and so on?	____	____	____	____	____
8. Do you avoid cramming the night before?	____	____	____	____	____
9. Do you get plenty of rest the night before the test?	____	____	____	____	____

Strategies Used to Prepare for a Test	1 Never	2 Infrequently	3 Generally	4 Frequently	5 Always
10. Do you try to do your best on every test you take?	____	____	____	____	____
11. Do you take tests without too much anxiety?	____	____	____	____	____
12. Do you find other people in your class to study with?	____	____	____	____	____
13. Do you arrive early to your classroom the day of the test?	____	____	____	____	____

General Test-Taking Strategies

	1 Never	2 Infrequently	3 Generally	4 Frequently	5 Always
14. Do you preview the test before writing anything?	____	____	____	____	____
15. Do you plan test-taking time? (How much time will you allow for each task?)	____	____	____	____	____
16. Do you make sure you are following directions by underlining key words?	____	____	____	____	____
17. Do you answer the easiest questions first?	____	____	____	____	____
18. Do you answer all questions (unless the directions say otherwise)?	____	____	____	____	____
19. Do you check all answers carefully? (This means reworking each question if time permits.)	____	____	____	____	____
20. Do you use all the time allotted for the test?	____	____	____	____	____

Strategies for Taking Specific Types of Tests

Strategies Used to Prepare for a Test	1 Never	2 Infrequently	3 Generally	4 Frequently	5 Always
21. Do you use specific strategies in taking objective tests such as multiple-choice, true/false, fill-in, and matching?	____	____	____	____	____
22. Do you use specific strategies to answer essay questions?	____	____	____	____	____
Subtotals:	____	____	____	____	____

Add the numbers you've written in each column to find your subtotals. Add your subtotals to find your final score: _____

How testwise are you? **Rating Scale**
22–44   Poor
45–66   Fair
67–88   Good
89–110   Excellent

Personal analysis: On another sheet of paper write a paragraph in which you analyze your strengths and weaknesses in the test-taking strategies specifically covered in the inventory above.

Budgeting Your Time When Taking Tests

One of the most important strategies for taking any kind of test is budgeting your time. Too often we hear students say that they knew the answers but ran out of time or that they made careless mistakes because they rushed. Since you want to get the most points for the time you spend, you should analyze each test and budget your time accordingly.

 braiN byte

The "big three" of Dr. Hillman's Breathe System should also improve your test taking by supplying your brain with sufficient oxygen and giving you a feeling of self-confidence. You've prepared your mind for the test by studying. Now prepare your body: Maintain proper posture, relax neck and shoulder muscles, and take cleansing breaths.

Preview the test.

1.   Determine the types of questions.
2.   Calculate the point value of questions.
3.   Look for questions you need to make notes about; if necessary, use a mnemonic or other review strategies you have learned.
4.   Locate easy questions to answer first.

Budget your time.

1.   When calculating the point value of questions, determine the percentage of the total score toward which it counts. (If it counts 30 points, it's worth 30 percent of a 100-point test.)
2.   From the total amount of time allowed for the test, subtract some time for preview and review. (If you have 60 minutes to take a test, you might subtract 5 minutes for previewing the test and 5 minutes for reviewing it. This would leave 50 minutes base time to take the test.)
3.   Calculate the percentage of the base time (time remaining after you've subtracted preview and review times) that you should allow for each question or set of questions. If a question counts for 30 percent of the test, multiply .30 (percent) × 50 (base time). Allow 15 minutes to answer that question. Use the entire time allotted for the test.

How much time would you allow for the following?

Total time for test: 2 hours

Time allowed for preview   _____

Time allowed for review   _____

2 essays (20 points each)   _____

25 multiple-choice (1 point each) _____

15 matching (1 point each)   _____

20 true/false (1 point each)   _____

Total time for test: 50 minutes

Time allowed for preview   _____

Time allowed for review   _____

20 true/false (1 point each)   _____

2 essays (10 points each)   _____

Matching (30 points)   _____

Fill in the blank (10 points)   _____

Short answer (20 points)   _____

Following Directions

One of the most common mistakes students make on tests is that they don't follow directions. It is important to follow directions carefully even if the test is timed. Never assume that you know what the directions say. For example, true/false questions may ask you to correct the false ones to make them true. As practice, take the following test.

Directions: Read all questions before answering anything. This is a timed test. Your instructor will tell you at the beginning how much time you are allowed. You *must* complete it in the given time.

1. Write your name and section number in the top right corner of this paper.

2. In the top left corner, write today's date in *numbers.*

3. Under today's date, write "Following Directions, Timed Test."

4. In the blank following this question, write the name of the day before yesterday.

   _____

5. If you have a written syllabus, check it and write today's assignment in the space below. If you do not have a syllabus, write your teacher's name backward.

6. If $3 \times 4 \times 2 = 25$, write *green;* if not, write *purple.* _____

7. Count the number of empty desks in this room. _____

8. Draw a house with two chimneys, two windows, and one door.

9. Write the first name of three people in this class in alphabetical order.

   1. _____ 2. _____ 3. _____

10. Stand and say in a very loud voice, "I have reached question 10. I am the leader in following directions."

11. Write the number of the day you were born, and subtract the number of the month you were born.

12. Spell the name of your hometown backward. _____

13. Circle one: True or false, following directions is easy?

14. Underline one: True or false, following directions is essential?

15. Now that you have read all the questions, do only questions 1, 2, and 3. Then turn your page over and wait for the rest of the class to finish.

Strategies for Taking Any Test

Some survival tips for taking tests were presented near the beginning of this book. Hopefully you have used them throughout the term.

Go back to the Survival Kit (pages 6 and 8), or go to the http://www.mtsu.edu/~studskl/teststrat.html site to find survival test skills. Carefully review the survival tips for taking tests. Then answer the following questions. Use your own paper. Because you want to have a summary sheet of test strategies when you finish, it is important to include enough information to let you know what each question was. The label in the margin system may be useful to you here.

1. Why should you preview your test before answering any questions?

2. What specifically does doing a "mind dump" involve?

3. Why is it important to read directions? Does this step just waste important time?

4. List several reasons why you would want to answer the easy questions first.

5. Why should you skip the harder questions and go back to them later?

6. Name several things you might do if a question is unclear.

7. Why is it important to use the entire test-taking time allotted?

brain byte

Apparently, testing gives the learner an opportunity to practice effective-learning procedures simultaneously. Tests do not have to be graded to be effective. It is the act of taking the test that is helpful.

The strategies in your summary sheet can be used for taking any test. Now, however, we consider some strategies you can use for specific kinds of tests.

Strategies for True/False Tests

No amount of guessing can replace knowing the answer. Nevertheless, you should be aware of strategies to use if you are not sure. While these strategies won't apply every time, they will make you aware of possible tricks used by test makers.

1. **Assume statements are true unless you know they are false.** (If you absolutely must guess, guess true. It is easier to write a true statement than a false one. Unless they make a real effort, test writers will usually have more true than false questions.)

2. **If any part of a statement is false, then the whole statement is false.** This is always the case. You should, then, carefully read each statement looking for any part that may be false.

    _____ George Washington, Abraham Lincoln, and Benjamin Franklin were U.S. presidents.
    While Washington and Lincoln were presidents, Franklin was not a president.

3. **True/false statements that give reasons tend to be false** (*because the reason is incorrect or there may be additional reasons.*)

    _____ Children today get lower grades because they watch too much television.

    (This may be one reason, but not the only reason.) Be wary of statements that include words such as **reason, because, due to,** or **since.** They may be indicators of reasons that could very well be false.

4. **A negative word or prefix** (*not, cannot, un-, dis-, il-, non-, in-*) used in the statement **does not make the statement false, but you should make sure you understand what impact the negative has on the statement.** It is a good idea to circle all negatives so that you are sure of what the statement says.

    _____ A koala bear is a kind of bear.

    _____ A koala bear is not a kind of bear.

    *The first statement is false, but the addition of **not** in the second makes it true.*

    Not is the most commonly used negative; however, you should also be on the lookout for prefixes that make a word negative. Fill in the blanks with the negative of the word given.

    1. Truthful   Untruthful
        _____

    2. Alcoholic   _____

    3. Direct   _____

    4. Saturated   _____

    5. Perfect   _____

    6. Responsible   _____

7. Agreeable _____

8. Legal _____

5. Simplify the question by getting rid of *double* negatives. Double negatives include two negatives. You can cross out both negatives without changing the meaning of the word, phrase, or statement they appear in. If a question says, "You won't be unprepared," change it to say "You will be prepared." If a question says, "This is not an imperfect method," change it to say, "This is a perfect method." If a sentence has three negatives, you may cross out two without changing the meaning of the statement.

6. If **general qualifiers** are present (*generally, probably, usually, many, sometimes*), there is a **good chance that the statement is true.**

7. If **absolute qualifiers** (*all, always, no, never, none, every, everyone, only, best, entirely, invariably*) are used, the statement is probably false.

Honda makes cars.

Honda makes **only** cars.

All pit bulls are aggressive.

Nobody reads the dictionary for fun.

Absolutes are words for which there are no exceptions—100 percent words. Learn the absolutes well. Otherwise you are likely to be confused. When you see absolutes in a true/false statement, you can be sure than 99 percent of the time the statement is false.

What mnemonic can you develop to remember the absolutes?

_____

_____

_____

Practice with Double Negatives. Read the following statements. Circle all negatives. If two negatives occur, eliminate both. You won't change the meaning; you will simply clarify the statement. Then read and decide if the statement is true or false.

_____ 1. Most students are not unwilling to leave class early.

_____ 2. It is not unusual for students to have math anxiety.

_____ **3.** It is not illegal not to drive on the left side of the road in the United States.

_____ **4.** Most students would not be dissatisfied with an F on an exam.

_____ **5.** The cost of a BMW is usually not inexpensive in comparison to the cost of a Yugo.

Qualifiers are words that limit or change the meaning of a word or sentence. If we are talking about a child doing his chores at home, we can start with the sentence, "He does his chores." You can qualify that sentence in several ways:

If we begin with the negative, we can say:

He *never* does his chores.
He did *none* of his chores.   These are **absolute** qualifiers. They mean 100 percent.
He did *no* chores.   *The child didn't do **any** chores—not even one.*

Then you can move toward the positive:

He *seldom* does his chores.
He did *few* of his chores.
He did *some* of his chores.
He *sometimes* does his chores.   These are ***general*** qualifiers. They do not include 100
He *generally* does his chores.   percent.
He did *many* of his chores.
He *usually* does his chores.
He did *most* of his chores.

When we get to the other end of the continuum, you get back to absolutes on the positive side:

He **always** does his chores.
He did **all** of his chores.   These are **absolute** qualifiers. They mean 100 percent.
He did **every** chore.   *The child did all the chores—every one.*

We need to understand about qualifiers because they make a great deal of difference in answering a true/false question.

no, never, none, nobody, only	[few, seldom, some, generally, many, usually, most]	always, all, every, best

$\longleftarrow$ ——— $\longrightarrow$

| 100%
Absolute | General | 100%
Absolute |

Practice with True/False Tests

Use the methods just discussed to determine whether the following statements are true or false. Write T on the lines in front of the true statements and F on the lines in front of the false statements. In the blank following each statement, explain the strategy you used to determine if the statement was true or false.

_____ 1. General William Tecumseh Sherman was the only Union Army general to enter Atlanta.

_____

_____ 2. We should eat protein for breakfast because it gets oxygen to the brain.

_____

_____ 3. Franklin D. Roosevelt said, "The only thing we have to fear is fear itself."

_____

_____ 4. As a general rule, one should study two hours for each hour of class time.

_____

_____ 5. July is never a winter month.

_____

_____ 6. A master schedule should never be changed during a semester.

_____

_____ 7. Calcutta suffers from poverty, overcrowding, and unemployment because it is one of the largest cities in the world.

_____

_____ 8. Short-term memory appears to function in the hippocampus as a clearing-house that selects chunks of data to remember.

_____

_____ 9. Most students drop out of college because they are not smart enough.

_____

_____ 10. One should always study the hardest subject first.

_____

_____ **11.** The label in the margin system should be used for all reading.

_____ **12.** An absolute qualifier will always make a true/false question false.

_____ **13.** In taking class notes, students are not unlikely to miss the point if they try to write down everything.

_____ **14.** A good study environment should include good lighting, a comfortable seat, quiet music, and plenty of food.

_____ **15.** A chunk is defined as an unfamiliar array of only seven pieces or bits.

_____ **16.** The reason that Hannibal was unsuccessful in his attempt to take Rome was that he couldn't get his equipment over the Alps.

_____ **17.** Left-brained students are always smarter than right-brained students.

_____ **18.** For most students, getting a good night's sleep is more important than cramming all night.

_____ **19.** Making a weekly schedule helps you because your instructor knows what you are doing.

_____ **20.** *Most, few, some, all,* and *rarely* are general qualifiers and usually make a statement true.

Strategies for Multiple-Choice Tests

1. **Realize that there is not always a perfect answer.** You must choose the best answer.

2. **Cross out the incorrect answers.** Incorrect answers are called *distracters.* Crossing them out will focus your attention on reasonable options.

3. **Read all possible responses.**

4. **Treat each option as a true/false question.** Read the stem and then the first answer. Read the stem again and then the second answer. Read the stem again and then the third answer. And so on. Apply the true/false strategies each time. By doing this, you will keep track of the question in the tangle of answers.

5. **Use test flaws only as a last resort.** Although there is no substitute for knowing the material, becoming familiar with certain tendencies can be of value when you do not know the answer. Such tendencies are often referred to as test cues or test flaws. Use test cues, or flaws only as a last resort. As a general rule, the following types of options tend to be *incorrect answers:*

   ■ **Options with absolutes** (*Can you name ten absolutes?*)

   _____   _____   _____   _____   _____

   _____   _____   _____   _____   _____

   ■ **Options with unfamiliar terms** (*Of course if you haven't read the assignment or listened in class, all terms may sound unfamiliar!*)

   ■ **Options with jokes and insults**

   ■ **Options with highest and lowest numbers** (*except on math quizzes*)

And the following types of options tend to be *correct answers:*

   ■ **Options that read "all of the above"** (*especially when you know that two options are correct*)

   ■ **Options with more complete or inclusive answers**

   _____ Physical attractiveness is likely to vary among
   a. Italians.   b. female bank tellers.
   c. high school cheerleaders.   d. women over thirty.
   (*Which group includes the most people?*)

   ■ **Options with one of two similar-looking answers**

   _____ In the brain, logical and linguistic functions are processed by
   a. the right hemisphere   b. the left hemisphere
   c. habeas corpus   d. the cerebellum

Practice with Multiple Choice

Use the strategies just discussed to select the correct answer to the following questions. Write a, b, c, or d on the line in front of the question. Use the line following the question to explain the strategy you used.

_____   **1.** Research has found that the ideal length of a nap
       a. is only fifteen minutes.
       b. is as long as your history professor is talking.
       c. is thirty minutes.
       d. One should never take naps.

_____

_____   **2.** A sonnet is a
       a. lyric poem of fourteen lines.
       b. love poem with twenty-five lines.
       c. seven-line rhyme.
       d. flowery hat.

_____

_____   **3.** Horsepower is a unit of power equal to
       a. about 746 watts.
       b. about 300 watts.
       c. about 30,000 watts.
       d. 800 watts.

_____

_____   **4.** An excise tax is a tax
       a. imposed on health clubs.
       b. imposed on goods, especially luxuries and cars.
       c. imposed only on diamonds.
       d. added to all incomes over $100,000.

_____

_____   **5.** Calvin Coolidge
       a. was vice president under Warren Harding.
       b. became president in 1923 when Harding died.
       c. was elected president on his own in 1924.
       d. All of the above

_____

_____   **6.** Potassium
       a. is never found in red meat.
       b. is the only chemical necessary for Ph balance.
       c. should never be combined with vitamin C.
       d. is abundant in many fruits and vegetables.

_____

_____ **7.** Once a long-term memory has formed, which factor interferes with retrieving it?
a. Clogging at the synapse
b. Deterioration of the neuronal pathways involved
c. Stress
d. All of the above

_____ **8.** During the fifth and sixth century, Germanics migrated to England. They were called
a. Angles.
b. Saxons.
c. Jutes.
d. Angles, Saxons, and Jutes.

_____ **9.** Henry Clay is classified as
a. a great boxer and poet.
b. a war hawk.
c. a war hawk and the Great Compromiser.
d. entirely responsible for the War of 1812 and the Treaty of Ghent.

_____ **10.** The most effective time to study for a lecture class is
a. before class.
b. after class.
c. right before you go to bed.
d. irrelevant; it is not necessary to study for this type of class.

_____ **11.** Prolonged stress produces high levels of cortisol which can
a. cause the hippocampus to shrink.
b. significantly reduce the production of neurons.
c. affect memory, mood, and mental functions.
d. All of the above

_____ **12.** Normal reading speed is
a. 1200 to 1500 words per minute.
b. 723 words per minute.
c. 200 to 300 words per minute.
d. 80 to 100 words per minute.

Strategies for Fill-In Questions

1. Read the question to yourself so that you can hear what is being asked.

2. If more than one answer comes to mind, write both in the margin. Come back later and choose the one you want.

3. Make sure that your choice fits in logically and grammatically.

4. Remember that your answer may require more than one word.

Practice with Fill-In Tests

1. One should answer _____ questions, unless you are penalized for wrong answers.

2. _____ , _____ , and _____ are three kinds of objective tests.

3. Answer the _____ questions first.

4. True/false statements that give a reason tend to be _____ .

5. True/false statements with absolutes will almost always be _____ .

6. The incorrect choices in a multiple-choice question are called _____ .

Strategies for Matching

With true/false questions you have a 50 percent chance of guessing the correct answer. With multiple choice a 25 percent chance before you begin to eliminate distracters. Although most students think that matching is one of the easier ways to take a test, your chances of guessing the correct answers are very small. Below are some strategies that you should use when you take matching tests.

1. Preview all of the possibilities before answering anything.

2. Determine whether an answer can be used more than once.

3. Answer the ones you are sure of first.

4. Cross out options as you use them.

5. Use logic to determine what is being asked for—a person? A place? A date?

Practice with Matching

Use the strategies for matching to match the nicknames to the colleges below. You may use each letter only once.

_____	1. Commodores	a.	Kentucky
_____	2. Fighting Irish	b.	Ohio State
_____	3. Terrapins	c.	UCLA
_____	4. Tarheels	d.	Georgetown
_____	5. Jayhawks	e.	Texas
_____	6. Bruins	f.	Vanderbilt
_____	7. Crimson Tide	g.	North Carolina
_____	8. Wildcats	h.	U of Connecticut
_____	9. Orangemen	i.	Maryland
_____	10. Hoyas	j.	Alabama
_____	11. Buckeyes	k.	Notre Dame
_____	12. Huskies	l.	Syracuse
_____	13. Green Wave	m.	Tulane
_____	14. Razorbacks	n.	Kansas
_____	15. Longhorns	o.	Arkansas

Virtual Field Trip:
Objective Tests

Visit http://collegesurvival.college.hmco.com/students and select "Hopper," or go to http://www.mtsu.edu/~studskl/3evirtual-fieldtrips.html.

Predicting Test Questions

One of the most important study skills you can develop is predicting what will be on a test. Knowing this with confidence can make your study time more effective as well as cut down on test anxiety. By using the label in the margin system for taking notes from lectures and textbooks, you have already begun to use the essential strategies needed to predict what will be on a test.

brain byte

Brain researchers talk about knowledge as being **"state bound,"** meaning that how and where we learn may be as important to the brain as what we learn. This is why taking a practice test (which simulates the real situation) is a great way to study. What does it say about cramming for an exam?

Here are some important guidelines to remember in predicting questions that will be on a test.

1. Notice clues to test questions from lecture material:
   a. What an instructor says and how he or she says it (nonverbal cues)
   b. Ideas that are repeated
   c. Ideas written on the board, overhead, or in a handout
   d. "This is important"; "You'll see this again."
   e. Questions the instructor asks

2. Clues to test questions from textbook material:
   a. Material in **bold** print
   b. Information in summary section
   c. Problems or questions at the end of chapters

3. Save all tests, quizzes, homework, and so on.

4. Find out if previous tests are available.

Examine the test-taking strategies on the previous pages. Look closely at the strategies described in the diagnostic inventory and strategies for any test: true/false, multiple-choice, and fill-in questions, and matching. Now predict ten true/false questions and five multiple-choice questions dealing with these strategies. Use the following page for your questions.

True/False Possible Test Questions Dealing with Test-Taking Strategies

_____ 1. _____

_____ 2. _____

_____ 3. _____

_____ 4. _____

_____ 5. _____

_____ 6. _____

_____ 7. _____

_____ 8. _____

_____ 9. _____

_____ 10. _____

Multiple Choice

_____ 1. _____
        a.
        b.
        c.
        d.

_____ 2. _____
        a.
        b.
        c.
        d.

_____ 3. _____
        a.
        b.
        c.
        d.

_____ 4. _____
        a.
        b.
        c.
        d.

5. _____

    a.

    b.

    c.

    d.

Strategies for Essay Tests

Many students dread essay exams and discussion questions. Whereas objective tests require you to choose the correct answer or fill in a specific blank, subjective tests require you to recall and to organize. The main idea is to make sure that the grader knows that you know the answer to the question. Leave nothing to chance.

brain byte

Leslie Hart argues that subjective tests are superior to objective tests because learners have to identify patterns and select strategies for using them.

Basic Strategies for Writing Answers to Essay Tests

Below is a list of strategies to use with essay tests. You will want to go back to the Survival Kit at the beginning of the book and reread and process into your long-term memory the checklist for essay tests. You can also find the checklist on-line at http://www.mtsu.edu/~studskl/ essay.html.

1. Make sure that you understand what the directions are asking you to do.

2. If possible, turn the question into a statement that becomes your thesis statement. For example, if the question asks you to discuss the reasons why America won its war for independence, your thesis statement could say: "There are six primary reasons why America won its war for independence."

3. To make sure you answer all parts, underline or circle key words or phrases, and number the parts asked for in the question.

4. Write well-organized answers. Plan just as if the answer were an essay for English class.
   a. Have a clear, but simple, thesis statement; don't waste time with an elaborate introduction.
   b. Plan your major points; don't take the chance that they will just happen.

   c. Make your major points stand out through the use of strong transitions: *first-, second-, most important, next-,* and so on.
   d. Have support for your major points.

5. Write complete answers.
   a. Assume your audience is one of your peers.
   b. Write more than you think you need (if you have time).

6. Budget your time, but if you run out of time, ask if extra time is allowed. If not, outline what you would have written, noting that you ran out of time.

7. **PROOFREAD, PROOFREAD, PROOFREAD!**

Compare this list to the checklist on page 9 of the Survival Kit or the list at http://www.mtsu.edu/~studskl/essay.html. List the similarities and differences between the two lists.

Direction Words

Often students lose points on essay tests, not because they don't know the answer but because they do not answer the question being asked. The key to what your professor is asking you to do is to understand exactly what the directions ask for. On pages 203–204 is a list of fifteen commonly used direction words.

Make flash cards to help you remember these direction words. Write a direction word on the front of the card and put the definition and examples on the back.

Direction Word	Definition	Example
1. Compare	Emphasize similarities but also present differences.	**Compare** the strategies used in taking true/false tests with those used in taking multiple-choice tests.
2. Contrast	Give differences only.	**Contrast** the functions of the left brain and the right brain.
3. Criticize	Give your judgment of good points; then give the limitations with evidence.	**Criticize** the label in the margin system for taking lecture notes.
4. Define	Give meaning but no detail.	**Define** objective tests.
5. Describe	State particulars in detail.	**Describe** your weaknesses as tested by LASSI.
6. Discuss	Give reasons pro and con with details.	**Discuss** what you have done to overcome your weaknesses that were pinpointed by LASSI.
7. Evaluate	Discuss advantages and disadvantages along with your opinion.	**Evaluate** the implementation of the online catalog in the library.
8. Give cause and effect	Describe the steps that lead to an event or situation.	**Give the cause** of our forgetting what we read in textbooks and the **effect** that the label in the margin system has on this forgetting.
9. Give an example	Give a concrete illustration from your book, notes, or experience.	**Give an example** of a reference book that you think will be helpful in other courses.
10. Illustrate	Give an example.	**Illustrate** how the principle of meaningful organization will help transfer information from short-term to long-term memory.
11. Justify	Prove or give reasons.	Most students will not use the label in the margin system for reading a textbook because it takes too long. **Justify** its use.
12. Relate	Show how things interconnect.	**Relate** the label in the margin system for reading textbooks to the label in the margin system for taking lecture notes.

Direction Word	Definition	Example
13. Summarize	Organize and bring together main points only.	**Summarize** what you have learned in this course.
14. Support	Back up a statement with facts and proof.	Researchers say that recitation is the most powerful means for transferring information from short-term to long-term memory. **Support** this statement.
15. Trace	Give main points from beginning to end of an event.	**Trace** ideas from when they first enter the brain to active memory.

It is important that you understand direction words used in essay questions. Use the strategies for matching tests to match the direction words with their definitions.

_____ 1. Trace

_____ 2. Summarize

_____ 3. Illustrate

_____ 4. Justify

_____ 5. Give cause and effect

_____ 6. Describe

_____ 7. Define

_____ 8. Criticize

_____ 9. Contrast

_____ 10. Compare

a. Show how a principle works through example.

b. Emphasize similarities but also present differences.

c. Give differences only.

d. Give judgment of good points and limitations using evidence.

e. Prove or give reasons.

f. Give meaning but no details.

g. State the particulars in detail.

h. List the points.

i. Describe the steps that lead to an event or situation.

j. List and describe.

k. Give an example.

l. Organize and bring together the main points only.

m. Give the main points from the beginning to the end of an event.

Applying the Direction Words

Below are descriptions of what different instructors want you to write on a test. Identify which direction words they are likely to use in their directions. There is a self-grading version of this exercise on-line at http://www.quia.com/tq/215781.html if you prefer.

_____ **1.** In your composition class, the instructor asks you to show how the modes of narration and description are alike and how they are different.

_____ **2.** In a political science class, you are asked to give your judgment of the good points of the electoral college system while acknowledging its limitations.

_____ **3.** Your study skills instructor asks for you to point out differences between your study habits now and your study habits at the beginning of the semester.

_____ **4.** In an algebra class, the professor asks you to give the meaning of the term *slope*.

_____ **5.** In a literature class, the professor asks students to depict in detail the setting of the novel *Sula* by giving particular details.

_____ **6.** An aerospace instructor asks students to give a detailed analysis (both pros and cons) of the reasons NASA was faced by problems during the 1980s.

_____ **7.** Your study skills instructor asks you to discuss the advantages and disadvantages of using the label in the margin system for reading textbooks.

_____ **8.** Your political science professor asks you to discuss the steps that led to the resignation of Richard Nixon and what the consequences were for the Republican party.

_____ **9.** Your nursing professor asks you to give concrete illustrations of the effects of smoking on human health.

_____ **10.** Your physical fitness teacher asks you to give an example showing the link between aerobic conditioning and good health.

_____ **11.** An education professor asks you to prove or give reasons why teachers should use the "whole language" method of teaching reading.

_____ **12.** Your psychology professor asks you to demonstrate how Freud's theories of childhood development interconnect with Jung's theories.

_____ **13.** Your biology professor asks you to organize and bring together the main points regarding the process of photosynthesis.

_____ **14.** Your history professor asks you to use facts to prove that the South was technologically unprepared to win the Civil War.

_____ **15.** Your music history professor asks you to briefly discuss the main composers of the Jazz Age from its beginning to its end.

Critical Thinking About Direction Words

Part of understanding what that direction word is asking you to do is to determine the level of thinking your answer requires: **knowledge, comprehension, application, analysis, synthesis,** or **evaluation.** Reexamine the preceding exercise. What level of thinking does each of the fifteen questions require?

Practice with Direction Words and Topic Sentences.   The first sentence of your answer to an essay question is crucial. It should show the grader both that you understand the question and how you will develop your answer. In addition, it becomes your guide as well. It keeps you on track. Pay particular attention to the direction word. You will pay a severe penalty if you know the material but answer the wrong question because you did not pay attention to what the question asked you to do.

For each question below, plan what your answer would say, and write a clear topic sentence showing both that you understand the question and how you will develop your answer.

1. **Compare** what you did (or will do) this Christmas with what you did last year.

   _____

   _____

   _____

2. **Contrast** your choice of television viewing with that of your parents.

   _____

   _____

   _____

3. **Evaluate** your computer skills.

   _____

   _____

   _____

4. The cost, time, and effort involved in getting a college education is enormous. **Justify** your decision to come to college.

_____

_____

_____

5. **Relate** what you have learned in this course to your other courses.

_____

_____

_____

6. **Summarize** how you use your time in a typical school week.

_____

_____

_____

7. **Trace** the steps necessary to register for next term.

_____

_____

_____

After planning what should be included in each of these seven answers, choose one and write a complete answer to the question. Use a separate sheet of paper to write your answer.

Before you attempt the exercise on page 208, you may need to refresh your memory on why students should review returned tests. You can check page 10 of this text or log on to http://www.mtsu.edu/~studskl/rtrned.html.

Writing Winning Essay Answers

The essay below was written by a student who has trouble writing essays. See if you can do a better job. To get full credit for this question, you need to do three things:

1. Read the student's essay and evaluate it by using the checklist in the Survival Kit at the beginning of the book. On a separate sheet, write your evaluation. How many of the twenty points should the student get credit for? You are the instructor. Explain to the student how he could have gotten the full twenty points' credit. Remember, in the Survival Kit, there is also a list of reasons you should review a test when it's returned. Did the student include enough of these reasons?

2. Take the same topic, "Why Students Should Review a Test After They Get It Back Graded," and plan major points and a thesis statement.

3. Following your plan, write your own essay (in correct essay form) on this same topic. Be careful not to make the same mistakes the student made.

Here is the student's essay:

Discuss: Why Students Should Review a Test After They Get It Back Graded (20 points)

Review means to go over it. That means you should go over tests when you get them back. Because its really important. It's important to review them so you'll know what you missed. Also what the teacher asked you on the next test. Picking up clues is important too. I'm not sure how much reviewing a test can help because I haven't tried it yet. You should review what you missed so you won't miss it again if the teacher ask it on the next text. I never thought about doing it because I am usually thinking about the grade I got. Oh, I almost forgot, you should review tests to see if you spent you're time right. And if the questions come from the lectures or the book or both. That's as important to you as getting a good grade. As I was saying, I haven't tried it yet but I'm sure it wil help me.

Comments:

Practice Evaluating Essay Questions

It's good for you to examine discussion questions from a grader's point of view so that you will better understand what the grader is looking for when your paper is graded.

Following are five answers to the same question asked on a study skills test. The question was to discuss how to write an effective answer to an essay question. You are the grader. The question is worth twenty points. Use the checklist as your guide for what to look for in the student's answer and what elements the answer should contain. In the blank, give your score, with the highest possible's being 20. Write your comments as to why the student received those points.

Student 1 Score _____

> To write an effective answer to an essay question includes several steps. The first step is to answer by rewriting the question in a complete sentence. The second step is to write in complete sentences your answer. The third step is to support you answer with examples and facts. The fourth step as to conclude with complete sentences. Those are the four steps to answering an essay question. With these steps it lets the reader know how the answers were developed.

Comments:

Student 2 Score _____

In order to write an effective answer to an essay question, you must know the topic. All ways answer the question being ask in the first sentence of the answer. Have a strong thesis statement. The thesis statement should be what the paper is about. When you begin the actually essay, you must have proper facts. Detail sentences should support any topics brought up in your paper. Last, you shouol sum up your paper. Not bring up new ideas. This is my idea of how one should write an effective essay.

Comments:

Student 3 Score _____

When writing an effective essay, there tends to be several steps that are involved. I am here to tell you how to write the answer to a test question when it has to be in essay from.

First make sure that you understand what has to be written because if you do not people tend to loose focus on what the assignment is and start to write on another subject. Second, do some type of brainstorming, like do a prewrite. Jot down things that come to you're mind on the particular subject that you are writing about. Then start writing and go back what you have written. Third always be clear on what you are writing and give a lot of detail. Teachers, usually like when you give a lot of detail. Last, but not least write a concluding statement summarize what you have said in you thesis statement.

Comments:

Student 4 Score _____

My instructor says it important to use the check list for answering essay questions in order to make sure I get the most points possible for what I know. It's a bunch of stuff to memorize, but after analyzing the list more carefully I think she may be right. I do need to understand what the question is asking otherwise I probably won't get any credit even if I know something about the topic. The best way to do this is to plan my answer and then show the grader both that I understand what the question is asking me to do and how I will answer it. The grader knows I know the answer and it provides a guide fo me to follow so I make sure I cover all the points and don't get off the subject. Major points should standout so that I know I've covered them and the grader can check off points he's looking for. If I don't support the major points. I come up with just a list. That's not good. I need to make sure my writing is readable and that I have checked mistakes. I know when it's a test situation I may make more mistakes and not even know I've made them. A concluding statement let's me double check that I answered the question and reminds the graded again that I knew what the answer is. The check list may be over kill, but if I want to get the most points for what I now, I probably will do better if I did everything on it.

Comments:

Student 5 Score _____

In order for someone to write an effective answer to a discussion question he must include at least these nine strategies that fall into the categories of developing, supporting and concluding the essay. The first category is to develop and plan your answer. You need to read the question over to see that you fully understand what is being asked of you. Next, you do any preliminary planning that needs to be done in order to organize your answer before you start and then you make the first sentence of your essay repeat the question and show how you will answer it. The second stage is to support your answer. You need to make sure that you list all your major points and they are supported by examples. You must also make sure that anyone who is not in this class would be able to read your essay and know what the discussion is about. The last and sometimes most important thing to do is conclude your essay. Now this area consist of several checklist. First, did you cover all the major points? Did your completely answer the question? Have you re-read over the essay and proofed for any spelling or grammar errors/ Most importantly you should make sure your handwriting is neat and legible for someone to read and understand, without guessing, what you are saying. If you can include most, if not all of these strategies in your essay then you should be able to write an exceptional answer to a discussion question.

Comments:

Virtual Field Trip:
Essay Tests

Visit http://collegesurvival.college.hmco.com/students and select "Hopper," or go to http://www.mtsu.edu/~studskl/3evirtual-fieldtrips.html.

Virtual Field Trip:

Dealing with Test Anxiety

Visit http://collegesurvival.college.hmco.com/students and select "Hopper," or go to http://www.mtsu.edu/~studskl/3evirtual-fieldtrips.html.

Questions to Ask Before an Exam

A few strategically asked questions may also help you to predict what will be on a test. The more you know, the more efficient your study time can be. Often, when an instructor announces a test or exam, students go into panic mode and forget to ask important questions. But it's right before an exam that you have an excellent opportunity to ask your instructor several important questions.

Here's a list of questions that would be good to ask before an exam. Choose the five that you think are most important, and explain why it would be strategic to ask such questions.

1. How many questions will be on the test?

_____

_____

2. What types of questions will be on the test?

_____

_____

3. What material will be covered?

_____

_____

4. How much will the test count toward the final grade?

_____

_____

5. Will the questions come primarily from the notes or the text?

_____

_____

6. Will partial credit be awarded for some answers?

_____

_____

7. How much time will we have for the test?

_____

_____

8. Will there be any extra credit?

_____

_____

9. What materials (books, notes, calculators, dictionaries, and so on) will we be able to use?

_____

_____

10. What outside material (handouts, readings, and so on) will be included on the test?

_____

_____

Final Exams

You should, of course, begin preparation for finals the first day of class. Most of us, however, need a bit of organizing to get ready for finals. The following study organizer may be just what you need for each of your classes to be used a week or so before finals. List each class you are taking and fill in the information asked for about each class. *Be very specific.* Make copies so that you will have one sheet for each class.

Class _____   Date and time of exam _____

Instructor _____   Office and telephone number _____

What percent of the final grade will the final exam count? _____

What will be covered on the final exam? (Be specific.)

1. _____

2. _____

3. _____

4. _____

5. _____

What kind of exam will this be (multiple-choice, true/false, essay, and so on)?

_____

What is the best way to study for this exam? (Be specific.)

_____

_____

I need to have **flash cards** covering:

1. _____

2. _____

3. _____

I will use these **mnemonics** (and why):

1. _____

2. _____

3. _____

Summary sheets will be useful to study (specific concepts):

1. _____

2. _____

Name and telephone number of a person in the class with whom I will study for at least an hour.

_____

Summary

To check to see if you have grasped the major points of this chapter on **strategies for taking tests,** answer the following questions:

What is the difference between *recognition* and *recall* when answering test questions?

▶

Name four specific strategies that you already use to *prepare* for tests.

1.

2.

3.

4.

Why is it important to budget your time when taking a test?

▶

Explain how to budget your time when you take a test.

▶

Why are there usually more true statements than false ones?

▶

Give three examples of statements that tend to be false.

1.

2.

3.

What are negatives?

▶

What is a double negative?

▶

What is the difference between a general qualifier and an absolute qualifier?

▶

What are four basic strategies to use with multiple-choice questions?

1.

2.

3.

4.

What options tend to be the incorrect choice?

▶

What options tend to be the correct choice?

▶

What are basic strategies for fill-in questions?

▶

What are basic strategies for matching tests?

▶

Name some clues used to predict test questions from lecture material.

▶

What clues can you use to predict test questions from textbooks?

▶

Why is it important to know the meaning of direction words?

▶

Describe what the first sentence of the answer to an essay question should do.

▶

How can you be sure that your answer is well organized?

▶

Describe what the first sentence of the answer to an essay question should do.

▶

What is a good guideline to use in deciding how much to write?

▶

What is a strategy to use if you run out of time?

▶

List some strategies to use when preparing for final exams.

▶

▪ What's your Advice?

LaNita, Bill, and Charlene have a mid-term exam next week in Dr. Watts' philosophy class, one of only two tests in the course for the entire semester. The difficulty of Dr. Watts' exams is legendary on campus, but he is the only instructor who teaches this course, a requirement in their major. Because it is important for them to do well, the three students decide on their first day of class to meet weekly for a study session. The students promise to take notes in class, label them after class, and keep up with reading assignments by writing possible test questions in the margins and underlining the answers in each paragraph. At their weekly study session, they compare their marked notes and texts and take turns answering questions out loud. At the end of each weekly session, LaNita is responsible for making a practice test for next time using that week's material. Bill's responsibility is to come up with as many visual study aids as he can for the material—comparison charts, maps, time lines, and so forth. Charlene's job is to create mnemonics and use her computer program to make flash cards or games, using the information for the week. Because they keep up with weekly sessions, their tasks are relatively simple. At the class period before the exam, Dr. Watts tells the students that the test will have several discussion questions asking students to compare or contrast various philosophies, trace development of certain philosophies, or discuss how certain philosophers might react to a statement. In addition there will be a multiple-choice section, a true/false section, and a matching section. They will have one hour and fifteen minutes for the test. When the students meet for a final study session, the three agree that they have prepared well but are worried about taking the test. LaNita says that she usually does great on the objective parts of a test but somehow fails to get full credit on the discussion parts even though she knows the material. For Bill and Charlene, it is just the opposite. They ask for your advice on **test-taking** strategies. Please make them a guide for taking the test.

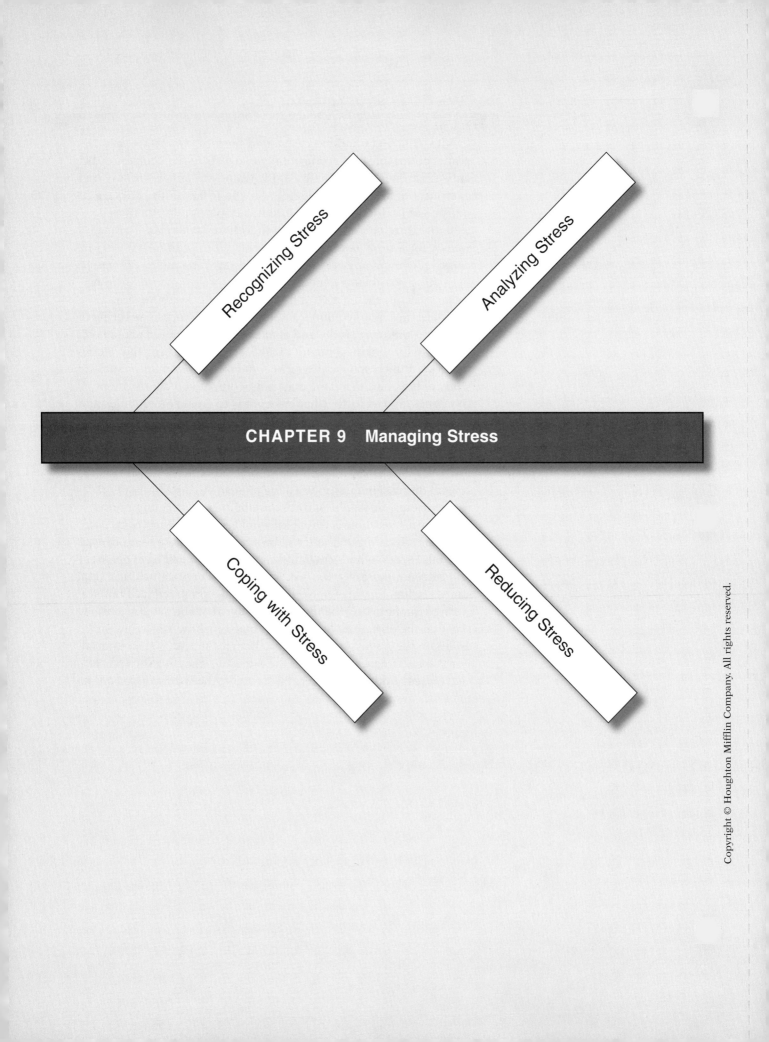

Recognizing Stress

Analyzing Stress

CHAPTER 9   Managing Stress

Coping with Stress

Reducing Stress

CHAPTER 9

Managing Stress

As a developing college student, you are learning how to manage your time, process information, and take tests: however, there is an additional factor that may determine your success as a college student. How well do you deal with stress? Have you developed strategies for dealing with the lack of concentration often caused by stress?

Stress: What Is It?

brain byte

Researchers O'Keefe and Nadel have found that positive forms of stress occur when we are challenged to rise to the occasion. Your body releases adrenaline and noradrenaline which actually heightens perception, increases motivation, and even enhances physical strength.

If you are not feeling stress at this point in the term, there is something wrong. Stress is completely normal and is our response to our changing environments. Therefore, not *all* stress is bad. There are as many different ideas about stress as there are people who experience stress in their lives. *Stress* refers to the way you react physically, emotionally, and mentally to stressors. *Stressors* are the many daily occurrences that require you to adapt to new situations and people. You may be going about your daily life and not realize the effect that stress is having on you. But the fact is, stress can make itself known in every aspect of a person's life. When you snap at your roommate, spouse, or children, when you have trouble concentrating, when you feel that you just want to be left alone, all may be symptoms of stress. These symptoms can be reflected in your health, your mental and emotional well-being, and your behavior. Let's look at a list of common symptoms of stress. Check those in the following table that apply to you.

221

Recognizing Possible Signs of Stress

	Health or Medical		Mental and Emotional		Behavioral
	Migraine or tension headache		Irritability		Sleeping badly
	Upset stomach diarrhea		Losing sense of humor		Snapping or shouting at those around you
	High blood pressure		Often on the verge of tears		Fiddling with your hair
	Shortness of breath		Crying spells		High-pitched or nervous laughter
	Loss of appetite		Feeling that you can't cope		Trembling, shaking, excessive blinking
	Frequent or lingering colds		Being suspicious of others		Finding it difficult to talk to people
	Acne or pimples		Difficulty concentrating		Having trouble completing tasks
	Cold sores on mouth		Difficulty making decisions		Overeating
	Dizziness		Making poor decisions		Drinking or smoking more than usual
	Lack of energy		Not being able to think		Reduced sex drive
	Dryness of the throat and mouth		Not being able to stay on task		Grinding the teeth or clenching the jaw

If you checked more than four or five of these, you are stressed and need to read further for help with your stress.

Analyzing Your Stress

In order to find an answer, it is helpful to know the problem. Likewise, in order to manage stress, it's helpful to know what causes it. You have learned from critical thinking that if you are going to solve a problem, you first need to determine exactly what the problem is. Remember step two, gathering information? Let's gather information about your stress.

Critical Thinking About **Stress**

When you think about stress in your daily life, what images, people, places, and so on, come to mind? List at least five causes of stress in your life.

1. _____

2. _____

3. _____

4. _____

5. _____

Step three in critically solving problems is to determine your options. Examine the major causes of stress in your life and try to determine what your options are for dealing with this stress. Choose one of the causes you listed, and list what you think some of your options are. Ask others to help if you are stuck.

Cause of stress: _____

Options I have for dealing with this stress:

1. _____

2. _____

3. _____

4. _____

brain byte

The body responds to negative stress by releasing the hormone cortisol. Too much cortisol negatively affects the hippocampus, which is very sensitive to the hormone. This weakens the brain's local memory and indexing systems. The hippocampus is the part of the brain that enables the body to fight disease, so the release of cortisol weakens the body's immune system.

The study strategies you have developed so far are ways of dealing with situations that are common for college students. Let's review some things you already know about relieving stress.

You have developed study strategies that use what you know about how the brain processes information in order to process information more efficiently.

You have developed a system for taking notes and reading textbooks.

You have developed strategies for studying for and taking tests.

You have developed a master schedule for help with time management.

You know how to write goals in order to solve stress-related problems.

You know how to use the Breathe System to relax and focus.

Are you using these strategies? Remember that if you have a plan or strategy for dealing with stressors, they are less likely to have the impact they might have had.

Developing a Plan of Action

Now return to the options you listed for dealing with one of the causes of your stress. Weigh each option carefully and choose one. Using what you know about goal setting, write a plan of action in the form of a useful goal.

Goal for dealing with _____

_____

Virtual Field Trip:
Let's Find Out More About Managing Stress

Visit http://collegesurvival.college.hmco.com/students and select "Hopper," or go to http://www.mtsu.edu/~studskl/3evirtual-fieldtrips.html.

The University Counseling Center at the University of North Carolina offers strategies for managing stress at http://caps.unc.edu/MStress.html (used with permission). Study the following ten commandments that are based on these strategies, then answer the questions that follow.

Ten Commandments for Managing Stress

1. **Thou shalt organize thyself.**
   Take better control of the way you're spending your time and energy so you can handle stress more effectively.

2. **Thou shalt control thy environment by controlling who and what is surrounding you.**
   In this way, you can either get rid of stress or get support for yourself.

3. **Thou shalt love thyself by giving yourself positive feedback.**
   Remember, you are a unique individual who is doing the best you can.

4. **Thou shalt reward thyself by planning leisure activities into your life.**
   It really helps to have something to look forward to.

5. **Thou shalt exercise thy body since your health and productivity depend on your body's ability to bring oxygen and food to its cells.**
   Therefore, exercise your heart and lungs regularly, a minimum of three days per week for fifteen to thirty minutes. This includes such activities as walking, jogging, cycling, swimming, aerobics, and so on.

6. **Thou shalt relax thyself by taking your mind off your stress and concentrating on breathing and positive thoughts.**
   Dreaming counts, along with meditation, progressive relaxation, exercise, listening to relaxing music, communicating with friends and loved ones, and so on.

7. **Thou shalt rest thyself as regularly as possible.**
   Sleep seven to eight hours a night. Take study breaks. There is only so much your mind can absorb at one time. It needs time to process and integrate information. A general rule of thumb: take a ten-minute break every hour. Rest your eyes as well as your mind.

8. **Thou shalt be aware of thyself.**
   Be aware of distress signals such as insomnia, headaches, anxiety, upset stomach, lack of concentration, cold/flu, excessive tiredness, and so on. Remember, these can be signs of potentially more serious disorders (for example, ulcers, hypertension, heart disease).

9. **Thou shalt feed thyself; thou shalt not poison thy body.**
   Eat a balanced diet. Avoid high-calorie foods that are high in fats and sugar. Don't depend on drugs and/or alcohol. Caffeine keeps you awake, but it also makes it harder for some people to concentrate. Remember, a twenty-minute walk has been proven to be a better tranquilizer than some prescription drugs.

10. **Enjoy thyself.**
    It has been shown that happier people tend to live longer, have fewer physical problems, and be more productive. Look for the humor in life when things don't make sense. Remember, the best treatment is from yourself.

Critical Thinking About
The Ten Commandments of Stress

Does the breaking of any of these commandments cause you stress?

_____

Which commandments do you routinely ignore? _____

Did you list any of the commandments' options for managing stress in the previous exercise? Explain.

_____

_____

_____

Coping Strategies for Alleviating Stress Symptoms

When stress is constant and unrelieved, it can become negative and even destructive. But you can break the cycle of negative stress by learning ways to help yourself relax. By taking the time to practice simple relaxation techniques on a regular basis, you can give yourself a chance to unwind and get ready for life's next challenge.

1. **Musical background tapes.** These can be purchased at most department or music stores in the cassette tape section. The content of these tapes ranges from soothing music to sounds of nature (oceans, thunderstorms, forest wildlife, and so on). You can also buy tapes that incorporate both music and nature sounds as well as those with a relaxation narrative.
2. **Breathe System.** The Big Three of Dr. Ralph Hillman's BREATHE System was presented in the Survival Kit. Hopefully it has become a habit. An overview of the system is presented here.

Breathe	Use the Big 3: (1) straighten your posture, elevate your rib cage; (2) relax your neck and shoulder muscles; (3) breathe by moving your ribs sideways and not raising your shoulders while inhaling to make calming breaths possible. Inhale completely (through your nose) and blow out (through your mouth) as much air as possible with each exhale.
Repeat	Take another calming breath, using the Big 3. Focus on the Breathing.

Emotion   Become aware of and identify your emotional condition and the emotions of others. Evaluate their effectiveness. Are those emotions working for or against you? Allow your emotional state to reduce in intensity or transform to a more effective emotional state.

Assess   Assess your actions and behaviors and those of others in the situation. Are those behaviors beneficial? Make the choice to change, regain personal control, and redirect your behavior to be more consistent with your goals. Focus on the Breathing.

Talk   Clarify what the wants/needs/concerns are by asking questions. Be careful how you ask the question. Use good voice quality, falling inflection, and don't let your voice reflect a negative emotional condition. Is what you are saying, feeling, and doing right now helping you achieve your goals? How may I help you? Focus on Breathing.

Hear   Focus on the concepts expressed or implied by the speaker (even if it is you). Look beneath the words to determine what is really being said. Continue to talk and listen as you seek additional options that might resolve this situation. Focus on Breathing.

Exit   Seek agreement about how to resolve this situation and return to the learning community, back to a place of security, calmness, and hope. Continue to Breathe.

Reprinted from DELIVERING DYNAMIC PRESENTATIONS: USING YOUR VOICE AND BODY FOR IMPACT by Ralph E. Hillman. Copyright © 1999. Reprinted by permission of the author.

3. **Progressive relaxation routine.** This is a three-step technique. It can be done while sitting or lying down and takes only fifteen minutes or so. It helps if you can practice the technique in a quiet, relaxing place. First, *tighten your hand muscles* and make a fist; then, notice how it feels. Your muscles are taut and strained, and your hand may even be trembling slightly. You may feel tension in your hand, wrist, and lower arm. Hold the tension for a few seconds before relaxing. Now, *release your hand*, relax your fist, and let the tension slip away. You may notice that your hand feels lighter than it did while your muscles were tensed and that your wrist and forearm also feel relieved of pressure. *Notice the difference* between how your hand felt when tensed and how it felt when you released the tension. Does your hand tingle or feel warm when relaxed? Did the throbbing you felt while tensed disappear when you relaxed? It is best to do this exercise on each of the major muscle groups of your body. The basic technique remains the same throughout:

Tighten the muscle, release the tension, then notice the difference. You can start with your hands, then progress to other muscles; or you can move from head to toe, tightening and relaxing the muscles in your face, shoulders, arms, hands, chest, back, stomach, legs, and feet.

4. **Autogenic scripts.** Autogenics is a progressive technique. You begin by concentrating on a mental suggestion such as "My left arm feels heavy and warm." As you concentrate on this command, try to feel your arm getting heavier and warmer. Then repeat the same command, focusing on your right arm, left leg, right leg, and so on. Try to practice this exercise for about ten minutes, twice a day, or whenever you feel stressed. *Sit comfortably,* loosen any tight clothing, close your eyes, and try to clear your mind. You may wish to breathe deeply for a few moments and repeat a peaceful suggestion such as "I feel quiet" or "My mind is at rest." *Mentally focus* on your left arm and repeat to yourself, "My left arm feels warm and heavy," until it begins to feel warmer and heavier. Then try the same command while focusing on your right arm, left leg, right leg, and so on, until you feel completely relaxed. *Breathe deeply and stretch* as you finish the exercise. Open your eyes, exhale slowly, and notice how you feel. As you become better and better at this technique, you'll be able to help your body relax anywhere, any time. Autogenics is a technique that requires practice, time, and commitment, but the benefits you gain are well worth the investment. Start by practicing autogenics twice a day for about ten minutes per session. Within four to eight weeks, you should be able to produce this relaxation response with as little as five minutes of concentrated effort. Even sooner you will find it easier and easier to help your body relax when you put your mind to it.

5. **Visualization.** Visualization can be thought of as a mental vacation, a license to daydream. You can produce feelings of relaxation simply by using your imagination. Visualization allows your imagination to run free. Try to visualize yourself feeling warm, calm, and relaxed. Picture a tranquil setting that has particular appeal for you, and try to imagine all of the details. Are you lying on a warm beach? How does the sun feel on your back? Do you hear waves lapping on the shore? Is there a fragrance in the air? Do you see sailboats on the water? Just by using your imagination, you can give yourself a mental vacation whenever you feel the need to take a moment to relax and enjoy life.

6. **Clearing your mind.** Giving yourself a mental break can help relax your body as well. When you clear your mind, you let your worries slip away. *Reduce distractions,* noise, and interruptions as much as possible as you begin this exercise. Try to set aside five to ten minutes daily to practice clearing your mind. *Sit comfortably,* loosen any tight clothing, kick off your shoes, and relax yourself. Then, close your eyes and begin to breathe slowly and deeply. *Mentally focus* on one peaceful word, thought, or image. If other thoughts should enter your mind, don't be discouraged; relax, breathe deeply, and try again. *Stretch and exhale* as you complete the

exercise. With practice, clearing your mind can help you feel refreshed, energetic, and ready to tackle the next challenge.

7. **Biofeedback.** If you are having difficulty zeroing in on your reaction to stress and your ability to relax, biofeedback may help. Certified biofeedback practitioners can show you how to listen to signals from your own body that indicate your level of stress or relaxation. External sensors placed on your body measure specific stress responses (such as perspiration and muscle tension) and translate these responses into signals that you can see or hear, such as lights or audible tones. Your challenge is to change these physical responses through relaxation, which alters the signals. Biofeedback can help you monitor the progress you are making in helping your body relax. It is often used in combination with other relaxation techniques such as deep breathing, autogenics, progressive relaxation, and visualization.

8. **Energy release activities.** Just about anything requiring physical activity will release energy. Get involved in a hobby or sport. Good old-fashioned exercise (jogging, weight lifting, calisthenics, and so on) also works wonders. Aerobic exercise or any exercise that keeps the heart pumping at elevated levels for twelve to thirty minutes is best. But don't fail to exercise just because you can't get in thirty minutes; lesser quantities do have a positive effect on stress.

9. **Talking it out.** Talking with a friend or counselor about a problem will prevent it from becoming bottled up inside, thus giving you a better chance of dealing with it rationally.

10. **Self-hypnosis.** Self-hypnosis can be learned from a professional therapist or hypnotist. It is a valuable tool in the development of a leisure lifestyle and can aid in the reduction of many specific unhealthy habits (overeating, smoking, phobias, and so on) as well as in general stress management.

11. **Laugh.** Many brain researchers have found that humor and laughter help relieve stress.

Name three specific situations that occur in your life in which you might find it necessary to use one of the techniques for alleviating stress discussed on pages 226–229.

1. _____

2. _____

3. _____

Analyze the eleven strategies for alleviating stress. List in order of probability of use five that you might try.

1. _____

2. _____

3. _____

4. _____

5. _____

Do you think you may need additional or individual help on stress management?

_____

Lifestyle Habits That Help Reduce Stress: Try a Few!

Stress can cause certain brain functions to literally shut down. Higher-level thinking skills and memory are most affected. A positive attitude and a positive lifestyle are key elements of stress management. Since stress involves both emotional and physical reactions to change, the better you feel in body and mind, the better you'll be able to deal with the stress in your life. When you learn to think positively, exercise, eat well, and rest regularly, you'll be taking care of the most important person you know—you. On the next page are a dozen lifestyle habits that help to reduce stress.

Read this list carefully. Choose *three* or *four* of the following habits that relate to your lifestyle. On the line below each of those habits, write about a time in your life that you *should have* used that habit.

1. Don't take on more than you can handle. Try to complete one task at a time.

    _____

2. Schedule quiet time and time for relaxation and planned exercise.

    _____

3. Be assertive and stand up for yourself—or no one else will. Learn to say no.

    _____

4. Distinguish between situations you **can** control and those you **cannot.**

    _____

5. Accept the fact that you can't be perfect and will not always be right.

    _____

6. Educate yourself about proper nutrition and how it can affect your mind and body.

    _____

7. Use time management to set priorities and allow enough time to complete a task. Eliminate something if too much is happening at once.

    _____

8. Don't make too many life changes at once.

    _____

9. Anticipate stressors when you know a change is coming.

    _____

10. Analyze your values and accept yourself for who you are.

    _____

11. Make efforts to develop close friendships and support systems.

    _____

12. Develop a stress-management program and stick to it!

    _____

Which suggestion do you need to pay most attention to?

_____

Summary

To see if you have grasped the major ideas of this chapter, answer the following questions:

What is stress?

▶

What are stressors?

▶

Name some common symptoms of stress.

▶

Name three things that cause stress in your life.

1.

2.

3.

What is your plan of action for dealing with one of your stressors?

▶

This chapter presents eleven coping strategies to alleviate stress symptoms. Discuss the four that you think will be most useful to you.

1.

2.

3.

4.

What's Your Advice?

Several students gathered in the hall before class. It is mid-term and everyone is talking about being stressed out. Most of the class, however, is managing to deal with stress. John is not sure that's possible for him. He never has time to do his class work. Besides, he thinks most of it is just busy work. His boss is constantly on his back to work more hours, and his parents are always nagging him about money. John's girlfriend complains that he doesn't spend enough time with her. His roommate is a bore, and there is always something broken in their rented house. If he doesn't pass all his classes, he will lose his financial aid. He has frequent headaches and can't seem to concentrate for more than five minutes at a time. He's smoking up to two packs of cigarettes a day and hasn't really slept well in what seems like months.

Obviously John needs more help than you can give him, but he would really like some suggestions from you of ways that you deal with *your* stress that might work for him.

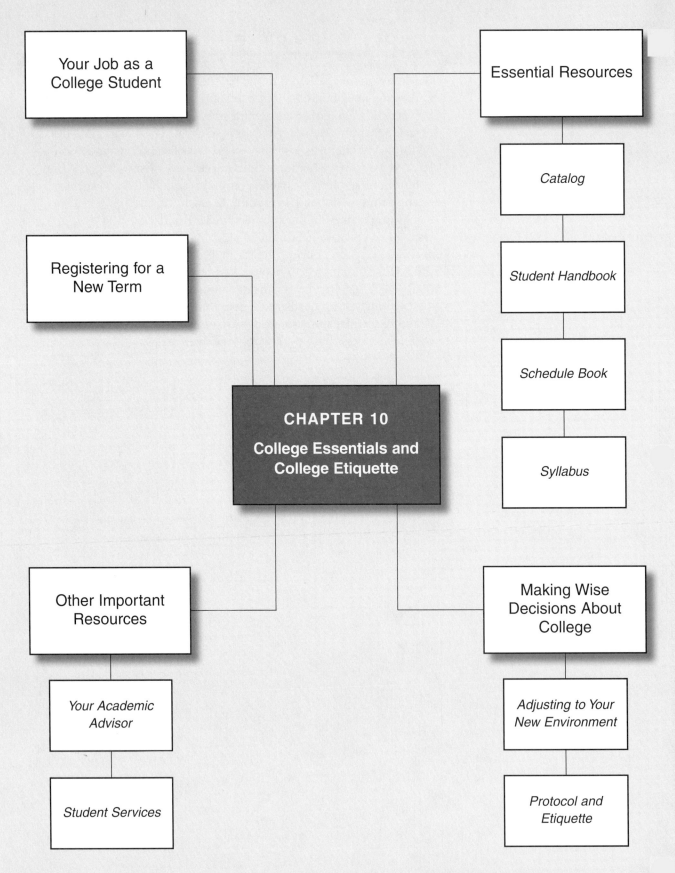

Your Job as a College Student

Registering for a New Term

CHAPTER 10

College Essentials and College Etiquette

Other Important Resources

Your Academic Advisor

Student Services

Essential Resources

Catalog

Student Handbook

Schedule Book

Syllabus

Making Wise Decisions About College

Adjusting to Your New Environment

Protocol and Etiquette

10

College Essentials and College Etiquette

As we discussed at the beginning of this book, in a learning strategies course, you need everything at once or even before you begin. That's why we began with the Survival Kit. We began our study with critical thinking, memory principles, and basic study skills. You have begun to master the basic study skills needed to gather, manage, and analyze the large amounts of information you have confronted. You should now have set in motion plans for setting goals, managing your time, and managing stress. You have examined your learning style. You are developing the tools and skills you need to be successful in your course work. Smart students, critical thinkers, make use of all the resources available to them. It's time to look at some other essentials—resources on your campus that you need to use. You are probably already using many of them. And while undoubtedly by now you have discovered what kind of behavior is expected of you, we shall review some college etiquette. Critical thinkers know how to make the best of each situation.

You are a college student. This is your job! Many of you are still working your old job, but beginning college is the same as beginning a new job. Each semester is a promotion and brings new responsibilities. Think of your first days on other jobs. In fact, jot down some things you remember about your first few weeks on the job. I'm sure you didn't just choose a place to work and say, "I think I'll work here today." Many of us approach college this way, however. For your job, someone interviewed you, and when you were hired, someone explained *exactly* what was expected of you, what procedures to use, how to work necessary equipment, and where to go to find out information you did not know. Often this is not the case at the beginning of college. Some of us plunged right in. You should approach college as you would a new job. Don't just wander in and begin work without knowing essential information. If you have not already done so, meet with an academic advisor. Discover how to register in the most efficient manner and which courses you really need to take. You are spending too much time, effort, and money not to do it right!

Can you find parallels with your new job as a college student? Use the space below to list parallels. The job side is begun for you. You will want to list others, however.

Job	College
You are expected to be there and on time.	
There are company rules to follow.	
You are expected to do your best.	
You have a boss who evaluates you.	
You find out what resources are available.	
You consult the expert when you are stuck.	
You must get along with fellow workers.	

Essential Resources

At most colleges and universities there are some essential resources that will provide your job description in addition to explaining how to get promotions.

The first essential resource you need is the ***college catalog.*** Because the catalog is changed periodically, the catalog for the year you enroll becomes your contract with the university. The catalog contains the rules, regulations, and procedures you are expected to follow. It corresponds to a company's policy manual. In addition, it contains the requirements for degrees and lists course descriptions. You need to know what is in your catalog. It is a reference book, and like most reference books, it will not be read cover to cover. However, it's a good idea to put it in a place where you will look at it often, both to become aware of policies and procedures and to understand your degree requirements. If you have declared a major, that section should be studied carefully. If you don't have a major yet, the catalog is a good source of information to help you decide on possible majors. When you register for classes, you consult the catalog for a description of the course you are registering for.

Using Your College Catalog

Consult your college catalog and find the following (put page numbers so you can find this again; you may need to use a separate sheet of paper for some of the questions):

Locate the academic calendar. What are the holidays for this semester?	
How do you drop or add a course?	
What is the significance of course numbers?	
What degrees are offered at your institution?	
What are the requirements for the degree you seek?	
Find the course description of one course that you are required to take and write a brief summary of that course.	
What grade point average do you need to graduate?	
What recreational opportunities are available on your campus?	
What are some of the student services offered on your campus?	

General Education or Core Curriculum Courses

One of the most important uses of the catalog is determining which courses to take and when to take them. Most colleges and universities have a required core curriculum often called general education or general studies courses. No matter what major, any student who graduates from that college or university must complete a required number of courses covering a broad area. According to the Association of American Colleges, college graduates should

> possess the marks of a generally educated person—that is, having such qualities as a broad base of knowledge in history and culture, mathematics and science, the ability to think logically and critically, the capacity to express ideas clearly and cogently, the sensitivities and skills to deal with different kinds of people, sophisticated tastes and interests, and the capability to work independently and collaboratively.[1]

College education should be both specialized (a major) and general, or broad (general education) because we experience the world whole, not in isolated parts as history or biology. We find that as many as two-thirds of college graduates work in areas unrelated to their majors. General education provides students with adaptive skills for an uncertain future.

The requirement of general education courses allows students to build a base of general knowledge often before they decide on a major.

[1]*Strong Foundations: Twelve Principles for Effective General Education Programs* (Washington, D.C.: Association of American Colleges, 1994, pp. ii–iii).

Here's where you may need to be careful in your choices of courses. Although there are usually many choices in an area of general studies, your major may require a particular course. By seeing an advisor, you can avoid taking extra courses. What follows is a chart loaded with useful things you can learn from your advisor. Students notoriously avoid seeing their advisor when, in fact, the services of your advisor may be one of the biggest bargains included in your tuition. Study "All I Ever Needed to Know I Learned from My Advisor" (permission granted by Laurie B. Witherow and Ginger A. Corley). Circle at least four things you might ask your advisor about.

All I Ever Needed to Know I Learned from My Advisor

• **What classes to take this semester, and next semester, and the next semester, and ...** • *Why I can't take forty hours if I can work forty hours* • **That I should study a minimum of two hours outside class for every hour in class** • *How many credits I need to graduate* • ***Information about graduate schools*** • How to get an overload • **Why I must take general studies classes that have nothing to do with my major** • *"Mr. Staff" isn't the hardest-working instructor on campus* • **How to withdraw from a class** • *An advisor writes a good recommendation letter* • ***How to change my major*** • What minors might be good for me • **Scholarships offered by my department** • *Why I shouldn't take all my classes in a row* • **When and where to file my upper-division and intent-to-graduate forms** • *What employers in my field are looking for* • ***What campus organizations would benefit me*** • Career information • **My advisor cares.**

A second resource you should have is your institution's **Student Handbook.** Handbooks usually list specific student resources and student organizations in addition to rules and regulations. Many colleges and universities have the handbook on-line.

Using Your Student Handbook

Consult your student handbook and find the following (be sure to put page numbers so you can find this again).

Where do you get a parking permit?	
Where can you replace a lost ID?	
Name two student organizations you might be interested in joining.	1. 2.
Where can you go for career counseling?	
Name three other things in the handbook and explain a situation that might arise where you would need to know this information.	1. 2. 3.

A third resource that you should keep is the current *schedule or registration book.* The schedule book will have the class schedule for that semester, payment instructions, important dates for that semester such as drop-and-add dates, and the final exam schedule. Don't think that because you have registered, you are finished with the book. Like the catalog, the schedule book contains information that you are not likely to find elsewhere. Read it carefully and save it. Because changes in classes or instructors may be made after the schedule is printed, you should double check offerings on-line whenever possible. Remember if you need an explanation for the course, the college catalog will be your source of information.

Using Your Schedule Book

Consult your schedule book for the following (be sure to insert page numbers so you can find this again):

How much did this class cost to take?	
When is the final exam for this class?	
What is the last day to officially drop this class?	
How will you get your grades at the end of the semester?	

The fourth resource to keep at all times throughout the semester is the *syllabus* for each class. The syllabus contains the rules and policies for that particular class. Not all classes will have the same grading scale, absence policy, or make-up policy. In addition, a syllabus will contain overall course requirements and perhaps class-by-class assignments. The syllabus should contain your instructor's office hours and telephone number. Students forget most of what went on the first day of class, so it's important to take notes and read your syllabus carefully both to refresh your memory and to understand policies that perhaps weren't discussed. The syllabus is your contract with your professor.

Using Your Syllabus

Consult the syllabus for this class to determine the following:

What is the absence policy?	
How is your grade determined?	
Is late homework accepted? Is there a penalty for late work?	
What are your instructor's name, telephone number, and office hours?	

Student Services

Are you missing out on some valuable resources just because you don't know they exist? Although most colleges try to keep the campus community aware of what they offer, it is difficult to keep up with all options.

Virtual Field Trip:
Your College Homepage

Visit http://collegesurvival.college.hmco.com/students and select "Hopper," or go to http://www.mtsu.edu/~studskl/3evirtual-fieldtrips.html.

Some Frequently Asked Questions (FAQs) by First-Year College Students or Transfers

I don't own a computer. Where can I use one?

Can I buy or rent one at a student rate?

Are there workshops or classes I can take to become more computer literate?

I don't have any financial aid. Where can I go to see if I qualify?

What if I get sick? What kinds of health services are available?

I am having trouble with my math, chemistry, and history. Are there tutoring services available?

Is there affordable childcare available on or near campus?

I think I may have a learning disability. Is there a place I can get help?

My professor suggested group study. Are there group study areas available?

I am having nonacademic problems. Is there help on campus?

I need a part-time job.

My professor says the more involved I get on campus, the more sense of belonging I will have. She says that this will contribute to my success as a student. What clubs or activities are available?

Where can I cash a check or use an ATM?

Where can I get photocopies made?

Is there public transportation available?

What is there to do on the weekends?

Your Grade Point Average

Your college requires you to have a certain amount of credit hours in certain areas in order to graduate. Each course you take is assigned the appropriate amount of credit hours. Your college or university also requires that you maintain a certain Grade Point Average (GPA) to stay in school or to qualify for certain programs. Thus it is important that you know how to calculate your grade point average. The chart below shows how to do this calculation. This chart uses a four-point system. Check your college catalog to see by which system your grades are calculated.

If a plus or minus system is used, your catalog will explain how to use it to figure your GPA.

How to Calculate Your GPA

The following is an explanation of how to calculate your GPA. You may want to use the chart to help you figure the examples on page 243.

1. List each graded course.
2. Enter the letter grade received.
3. Enter the grade point value (A = 4, B = 3, C = 2, D = 1, F = 0).
4. Enter course credit hours.
5. Multiply line items from column 3 by line items in column 4, and put the product in column 5.
6. Add column 4 to get total credit hours.
7. Add column 5 to get total quality points.
8. Divide the quality points by the number of credit hours to get your grade point average.

1	2	3	4	5
Name of Course	Letter Grade	Letter Grade Value	Credit Hours for Course	Quality Points
			×	=
			×	=
			×	=
			×	=
			×	=
			×	=
		Total		

$$\frac{quality\ points}{credit\ hours} = \text{GPA}$$

Consult your college catalog to find out how your university figures grade point averages.

Grade Point Average Practice

Figure John's grade point averages for the fall and spring terms. Carry the averages to hundredths; do not round out.

Fall Term Course	Hours Credit	Grade
Math 141	3	C
Hper 107	1	A
Dse 080	3	B
Spee 220	3	B
Dss 080	3	B
Psy 111	3	D

Grade point average for fall term: _____

Spring Term Course	Hours Credit	Grade
Art 101	3	A
Dsm 085	3	B
Biog 112	4	D
ROTC	1	C
Eng 111	3	C

Grade point average for spring term: _____

Now figure what John's *cumulative* (fall plus spring) grade point average is. The formula is the same: *total* quality points divided by *total* credit hours.

Cumulative grade point average: _____

Add the following courses for the summer term and compute John's cumulative GPA—his average for all three terms, not just his summer GPA.

Course	Hours Credit	Grade
Phy sci 100	3	B
Eng 112	3	C

Cumulative grade point average: _____

Virtual Field Trip:

Check Your GPA

Visit http://collegesurvival.college.hmco.com/students and select "Hopper," or go to http://www.mtsu.edu/~studskl/3evirtual-fieldtrips.html.

Higher Education

You have already discovered that there is a great deal of difference in the demands made on you as a high school student or an employee and the demands made on you as a college student. Stop and make a list of the differences you have found that affect you. Then examine what other students have said.

Critical Thinking About **Higher Education**

Below is a list of differences students have noted both between higher education and high school and between higher education and work. Choose at least four of these and comment on how you have learned to handle them. Be specific. If you have not been able to handle them, set specific goals to work toward.

1. There is more reading to do.

2. The college campus is larger. It's hard to know what's available and who to see.

3. College classes are larger, and classmates more diverse.

4. I have less free time in college.

5. I have more responsibilities in college.

6. College seems more impersonal.

7. I have more financial pressures in college.

8. College professors give fewer tests and are less tolerant of excuses.

9. There are so many courses offered at the college that I don't know what to take or when to take them.

10. Most classes at the college last for only one term (semester or quarter).

What difference *not* noted above has been most difficult for you?

Which five do you think are the most important? Explain why. (You may need to use a separate sheet of paper.)

brain byte

In *How People Learn*, John Bransford says that the goal of education today should be "helping students develop the intellectual tools and learning strategies needed to acquire the knowledge that allows people to think productively about history, science and technology, social phenomena, mathematics and the arts." He suggests that fundamental understanding about all subjects, including how to ask questions about many subject areas, is a major factor in understanding the principles of learning that people need to develop in order to become lifelong learners.

Taking Responsibility

Professors expect you to **take responsibility** for your own learning.

1. They will be there to lead the class, but you must make the effort to learn.
2. You must take it upon yourself to do whatever it takes (required or not) to learn the material.
3. You must realize that the work you do will result in the grade you get.

What are some things you have discovered that you wish someone had told you the first day on your new job as a student?

1.

2.

3.

Your professors are human, so they are always forming opinions. You need to be aware that the impression you make can have an effect on your grade. Even the way you sit and where you sit communicates something to your professor. Three good rules to follow are:

1. Get to know the professor personally.
2. Be prepared for class.
3. Be an active part of class.

Discuss how these can be accomplished.

Most of your professors will have responsibilities other than teaching your class. If you wish to talk to your professor, you should probably make an appointment during office hours. The professor's office hours are usually included in the syllabus. Check with each professor to see what his or her policy for student appointments is. If you just drop by, you may be disappointed to find another student has scheduled an appointment.

The quality of your work is also important. Your assignments and the way you turn them in tell the instructor a great deal about you and how much you care about the course. It doesn't matter what the assignment is; you should make an effort to complete it on time and fully. The more information you can give, the better. Getting by is not good enough in college. Not understanding is never an excuse in college, nor is not having enough time.

Look at the assignment you had due for today. Is it neat? Is it complete? Did you do your best? Write a few sentences describing the impression this assignment would make on the instructor.

_____

_____

_____

_____

_____

College is difficult and you need to be aware of everything that can help you. On a separate sheet of paper, write a paragraph on what kind of behaviors you modeled in class today (this includes assignments). What did your behavior say about you as a student?

You can't just *attend* college and expect to be successful. Less than 24 percent of Americans over the age of twenty-five have earned a college degree. It's not easy. There are certain expectations and responsibilities that go hand in hand with higher education. You have already discovered that there are many differences between the world of higher education and what you were doing last year.

Evaluating Your Classroom Savvy

Just as on the job you do and act a certain way if you are to be successful, there are also expectations about you as a college student. Here are a few behaviors that are expected of you as a college student. Put a plus (+) sign beside the behaviors that you already do well and a minus (–) sign beside the ones you need to improve: As you evaluate the behaviors you exhibit, analyze **why** each behavior is important.

_____   **1.** Attend every class.

_____   **2.** Come to class prepared.

_____   **3.** Be alert and attentive in class.

_____   **4.** Participate in class discussions.

_____   **5.** Show an interest in the subject.

_____   **6.** Ask questions when you don't fully understand.

_____   **7.** Seek outside sources if you need clarification.

_____   **8.** Take advantage of all labs, study sessions, and outside help.

_____   **9.** Set up meetings with your professors to discuss your progress.

_____   **10.** Go the extra mile with all papers and assignments.

_____   **11.** Always be on time for class.

_____   **12.** Take notes.

_____   **13.** When you must miss a class, make sure you find out exactly what you missed, make up the work, and come prepared for the next class.

_____   **14.** Comment on lecture material.

_____   **15.** Get to know your professors.

_____   **16.** Set goals and objectives for your classes.

_____   **17.** Evaluate yourself.

_____   **18.** Make friends in each of your classes.

_____   **19.** Have a positive attitude toward the professor and the class.

Nonsavvy Behavior

Now let's have a little fun. Your task is to come up with a list of **non-savvy** behaviors you have noticed in the classroom. See if you can list ten nonsavvy things that you have seen happen this semester. You may also want to ask your professors to add to your list. Let me start you off with some obvious ones.

1. Coming in late for class

2. Copying homework or cheating on a test or other assignments

3.

4.

5.

6.

7.

8.

9.

10.

You hold more power in the classroom than you may realize. Ask any professor. He will tell you that the students in the class significantly affect the delivery of information. By coming prepared, sitting up front, paying attention, taking notes, making eye contact, nodding when you agree or understand, asking questions when you are confused, you actually change the professor's enthusiasm and approach to the class. Think about classes that you are taking now. The best instructors have the best students. I can't be an exciting instructor without your cooperation.

Registering for a New Term

Now that you have almost completed the term, let's do some thinking about next term before you just sign up for new classes. You want to begin planning for the next term early. The day before or even several days before you register is not early enough.

■ Consider your responsibilities outside college that may put constraints on your choice of classes. (List things you should consider.)

■ Given these constraints, what is a reasonable course load for you? Will this make a difference in when you can take classes?

■ Carefully study your options. Read the catalog to see what your logical choices are both in general education and in requirements for your major. (List the options you have.)

■ Taking the right mix of classes is also important. You don't want all courses that require a great deal of reading. If math is difficult for you, you don't want all math-related courses. What classes are you considering for next semester? Is there a mix of types of classes and time required for each course?

- If possible, talk to other students who have taken the classes you are considering. Many students say this is the best way to get a feel for what the classes will be like. Remember, however, your learning style preferences and work ethic may be different from the students you ask.

- Seek the opinion of experts. Consult with your advisor. Your time and money are too valuable to just take the advice of another student or to guess. (Who is your advisor?) What are some questions you should ask? If you are in doubt about what is involved in a course you are considering, talk with the professor.

After studying your catalog, your schedule book, and talking with your advisor, make a plan for the next semester or two.

Virtual Field Trip:

College Life

Visit http://collegesurvival.college.hmco.com/students and select "Hopper," or go to http://www.mtsu.edu/~studskl/3evirtual-fieldtrips.html.

Summary

Explain several essentials found in these four important resources.	1. **College catalog** 2. **Student handbook** 3. **Schedule or registration book** 4. **Class syllabus**
What are core curriculum or general education courses?	▶
Why are they required?	▶
What are other academic resources and student services you feel are essential to your success as a college student?	▶
List what you consider three important reasons for consulting with an academic advisor.	1. 2. 3. 4.
Explain how to compute a GPA.	▶
List five behaviors that are characteristic of successful students.	1. 2. 3. 4. 5.

What are three good rules to follow when dealing with professors?

1.

2.

3.

List some things you should consider before registering for a new term.

▶

What's Your Advice?

Your friend and co-worker, Tara, has decided that she wants to attend your college next semester. To put it mildly, she's a bit overwhelmed. She is the first in her family to attend college and you are one of the few people she can talk to about her fears. She doesn't know what her major will be. In fact, she's not even sure she knows what a major is. The whole idea of credit hours is unclear to her, and she doesn't know how to go about choosing what classes to take or how many to take. She has heard people talking about associate, bachelor, and master's degrees. She is certainly not sure what that's all about. It's been ten years since she graduated from high school, and she really wants to know what a college class is really like. What would a professor expect from her? How much homework will she have? She would really like to continue working at least part-time. Will she be able to do that? Will she need to buy a computer? These are just some of the things she is worried about. What can you tell Tara that will help her feel more comfortable? What practical suggestions do you have for helping her to be successful?

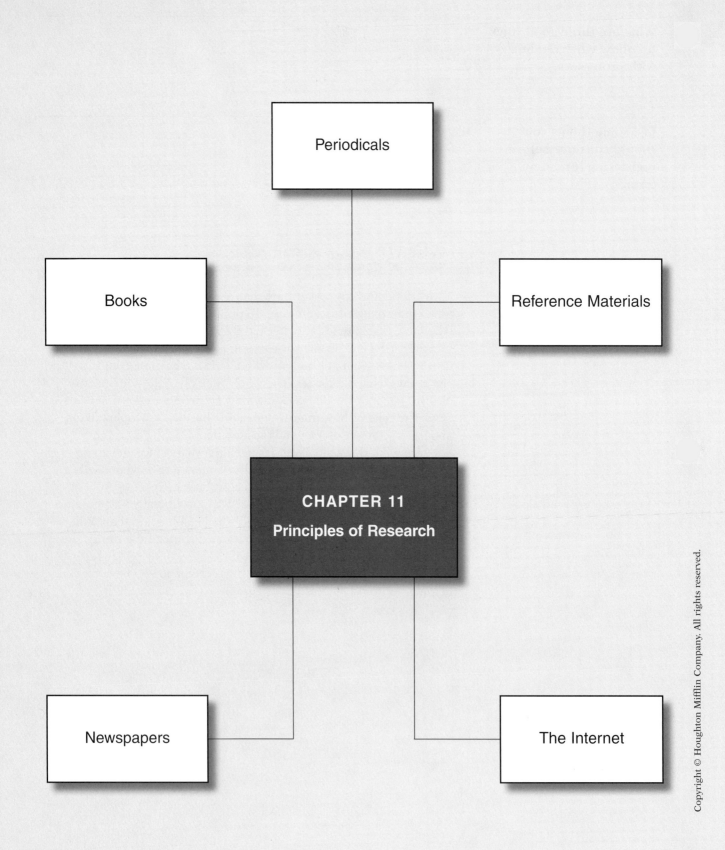

Periodicals

Books

Reference Materials

CHAPTER 11
Principles of Research

Newspapers

The Internet

CHAPTER **11**

Principles of Research

Using the Resources in the Library

Each college library is unique. But there are basic resources in all libraries that you will need to use with proficiency, no matter how large or small or technologically up to date your library is. If you have not already done so, take time to learn both what is available in your library and how to access it, so that when you need it, you won't have to stop and learn them. On some campuses, there is a library orientation. In addition, there will probably be handouts and printed instructions, or you can ask the librarians to help you. Do not hesitate to ask. You are certainly not the first or only student who ever needed help.

Using Databases

When using the library, you will use many different databases. It is important that you have a concept of what a database is. A database is a collection of information usually gathered for the purpose of organizing like information into one place. The telephone book for your city is a database of the telephone users in that area with telephone numbers and addresses. The database that tells you what books and periodicals your library has is the card catalog, which is electronic in most libraries today. In the library you will also use databases for finding articles in journals and magazines and newspapers or databases for finding information about certain subjects such as education, medicine, or psychology.

Books

There are various sources of information in any library. The one we usually think of first is *books*. When you use a book for research, you want to check the date it was written and the credentials of the author. For example: Is it important that the information in the book be up to date? What is the author's background? What makes him or her an expert on

253

the subject? Remember that when you use a book in your research, you will need to document it. Be sure to write down the entire title, the author's name, and the date and place of publication as well as the publisher's name. Also note what pages you use. Doing so will save you valuable time when you document your research.

Finding Books

The traditional way to see if the library has a certain book or books by a certain author or on a certain subject is to use the card catalog. The library has at least three cards for each book, so you can find a book by subject, author, *or* title. Most college libraries have computerized their database and have an on-line catalog. Because so many people use them, on-line computer databases are generally user friendly. You will need to determine how to use your library's system and then practice a bit to make sure you understand how to make it work for you.

Answer the following basic questions about your library.

1. What system is used to catalog the books (Dewey decimal or Library of Congress)?

   _____

2. What is the best method for determining if your library has a book (card catalog or computerized on-line catalog)?

   _____

3. Is there a traditional card catalog? _____

4. What are the basic on-line catalog commands for the following?

   To begin a search _____

   To find a list of commands or other help _____

   To find books on a certain subject _____

   To find books by a certain author _____

   To find a book by its title _____

   To find a book if you know only part of its title _____

   To limit the choices by publication date _____

   To check the availability of a book _____

5. Only books are listed in the traditional card catalog. What is included in the computerized on-line database?

_____

6. Can the computerized on-line catalog be accessed from outside the library? (If so, how?)

_____

Using the Computerized On-Line Catalog

Use the computerized catalog in your library to find the following (if your library database is not computerized, use the card catalog):

Find a book about _time management._

_____   Title

_____   Author

_____   Call number

_____   Number of pages

_____   When published

_____   Where published

_____   Publisher

_____   Is it illustrated?

_____   Does it have a bibliography?

_____   Is it currently available for checkout?

_____   How do you check it out?

How many books does your library have by John Steinbeck? _____

Choose one and answer the following:

_____   Title

_____   Call number

_____   Number of pages

_____   When published

_____ Where published

_____ Publisher

_____ Is it currently available for checkout?

Does your library have *I Know Why the Caged Bird Sings?* _____

If yes, answer the following:

_____ Author

_____ Call number

_____ Number of pages

_____ When published

_____ Where published

_____ Publisher

_____ Is it currently available for checkout?

_____ How do you check it out?

    For more specific kinds of books and background information, consult encyclopedias and other reference materials. Don't stop with the general encyclopedias; check the on-line catalog or ask your librarian for reference materials that might be useful.

Enter *encyclopedia* as a keyword search into the on-line computer. How many books are on the list?

_____

List several that are interesting to you.

Essay Index

You may find that there are no entire books on the topic you need to research but, instead, an essay or chapter about it in a book. For example, scholarly books often contain essays or chapters that may not appear in a subject or term search on the book database. The *Essay and General Literature Index*[1] is a useful reference that will help you ferret out hard-to-find subjects and spare you the need to look in indexes and tables of contents. The *Essay Index* is an author and subject index to essays in collections with a particular emphasis on humanities and social sciences. It is published semiannually in a paperbound issue and appears as a hardbound cumulative index every five years.

Practice with the Essay Index

Your subject is **rape in literature.** Search *two* different volumes of the *Essay and General Literature Index* to find resources. Complete the following:

Volume of the *Essay Index* _____

Author of essay on rape in literature _____

Title of essay on rape in literature _____

Found in what book? _____

Page numbers _____

Does your library have this book? _____

Volume of the *Essay Index* _____

Author of essay on rape in literature _____

Title of essay on rape in literature _____

Found in what book? _____

Page numbers _____

Does your library have this book? _____

You will explore several specific reference books at the end of this chapter. For now, however, let's examine the more general category of periodicals.

[1]H. W. Wilson Company.

Finding Periodicals

A second source of information is periodicals, so called because they come out periodically: weekly, monthly, annually, and so on. Magazines and scholarly journals are considered periodicals. Your library probably subscribes to thousands of periodicals. One reason for using periodicals in your research is that they are often more up to date than books; another is that the articles take less time to read than a book. Most libraries have copies going back to the early publication of the periodicals, either physically bound or on microfilm. If you want a historical view of an event, don't forget to research periodicals from the era in question.

Before databases were computerized, researchers used indexes such as the *Readers' Guide to Periodical Literature* to find periodical articles on their subject. The *Readers' Guide* indexes 300 popular magazines in yearly volumes. Other indexes such as the *Education Index, Humanities Index,* and *Social Sciences Index* are more subject-specific.

If your library doesn't have an electronic database such as Infotrac, EdscoHost, and ProQuest Direct (all of which are expanded academic indexes such as InfoTrac® OneFile or EBSCO's Academic Search™ Premier), the *Readers' Guide* is a good place to begin your search for periodical articles. Because most electronic databases begin around 1980, you will also need to use *Reader's Guide* or other hard copy indexes.

Practice with the **Readers' Guide**

Locate the *Readers' Guide* in your library. Describe where it is and what it looks like.

_____

Choose *one* of the following subjects and find *two* articles about it in the *Readers' Guide.* As with books, you will need to write all your documentation the first time. It may be difficult and time consuming to try to locate the information you need at a later time. Be sure to note that you will locate the article *by the title of the periodical, not the title of the article.*

Dyslexia   Anthrax   Subways   NCAA rules and regulations   Memory and Learning

_____ Subject (Article 1)

_____ Subheading (if any)

_____ Title of article

_____ Author of article (if any)

_____ Title of periodical

_____ Volume of periodical (appears before the colon)

_____   Page number (appears after the colon)

_____   Date of periodical

_____   Subject (Article 2)

_____   Subheading (if any)

_____   Title of article

_____   Author of article (if any)

_____   Title of periodical

_____   Volume of periodical (appears before the colon)

_____   Page number (appears after the colon)

_____   Date of periodical

If your library has a computerized database either in-house or through the Internet, you will find that your research base is extensive. For example, the *Readers' Guide* indexes 300 popular periodicals; Infotrac OneFile, however, indexes over 6,000 periodical titles and includes the full text of over a million articles. When you use the *Readers' Guide* you must look separately at each yearly volume and then locate a hard copy of the periodical. When you use an electronic database, you direct the search to cover the years you want to research.

Locate the electronic database in your library and answer the following questions.

_____   Name of the database?

_____   What specifically is indexed—how many periodicals,

_____   what kind, what years, and so on?

_____

_____   How do you access the database?

Practice Using Electronic Databases for Periodicals

Use the **electronic database** (*Infotrac OneFile* or the electronic database in your library) to find two articles on the **same subject** you chose in the *Readers' Guide* exercise:

Dyslexia **Anthrax** **Subways** **NCAA rules and regulations** **Memory and Learning**

_____ Subject

_____ Subheading (if any)

_____ Title of article

_____ Author of article (if any)

_____ Title of periodical

_____ Volume of periodical

_____ Page number

_____ Date of periodical

_____ Is an abstract or the text available on-line?

_____ Subject

_____ Subheading (if any)

_____ Title of article

_____ Author of article (if any)

_____ Title of periodical

_____ Volume of periodical

_____ Page number

_____ Date of periodical

_____ Is an abstract or the text available on-line?

Your library will have other important databases, some on-line, some on CDROM, and some as hard copy. Choose two of the following majors and list as many databases and resources you can find on your campus. Then use one of the databases you found to research a subject of interest in that category.

Accounting	Engineering tech.	Nursing
Aerospace	Fashion/design	Nutrition/food science
Agriculture	Foreign languages	Philosophy
Anthropology	Geography	Physics
Art	Geology	Political science
Biology	History	Psychology
Business	HPERS	Radio/TV/photography
Chemistry	Journalism	Recording industry
Computer science	Law	Social work
Criminal justice	Literature	Sociology
Current issues	Mathematics	Theater
Education	Music	Women's studies

Finding Newspapers

A third source of information you may need to use in your research is newspapers. The advantage of using newspapers is that they are more current than periodicals and give a slant to information that is slightly different from that in books or periodicals. Most libraries subscribe to several major newspapers and have back copies on microfilm. The most common way to find a newspaper article on your subject is to use an index such as the *New York Times Index* or *London Times Index*. Your library will probably have several electronic newspaper databases on-line. National Newspaper Index, Poole's Plus and LexisNexis UNIVerse are a few. LexisNexis covers general news and information, and legal, business, and medical resources. It gives mostly full-text access to newspapers and magazine articles, state and federal law, company financial information, industry news, and more. If you don't find full text on-line, you will have to read the article on microtext. You may find a digest form of significant news in *Facts on File*. *Facts on File* is usually found in the reference section of the library.

Practice Using Newspaper Sources

As practice using newspaper sources, use the same subject you used for periodicals from the following and find two news articles about that subject from different newspaper databases. Use *Facts on File* for the third database.

Dyslexia   Anthrax   Subways   NCAA rules and regulations   Memory and Learning

_____   Newspaper database

_____   Newspaper

_____   Headline of article

_____   Date of article

_____   Page of article

Short summary of article:

_____   Newspaper database

_____   Newspaper

_____   Headline of article

_____   Date of article

_____   Page of article

Short summary of article:

For most of your research projects, you will use primary resources in the form of books, periodicals, and newspapers. It is always a good idea to consult with the professor who assigned the topic or project for suggestions. Again, be sure to write down all information you will need to document your sources.

Using the Internet for Research

The World Wide Web, a powerful Internet access tool, is a virtual reference desk. There is probably a way to access the Internet on your campus. But because technology is handled differently on each campus, you may have to find out what is available to you as a student. Ask your librarian, the office of information technology, or student services about how to access the Internet on your campus. By using a web browser, such as Netscape's Navigator or Microsoft's Internet Explorer, or a commercial information service, such as CompuServe, America Online, Prodigy, Genie, or Delphi, you should be able to find up-to-date information on almost any subject.

Once you log on to your Internet provider, unless you know the URL of a specific site, you will use a search engine to locate sites that are related to your subjects. You may already be familiar with some search engines such as Google, AltaVista, Excite, Yahoo, AOLFind, HotBot, and Lycos. New search engines appear almost daily. In a recent random check, I located more than 15,000 search engines. A search engine is a type of software that creates indexes of databases or Internet sites on the basis of the titles of files, keywords, or the full text of files. The search engine has an interface that allows you to type what you're looking for into a blank field. It then gives you a list of the results of the search. When you use a search engine on the Web, the results are presented to you in hypertext; this means you can click on any item in the list to get the file. Some sites allow you to use more than one search engine at a time. After using various search engines, you will find one or two that you prefer. Although the results will be similar, each search engine will probably identify some hits that are different.

A very important fact to remember is that a search cannot read your mind or weed out information you need. The search engine simply tries to locate sites that contain your search word, and these sites may or may not be relevant. The search engine Excite came up with 1,900,922 hits to my search for *time management*. The engine located anything with the word *time* or *management*. Critical thinking is extremely important in both performing and limiting a search and when evaluating the usefulness of a site on the Internet. It's tempting to just get on the Web and surf. But you can waste a great deal of time if you don't know what you are doing. Before you use any search engine, click on the *search tips* or *help* link for the engine you have chosen. Even if you have frequently used the Internet for research, you will find time savers and ways to minimize the number of hits you get that are not relevant to your search.

Virtual Field Trip:
Internet Searches

Visit http://collegesurvival.college.hmco.com/students and select "Hopper," or go to http://www.mtsu.edu/~studskl/3evirtual-fieldtrips.html.

Practice Using the Internet

As practice using the World Wide Web as a resource, use the same subject you used to practice finding periodicals and news articles. Find four web sites that will give you information about the subject from the following.

Dyslexia   Anthrax   Subways   NCAA rules and regulations   Memory and Learning

Subject _____

1. Web site address: _____
   Description of what found:

2. Web site address: _____
   Description of what found:

3. Web site address: _____
   Description of what found:

4. Web site address: _____
   Description of what found:

The databases you use in the library for books, journals, and other resources have been reviewed, evaluated, and selected by scholars, but what about the sites on the Internet? The fact is that anyone can put virtually anything on the Internet. It doesn't have to be truthful, reliable, or accurate.

Virtual Field Trip:
Evaluating Sites

Visit http://collegesurvival.college.hmco.com/students and select "Hopper," or go to http://www.mtsu.edu/~studskl/3evirtual-fieldtrips.html.

Which Database?

Before you begin this exercise, make a list of the following:

Database you use to locate books _____

Database you use to locate periodical articles _____

Database you use to locate newspaper articles _____

Database you use to locate subject-specific indexes _____

Internet Browser _____

Knowing which database to use is the most efficient way for you to use resources; it will save you many hours in the library or on-line. Analyze the following and tell what the best database to use in your library is:

1. You need to know if your library has a book or books about astronomy.

2. You are looking for some general periodical articles about global warming.

3. You want to find a book by George Eliot.

4. Your education professor has asked you to research technology in the classroom.

5. For your nursing classes you need technical information about juvenile diabetes.

6. You want information about Alicia Keys.

7. You need the call number for *Benet's Reader's Encylopedia*.

8. You want information about a recent accident in London.

9. You want weather information about your favorite ski resort.

10. You need general periodical articles about the candidates for the senate in your state.

Quick References

Several terms ago, I conducted a survey of colleagues who teach general studies courses on my campus. I asked them which library reference books their students use most often. In the list that follows are the eight reference books cited most often by my colleagues. These reference books should be in any library. For each of them I have provided a brief explanation of the purpose of the book and one or more examples of information that can be found in the book.

Your assignment is to locate each book in your library and after investigating the index and contents, pretend that you are an instructor. Write a question that you want your students to answer by using the book and include the answer. Use the most recent copy you can find.

1. Joseph Nathan Kane's *Famous First Facts* records first happenings, discoveries, and inventions in the United States. You could use this book to find out who was the first African American woman to be awarded a medical degree.
   Call number _____
   Your question and answer:

2. The *World Almanac and Book of Facts* is probably the most comprehensive and most frequently used U.S. almanac of miscellaneous information. It is published yearly. You might use it to discover the world's tallest building, the zip code of a certain city, or the parent company for Jim Beam whiskey.
   Call number _____
   Your question and answer:

3. The *Statesman's Yearbook* contains information on the countries of the world (large and small) including history, area and population, constitutional government, defense, international relations, economy, energy and natural resources, industry and trade, communications, justice, religion, education, and welfare. It is published yearly, so it often contains the most up-to-date information on a country. You might use *The Statesman's Yearbook* to determine the currency of Greece, the official language of Malta, or the area in square miles of Rwanda.
   Call number _____
   Your question and answer:

4. *The Congressional Directory* contains biographical sketches of members of the U.S. Congress, the president's cabinet, a section on the diplomatic and consular service, and small maps showing congressional districts. You might use the most current to find who is your U.S. representative.
   Call number _____
   Your question and answer:

5. The *Statistical Abstract of the United States* as prepared by the chief of the Bureau of Statistics is a standard summary of statistics on the social, political, and economic organization of the United States. It is published annually. Use this reference to determine the median family income in the United States or the life expectancy for a white female born in 1960.
   Call number _____
   Your question and answer:

6. The *United States Government Manual* is the official handbook of the federal government. It contains comprehensive information on the agencies of the legislative, judicial, and executive branches of government. In it you can find out who the secretary of the interior is or the chairperson of the Tennessee Valley Authority.
   Call number _____
   Your question and answer:

7. *Benet's Reader's Encyclopedia* contains short articles on writers, scientists, and philosophers of all countries and periods, as well as literary expressions and terms, and plots and characters of famous works. It is a reference that will be extremely useful in a literature course. In it you can determine the pen name of Charles Lamb or find an explanation of existentialism.
   Call number _____
   Your question and answer:

8. *Bartlett's Familiar Quotations* is arranged chronologically by authors with exact reference to the source of each quotation. The index contains an average of four to five entries for each quotation. You can use it to find a quote about mothers or to find out who said, "We live and learn, but not the wiser grow."
   Call number _____
   Your question and answer:

Biographical Resources

Often you will need to find biographical information about someone but don't know where to start. A good place to begin is the *Biography and Genealogy Master Index (BGMI)*. This multivolume set guides researchers to more than 3,200,000 listings of biographies in over 350 current *Who's Who* and other works of collective biography. It is updated by cumulative and yearly supplements. Although the *BGMI* itself gives no biographical information, it enables the user to determine which edition of which publication should be consulted for biographical information. It may refer you to biographical dictionaries, subject encyclopedias, volumes of literary criticism, or other indexes. Your library may have an electronic version of *BGMI*, or you may log on to an on-line version at: http://galenet.gale.com/m/mcp/db/bgmi/.

Directions:

1. Choose one of the people listed below.

2. Locate them in the *Biography and Genealogy Master Index*.

3. List all the sources referred to by *BGMI*. Be sure you list the entire name of the publication, not just the abbreviation (see inside of the cover).

4. Find the person in at least one source listed.

5. List four facts about that person and the source of your information.

Sam Donaldson	Maya Angelou
Arnold Palmer	Donald Trump
Noam Chomsky	Barbara Walters
Jean Piaget	Ralph Lauren

Name _____ Source consulted _____

Sources Listed in BGMI	*Four Facts and Source*
	1.
	2.
	3.
	4.

Exercise for Quick References

Matching: To test how well you remember what is in each of the reference books, match the question to the book that would be most useful in finding the answer.

a. *Kane's Famous First Facts*
b. *World Almanac*
c. *Statesman's Yearbook*
d. *Congressional Directory*
e. *Statistical Abstract of the United States*
f. *United States Government Manual*
g. *Bartlett's Familiar Quotations*
h. *Benet's Reader's Encyclopedia*
i. *Biography and Genealogy Master Index*

Using the above list, where would be the most efficient place to find the answers to the following questions? Put the letter in the blank.

_____ **1.** Who are the two main characters in Toni Morrison's *Jazz*?

_____ **2.** For what is Andy Warhol famous?

_____ **3.** What is the source of this quote: "All animals are equal, but some animals are more equal."

_____ **4.** What are the trends in the cost of postsecondary education?

_____ **5.** What U.S. government department issues passports?

_____ **6.** Where was the first ice cream cone served?

_____ **7.** What is the currency in Bhutan?

_____ **8.** What are the names of the planets in our solar system?

_____ **9.** How many representatives does California have in Congress?

Virtual Field Trip:
Citing Sources

Visit http://collegesurvival.college.hmco.com/students and select "Hopper," or go to http://www.mtsu.edu/~studskl/3evirtual-fieldtrips.html.

▪ Summary

Name four types of resources you should use for research.	1.
	2.
	3.
	4.
What is a database?	▶
What is the primary database in your library for books?	▶
In your library what is the primary database for *general* periodicals?	▶
What are some databases for *subject-specific* periodicals?	▶
What advantages may periodicals have over books?	▶
Name two databases you can use to find articles from newspapers.	1.
	2.

Choose one search engine and explain how to use it to perform a subject search on the Internet.

▶

What are four things you should consider when evaluating a web site?

1.

2.

3.

4.

■ **What'J Your Advice?**

Nathan is beginning college after working in sales for ten years and enjoying the challenge. In his English class he has been assigned a research paper. The paper must have at least eight sources, including a minimum of two books, two periodical articles, one newspaper article, and one authoritative Internet source. From his instructor's suggested topics, he has chosen a subject that interests him. However, when he goes to the library, panic sets in. He has not been in a library in ten years and has no idea where to begin. You find a worried Nathan in front of the library. Please make Nathan a list of which databases are available in your library for books, periodicals, and newspapers, and give suggestions for using them efficiently. You will also need to suggest a search engine or two he might use to find an Internet article and explain how to tell if it's "authoritative."

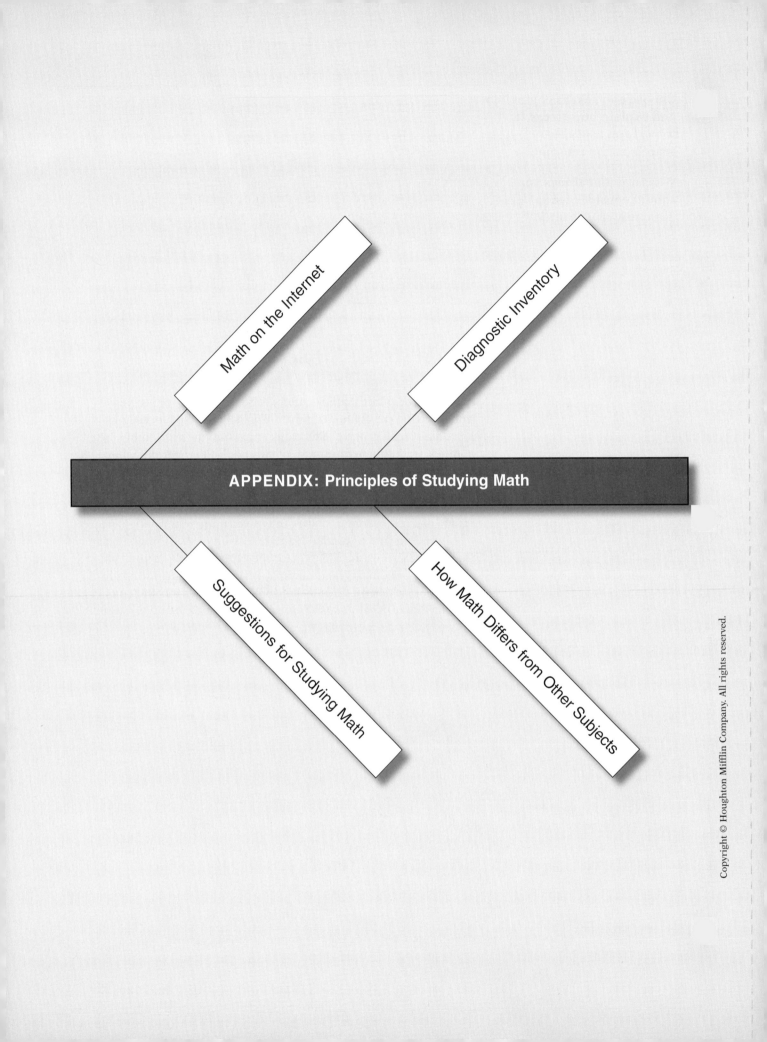

Math on the Internet

Diagnostic Inventory

APPENDIX: Principles of Studying Math

Suggestions for Studying Math

How Math Differs from Other Subjects

APPENDIX

Principles of Studying Math

The study skills principles discussed in this workbook are applicable to any subject. Many students, however, seem to have difficulty applying these principles to math, so this appendix is offered to students who need to examine math study skills specifically. The appendix begins with a diagnostic inventory. Be honest in your evaluation of your math study skills. You may find that your problem is not the math itself but, rather, the fact that you are not applying effective study skills to the math. Once you have evaluated your math study skills, choose several of the items that you scored particularly low on and set some goals for improving them. The inventory is followed by two charts to help you further your math study skills, "How Math Is Different from Other Subjects" and "Suggestions for Studying Math," and links to a dozen helpful Internet sites via Virtual Field Trips.

Math Study Skills: Diagnostic Inventory

Rate your achievement of the following statements by rating yourself **3** for **almost always, 2** for **sometimes, 1** for **almost never, 0** if you have never even thought about doing what the statement says.

Selecting a Math Class

_____ 1. I schedule my math class at a time when I am mentally sharp.

_____ 2. When I register for a math class, I choose the best instructor for me.

_____ 3. If I have a choice, I select a math class that meets three or four days a week instead of one or two.

_____ 4. I schedule my next math class as soon as possible after I have completed the current course.

_____ 5. I am sure that I have signed up for the correct level math course.

273

Time and Place for Studying Math

_____ **6.** I study math every day.

_____ **7.** I try to do my math homework immediately after math class.

_____ **8.** I have a specific time to study math.

_____ **9.** I have a specific place with few distractions to study math.

_____ **10.** I do my math homework in the lab where I can get help.

_____ **11.** I am careful to keep up to date with my math homework.

_____ **12.** I study math at least eight to ten hours a week.

Study Strategies for Math Class

_____ **13.** I read my math textbook before I come to class.

_____ **14.** If I have trouble understanding the textbook, I find an alternative text.

_____ **15.** I take notes in math class.

_____ **16.** I am careful to copy all the steps of math problems in my notes.

_____ **17.** I ask questions when I am confused.

_____ **18.** I go to the instructor or lab when I am confused.

_____ **19.** I try to determine exactly when I got confused and exactly what confused me.

_____ **20.** I review my notes and text before beginning homework.

_____ **21.** I work problems until I understand them, not just until I get the right answer for homework.

_____ **22.** I use flash cards for formulas and vocabulary.

_____ **23.** I develop memory techniques to remember math concepts.

Math Tests

_____ **24.** I preview the test before I begin.

_____ **25.** Before I begin taking the test, I make notes on the test of things such as formulas that I might need or forget.

_____ **26.** I begin with the easy questions first.

_____ **27.** I take the full amount of time allotted for the test.

_____ **28.** I carefully check or rework as many problems as possible before I turn in my test.

_____ **29.** When tests are returned, I keep a log of the types of mistakes I made—concept errors, application errors, careless errors.

_____ **30.** I keep up to date so that I don't have to cram the night before a test.

Anxiety

_____ **31.** I believe that I can succeed in math class.

_____ **32.** I have study partners in my math class.

_____ **33.** I take practice tests.

_____ **34.** I know several good relaxation techniques.

_____ **Total score**

Scoring

Total your score from all three pages.

If your score is 90–103, give yourself an **A.** You are using the study skills you need in order to be successful in math.

If your score is 80–89, give yourself a **B.** You are using good math study skills. Choose a few strategies to work on each day, and you will be well on your way to an A.

If your score is 70–79, give yourself a **C.** Your study skills are average. If you want an A, choose one or two strategies in each category to work on until you are using most of the strategies described in the inventory.

If your score is below 70, you are probably having a difficult time in math class. Math may not be your trouble! More than likely, your main problem is the study strategies you are using (or not using). *Make* yourself do as many of the thirty-four things listed as you can.

How Math Is Different from Other Subjects

1. Math requires different study processes. In other courses, you learn and understand the material, but you seldom have to *apply it*. You have to do the math problems.
2. Math is a linear learning process. What is learned one day is used the next, and so forth. (In history, perhaps you can learn Chapter 2 and not 3 and do OK on Chapter 4. In math, you must understand the material in Chapter 1 before you can go on to Chapter 2.)
3. Math is much like a foreign language. It must be practiced *every day,* and often the *vocabulary* is unfamiliar.
4. Math in the university is different from math in high school. Instead of going to class every day, in college you go only two or three times a week. What took a year to learn in high school is now covered in only fifteen weeks or less.

Critical Thinking About Studying for Math

Given the four differences above, make a list of specific study strategies you will use in studying math.

1. _____

2. _____

3. _____

4. _____

5. _____

Suggestions for Studying Math

Reasons people have math anxiety	1. People don't try to understand; they just memorize. 2. They are underprepared—*math is cumulative.*
How to study math	1. Keep up—review notes after class. 2. Take good notes—put everything from the board on paper. 3. Read the text—and if you don't understand, get help. 4. Get a study friend. 5. Have a set time to complete your math homework. Treat it as a scheduled class. The math lab is a good place to do homework.
How to study for math exams	1. Start at day one—do your homework. 2. Memorize formulas—use flash cards. 3. Rework problems that you missed on the homework.

Math is problem solving	1. Read the full question.
	2. Analyze and compute.
	3. Given/Find/Need:
	  ■ What's given?
	  ■ What do you need to find?
	  ■ What do you need to do?
	4. Draw pictures—they can simplify the problem.
	5. Use a calculator—do the calculations twice.
	6. Check your results—do the problem again another way.

Virtual Field Trip:
Improving Your Math Skills

Visit http://collegesurvival.college.hmco.com/students and select "Hopper," or go to http://www.mtsu.edu/~studskl/3evirtual-fieldtrips.html.

Principles for Optimal Learning

Brain-Compatible Strategies for Memory and Learning

Chudler, Eric. "A Computer in Your Head." *Odyssey.* March 2001.

Ford, Martin. *Motivating Humans.* Newbury Park, CA: Sage Publications, 1992.

Hart, Leslie. *Human Brain and Human Learning.* White Plains, New York: Longman, 1983.

Hillman, Ralph. *Delivering Dynamic Presentations: Using Your Voice and Body for Impact.* Boston: Allyn and Bacon, 1999.

Hopper, Carolyn. *Practicing College Study Skills: Strategies for Success,* 2nd ed. Boston: Houghton Mifflin, 2001.

Howard, Pierce. *The Owner's Manual for the Brain: Everyday Applications from Mind-Brain Research,* 2nd ed. Austin: Bard Press, 2000.

Jensen, Eric. *Brain-Based Learning.* San Diego: The Brain Store, 1995.

———. *Completing the Puzzle: The Brain-Compatible Approach to Learning.* San Diego: The Brain Store, 1997.

———. *The Learning Brain.* San Diego: The Brain Store, 1995.

———. *Super Teaching,* 3rd ed. San Diego: The Brain Store, 1998.

Locke, E. A., and Gary Latham. "Work Motivation and Satisfaction: Light at the End of the Tunnel." *Psychological Science* 1 (1990): 240–246.

Markowitz, Karen, and Eric Jensen. *The Great Memory Book.* San Diego: The Brain Store, 1999.

National Research Council. *How People Learn: Brain, Mind, Experience and School.* Washington, DC: National Academy Press, 1999.

O'Keefe, J., and L. Nadel. *The Hippocampus as a Cognitive Map.* Oxford: Clarendon Press, 1987.

Simon, Herbert. Observations on Sciences of Science Learning. Paper Prepared for Committee on Developments in the Science of Learning for the Sciences of Sciences Learning: An Interdisciplinary Discussion. Department of Psychology, Carnegie Mellon University, 1996.

Wurtman, Judith. *Managing Your Mind and Mood Through Food.* New York: Harper-Collins, 1986.

INDEX

Master Schedule Worksheet

	Sun	Mon	Tue	Wed	Thu	Fri	Sat
7–8							
8–9							
9–10							
10–11							
11–12							
12–1							
1–2							
2–3							
3–4							
4–5							
5–6							
6–7							
7–8							
8–9							
9–10							
10–11							
11–12							

Master Schedule Worksheet

	Sun	Mon	Tue	Wed	Thu	Fri	Sat
7–8							
8–9							
9–10							
10–11							
11–12							
12–1							
1–2							
2–3							
3–4							
4–5							
5–6							
6–7							
7–8							
8–9							
9–10							
10–11							
11–12							

Master Schedule Worksheet

	Sun	Mon	Tue	Wed	Thu	Fri	Sat
7–8							
8–9							
9–10							
10–11							
11–12							
12–1							
1–2							
2–3							
3–4							
4–5							
5–6							
6–7							
7–8							
8–9							
9–10							
10–11							
11–12							

Master Schedule Worksheet

	Sun	Mon	Tue	Wed	Thu	Fri	Sat
7–8							
8–9							
9–10							
10–11							
11–12							
12–1							
1–2							
2–3							
3–4							
4–5							
5–6							
6–7							
7–8							
8–9							
9–10							
10–11							
11–12